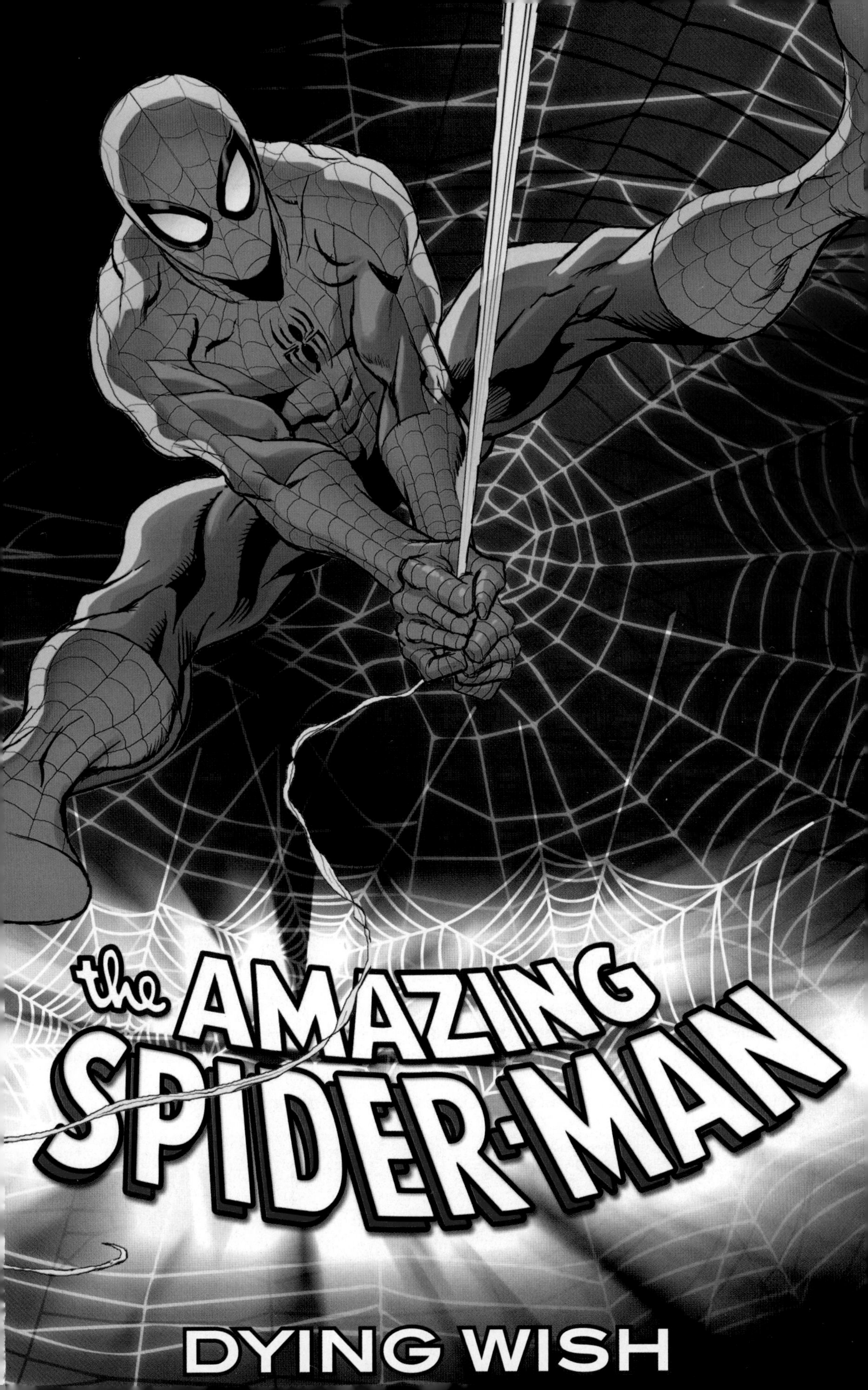
the AMAZING SPIDER-MAN
DYING WISH

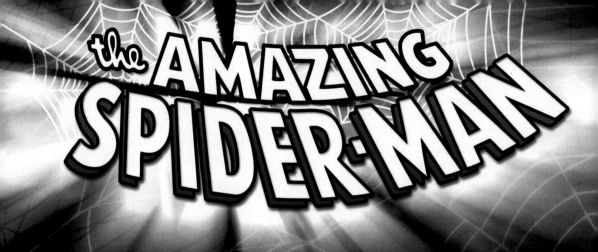

the AMAZING SPIDER-MAN

DYING WISH

AMAZING SPIDER-MAN #698
Writer: **DAN SLOTT** • Artist: **RICHARD ELSON**
Inker: **KLAUS JANSON**
Colorist: **ANTONIO FABELA**
Cover Art: **PAOLO RIVERA**

AMAZING SPIDER-MAN #699-700
Writer: **DAN SLOTT** • Penciler: **HUMBERTO RAMOS**
Inker: **VICTOR OLAZABA**
Colorist: **EDGAR DELGADO** • Cover Art: **PAOLO RIVERA** (#699) & **MR GARCIN** (#700)

"SPIDER-DREAMS"
Writer: **J.M. DEMATTEIS** • Artist: **GIUSEPPE CAMUNCOLI**
Penciler: **SAL BUSCEMA** • Colorist: **PAOLO RIVERA**

"DATE NIGHT"
Writer: **JEN VAN METER** • Artist: **STEPHANIE BUSCEMA**

Letterer: **CHRIS ELIOPOULOS** • Assistant Editor: **ELLIE PYLE** • Senior Editor: **STEPHEN WACKER**
Special thanks to Sana Amanat, Tom Brennan, Jeanine Schaefer & Cory Sedlmeier

Collection Editor: **JENNIFER GRÜNWALD**
Assistant Editors: **ALEX STARBUCK** & **NELSON RIBEIRO** • Editor, Special Projects: **MARK D. BEAZLEY**
Senior Editor, Special Projects: **JEFF YOUNGQUIST** • SVP of Print & Digital Publishing Sales: **DAVID GABRIEL**

Editor in Chief: **AXEL ALONSO** • Chief Creative Officer: **JOE QUESADA** • Publisher: **DAN BUCKLEY** • Executive Producer: **ALAN FINE**

SPIDER-MAN: DYING WISH. Contains material originally published in magazine form as AMAZING SPIDER-MAN #698-700. First printing 2013. Hardcover ISBN# 978-0-7851-6523-1. Softcover ISBN# 978-0-7851-6524-8. Published by MARVEL WORLDWIDE, INC., a subsidiary of MARVEL ENTERTAINMENT, LLC. OFFICE OF PUBLICATION: 135 West 50th Street, New York, NY 10020. **Printed in the U.S.A.** ALAN FINE, EVP - Office of the President, Marvel Worldwide, Inc. and EVP & CMO Marvel Characters B.V.; DAN BUCKLEY, Publisher & President - Print, Animation & Digital Divisions; JOE QUESADA, Chief Creative Officer; TOM BREVOORT, SVP of Publishing; DAVID BOGART, SVP of Operations & Procurement, Publishing; RUWAN JAYATILLEKE, SVP & Associate Publisher, Publishing; C.B. CEBULSKI, SVP of Creator & Content Development; DAVID GABRIEL, SVP of Print & Digital Publishing Sales; JIM O'KEEFE, VP of Operations & Logistics; DAN CARR, Executive Director of Publishing Technology; SUSAN CRESPI, Editorial Operations Manager; ALEX MORALES, Publishing Operations Manager; STAN LEE, Chairman Emeritus. For information regarding advertising in Marvel Comics or on Marvel.com, please contact Niza Disla, Director of Marvel Partnerships, at ndisla@marvel.com. For Marvel subscription inquiries, please call 800-217-9158. **Manufactured between 12/24/2012 and 2/4/2013 (hardcover), and 12/24/2012 and 8/5/2013 (softcover), by R.R. DONNELLEY, INC., SALEM, VA, USA.**

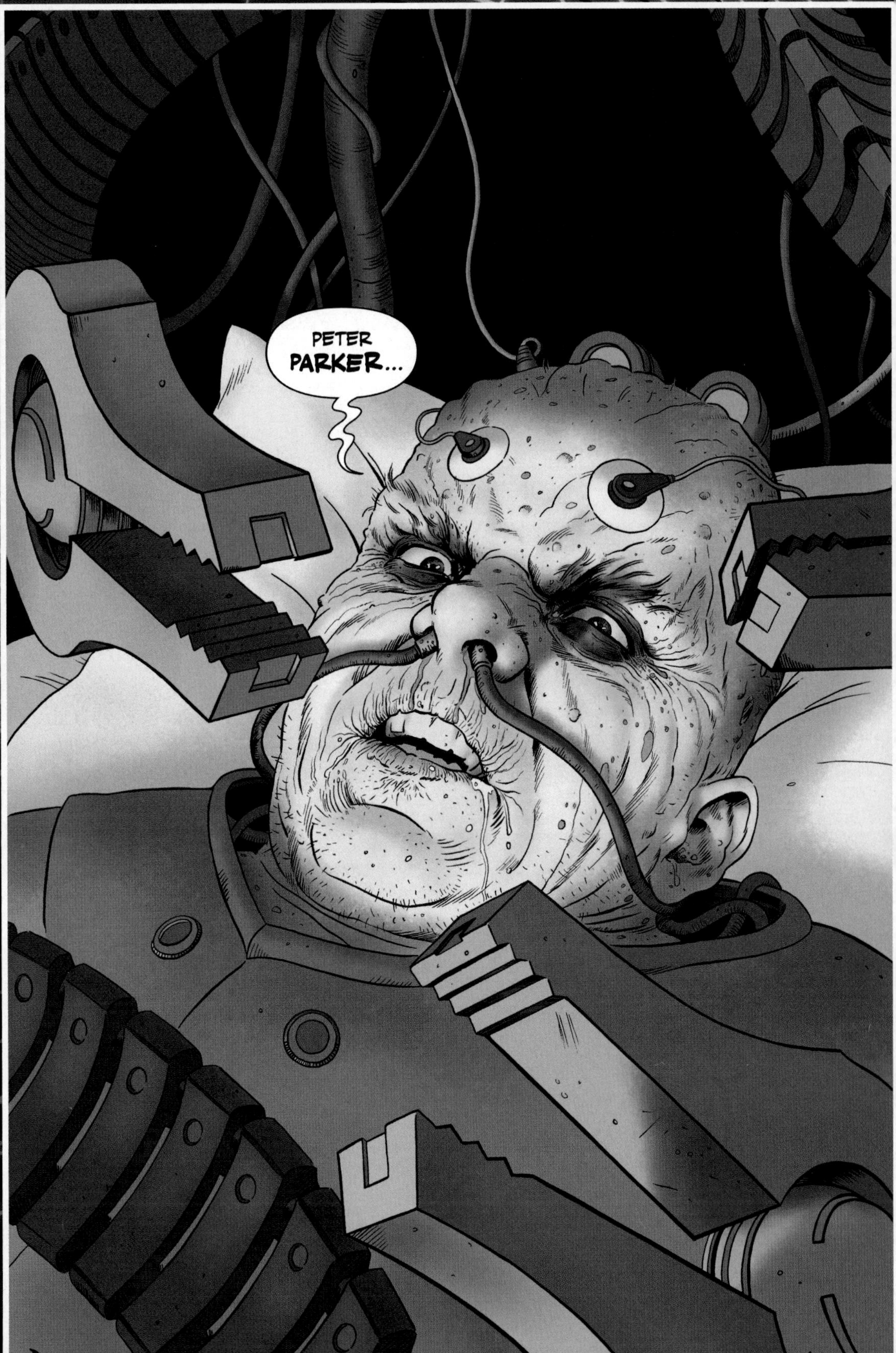
PETER PARKER...
RIVERA

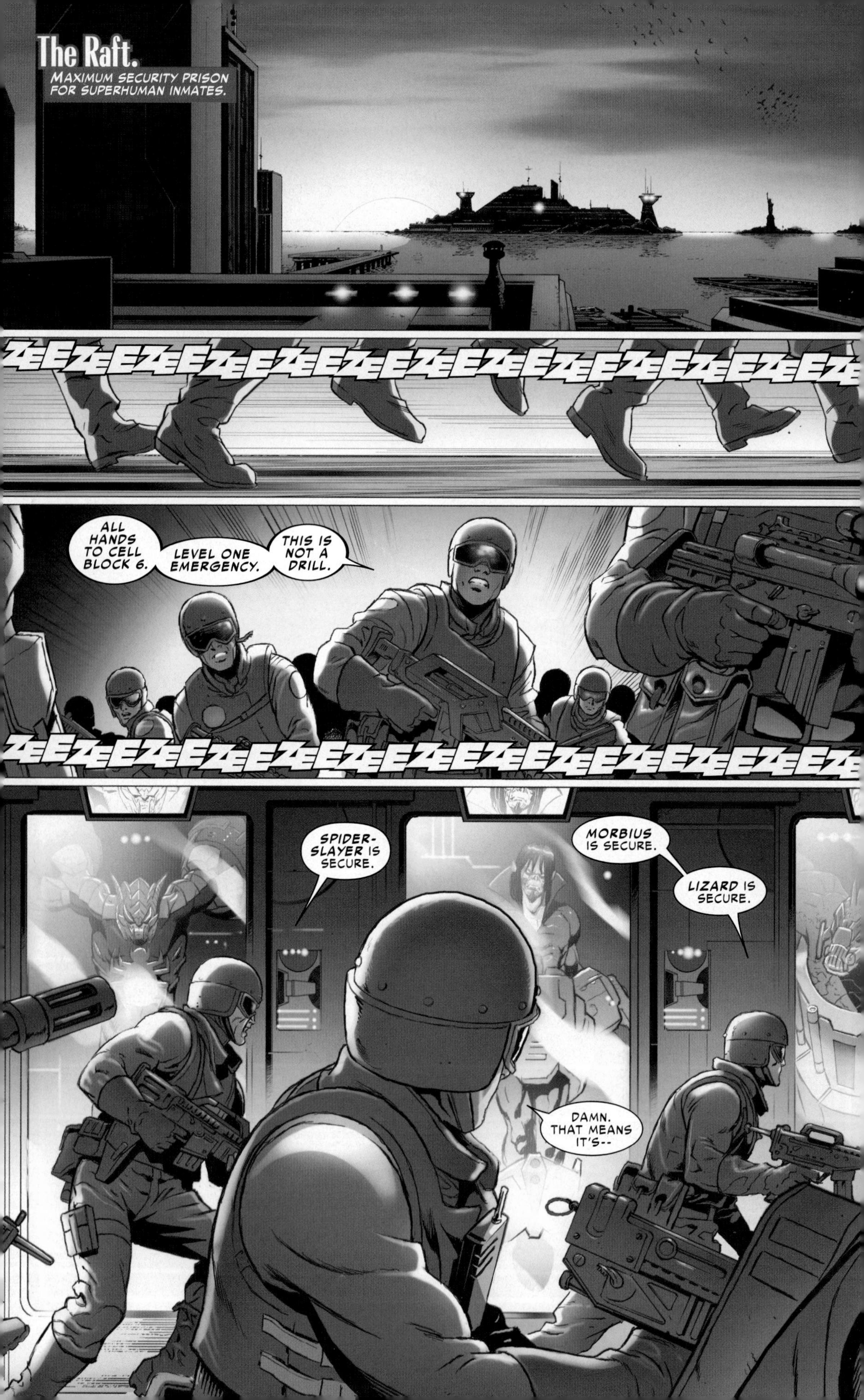
The Raft.
MAXIMUM SECURITY PRISON FOR SUPERHUMAN INMATES.
ZEEZEEZEEZEEZEEZEEZEEZEEZEEZEEZEEZEEZEE
ALL HANDS TO CELL BLOCK 6.
LEVEL ONE EMERGENCY.
THIS IS NOT A DRILL.
ZEEZEEZEEZEEZEEZEEZEEZEEZEEZEEZEEZEEZEE
SPIDER-SLAYER IS SECURE.
MORBIUS IS SECURE.
LIZARD IS SECURE.
DAMN. THAT MEANS IT'S--

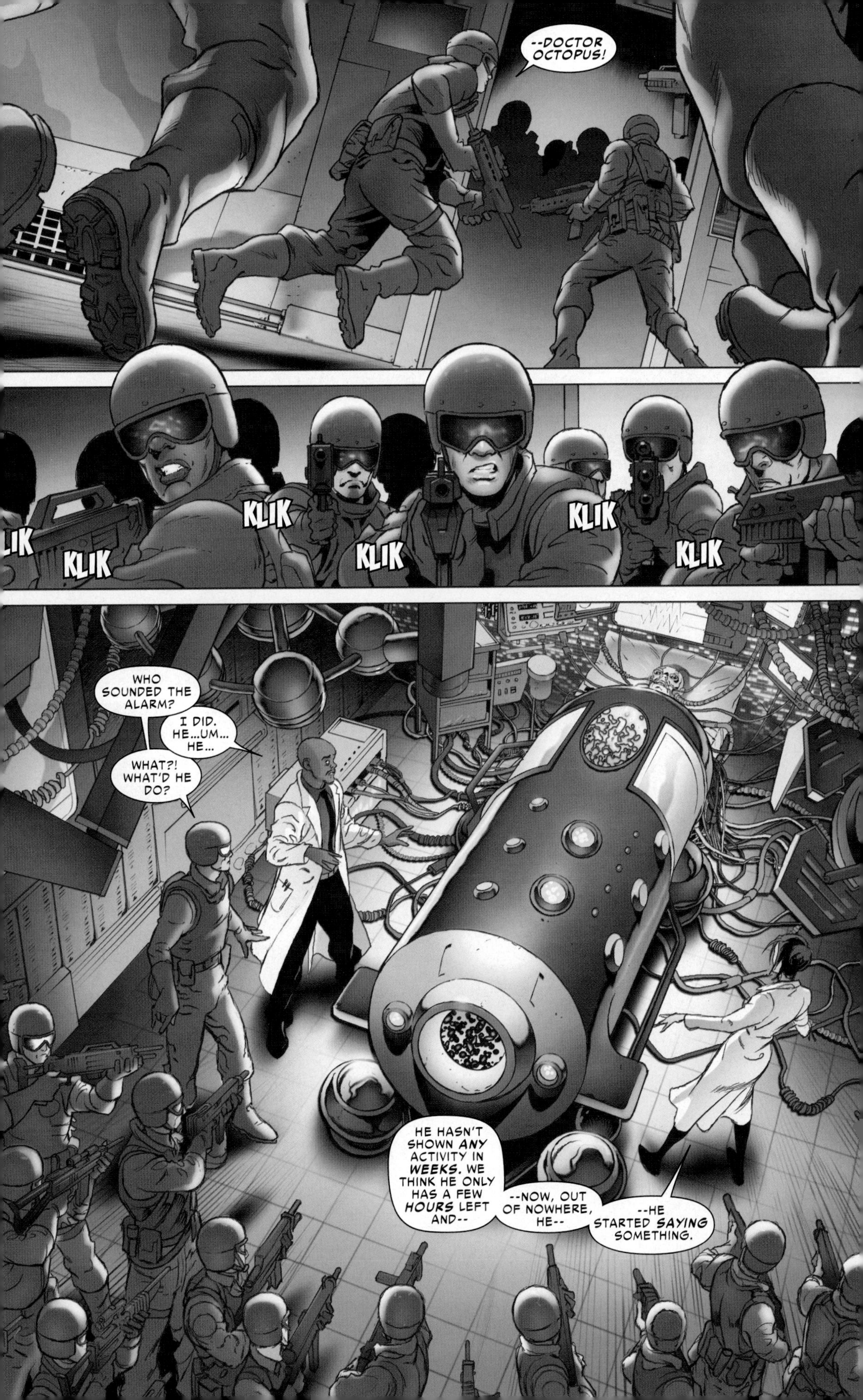
--DOCTOR OCTOPUS!
KLIK
KLIK
KLIK
KLIK
KLIK
KLIK
WHO SOUNDED THE ALARM?
I DID. HE...UM... HE...
WHAT?! WHAT'D HE DO?
HE HASN'T SHOWN ANY ACTIVITY IN WEEKS. WE THINK HE ONLY HAS A FEW HOURS LEFT AND--
--NOW, OUT OF NOWHERE, HE--
--HE STARTED SAYING SOMETHING.

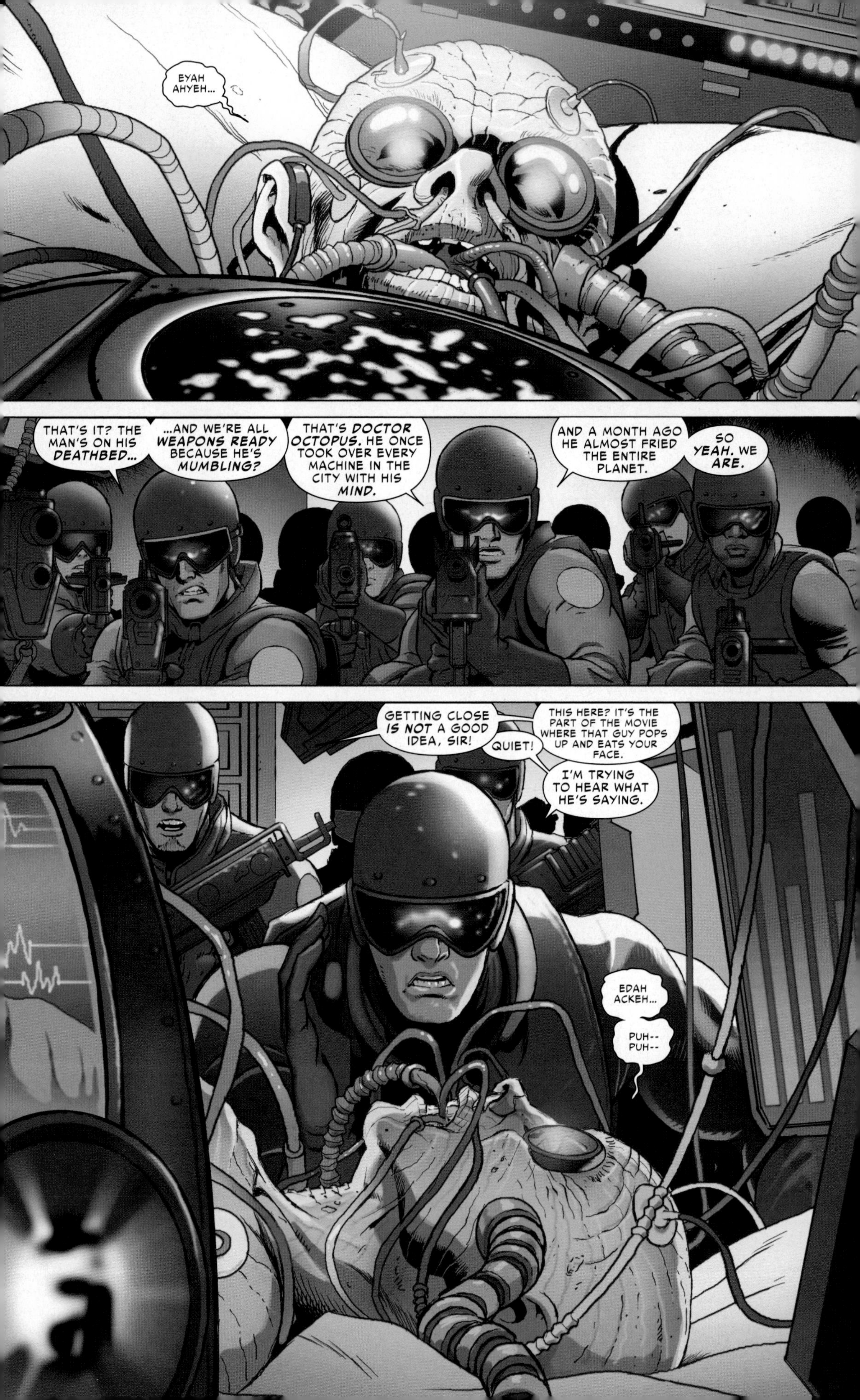
EYAH AHYEH...
THAT'S IT? THE MAN'S ON HIS DEATHBED...
...AND WE'RE ALL WEAPONS READY BECAUSE HE'S MUMBLING?
THAT'S DOCTOR OCTOPUS. HE ONCE TOOK OVER EVERY MACHINE IN THE CITY WITH HIS MIND.
AND A MONTH AGO HE ALMOST FRIED THE ENTIRE PLANET.
SO YEAH. WE ARE.
GETTING CLOSE IS NOT A GOOD IDEA, SIR!
THIS HERE? IT'S THE PART OF THE MOVIE WHERE THAT GUY POPS UP AND EATS YOUR FACE.
QUIET!
I'M TRYING TO HEAR WHAT HE'S SAYING.
EDAH ACKEH...
PUH-- PUH--

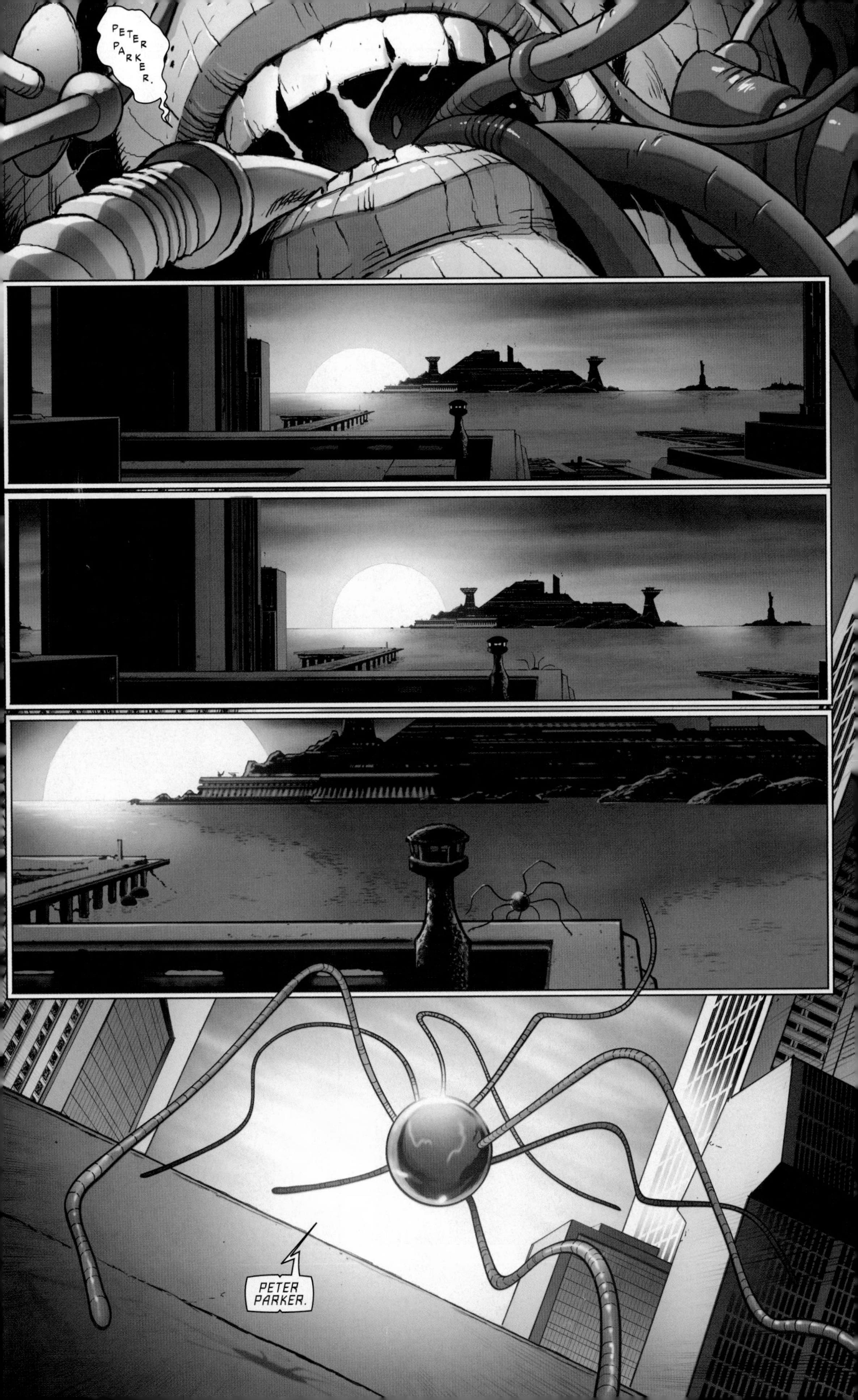
PETER PARKER.
PETER PARKER.

DAILY BUGLE

FINAL ★★★★

NEW YORK'S FINEST DAILY NEWSPAPER

SINCE 1897
★★★★
$1.00 (in NYC)
$1.50 (outside city)

INSIDE: CAPTAIN MARVEL IN DEEP WATER; VENOM CLEANS UP CARNAGE; HAWKEYE'S DIRTY LAUNDRY ON TAPE

DOC OCK ON DEATHBED

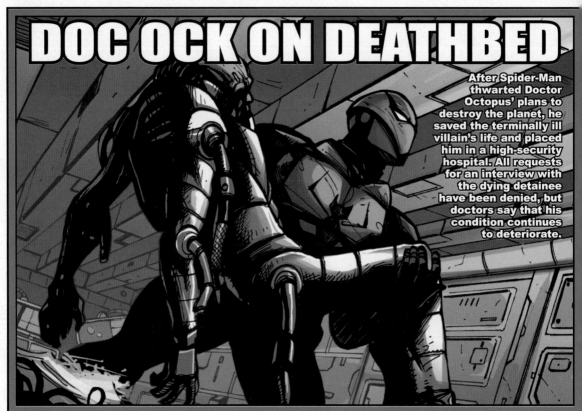

After Spider-Man thwarted Doctor Octopus' plans to destroy the planet, he saved the terminally ill villain's life and placed him in a high-security hospital. All requests for an interview with the dying detainee have been denied, but doctors say that his condition continues to deteriorate.

DOC OCK TECH STILL FLOATING

Witnesses claim Doctor Octopus' octobots are still clicking around the city, despite assurance from the Avengers. Is your home safe?

MJ'S CLUB GETS FIVE STARS

Style Section

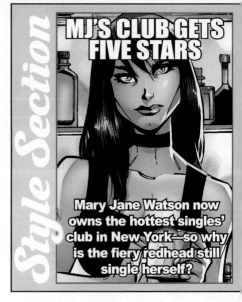

Mary Jane Watson now owns the hottest singles' club in New York—so why is the fiery redhead still single herself?

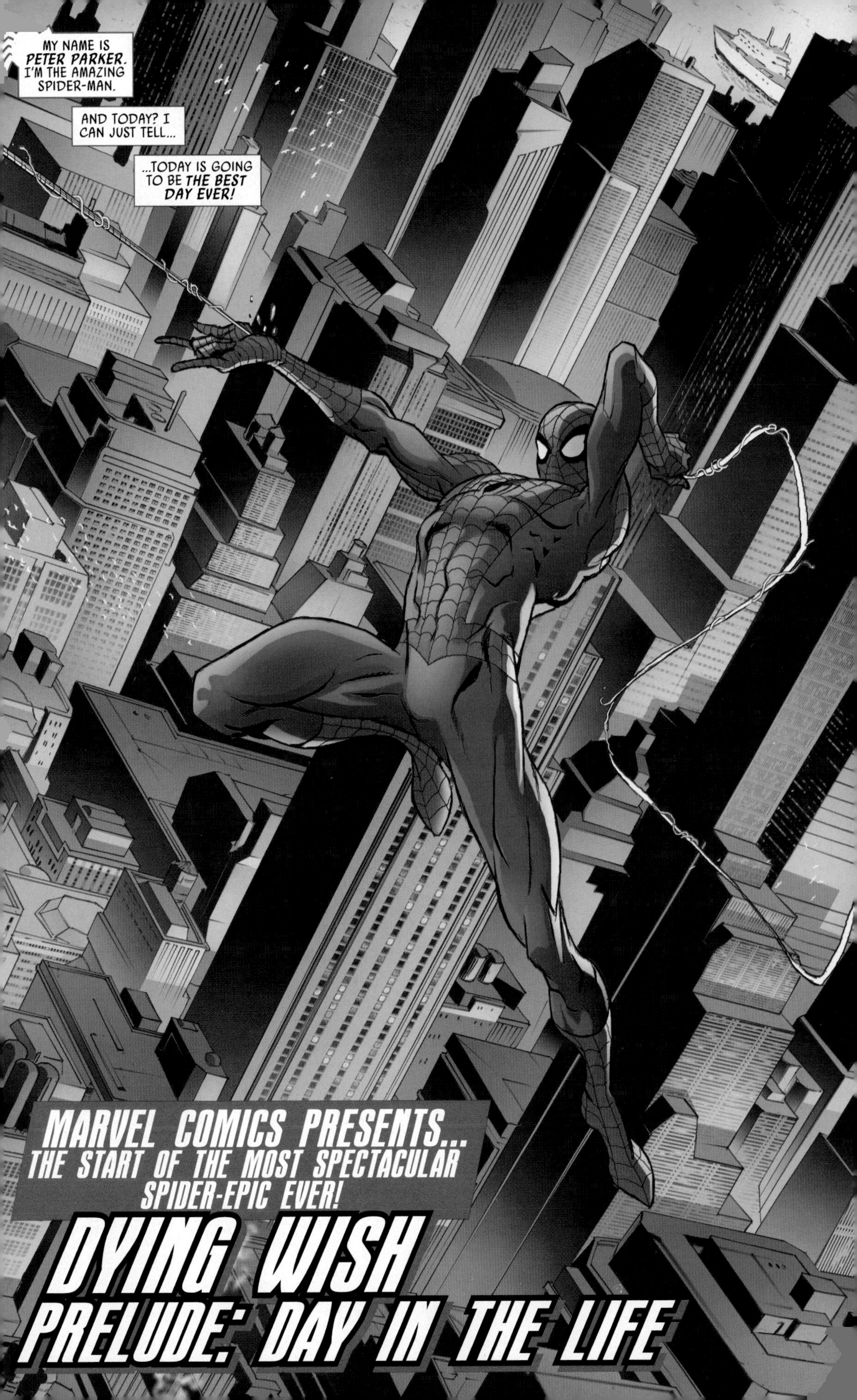
MY NAME IS PETER PARKER. I'M THE AMAZING SPIDER-MAN.
AND TODAY? I CAN JUST TELL...
...TODAY IS GOING TO BE THE BEST DAY EVER!
MARVEL COMICS PRESENTS... THE START OF THE MOST SPECTACULAR SPIDER-EPIC EVER!
DYING WISH
PRELUDE: DAY IN THE LIFE

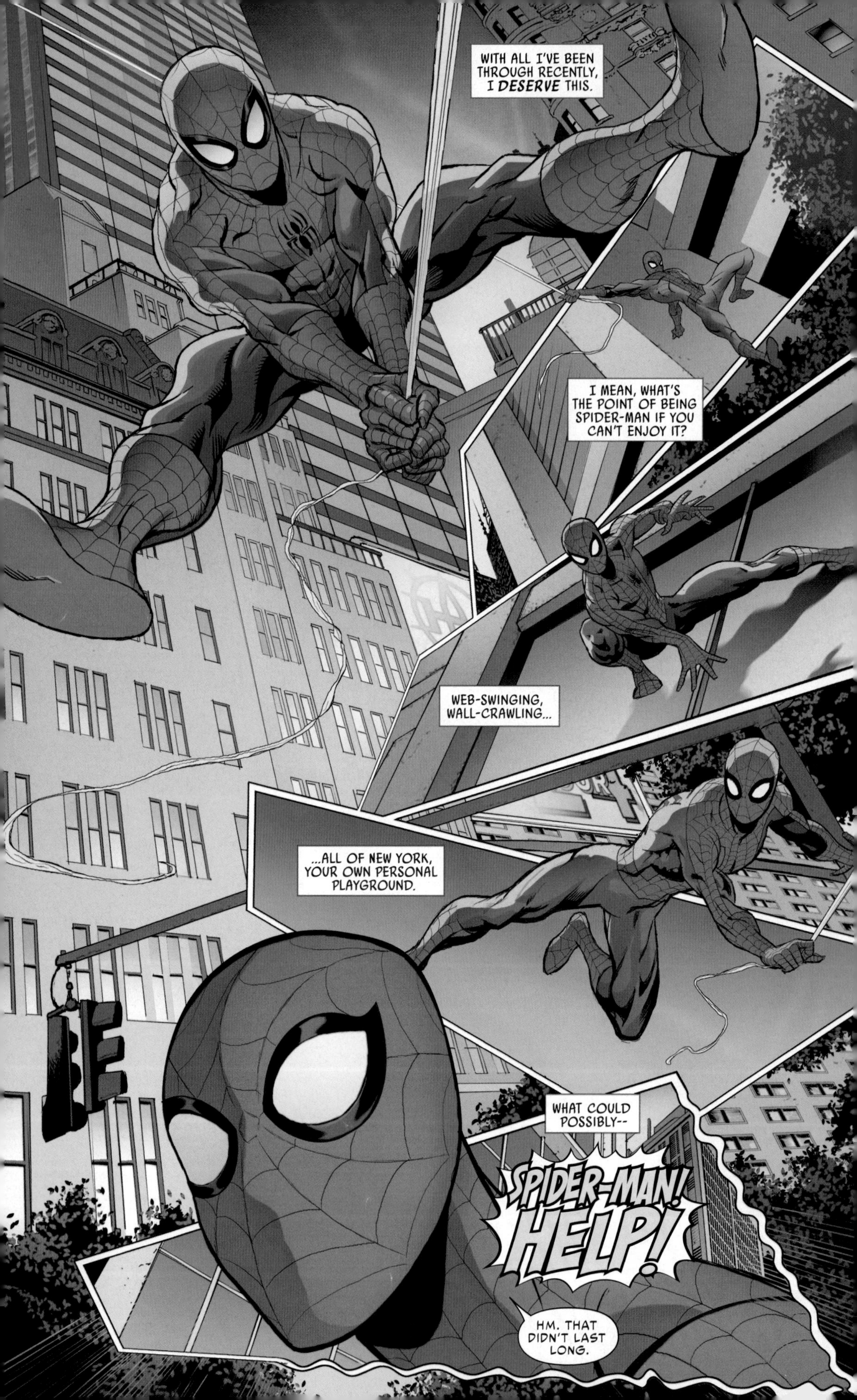
WITH ALL I'VE BEEN THROUGH RECENTLY, I *DESERVE* THIS.
I MEAN, WHAT'S THE POINT OF BEING SPIDER-MAN IF YOU CAN'T ENJOY IT?
WEB-SWINGING, WALL-CRAWLING...
...ALL OF NEW YORK, YOUR OWN PERSONAL PLAYGROUND.
WHAT COULD POSSIBLY--
SPIDER-MAN! HELP!
HM. THAT DIDN'T LAST LONG.

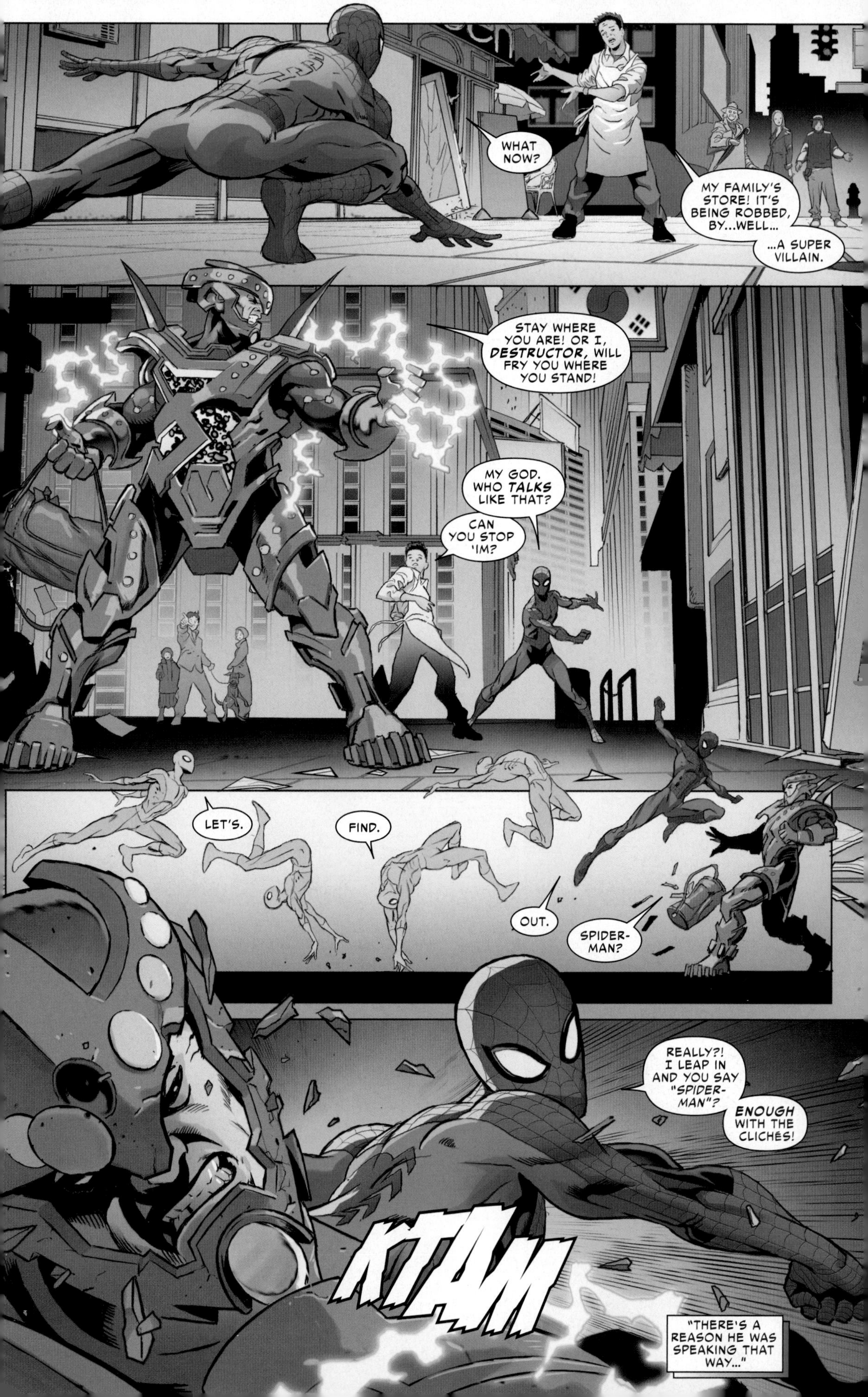
WHAT NOW?
MY FAMILY'S STORE! IT'S BEING ROBBED, BY...WELL...
...A SUPER VILLAIN.
STAY WHERE YOU ARE! OR I, DESTRUCTOR, WILL FRY YOU WHERE YOU STAND!
MY GOD. WHO TALKS LIKE THAT?
CAN YOU STOP 'IM?
LET'S.
FIND.
OUT.
SPIDER-MAN?
REALLY?! I LEAP IN AND YOU SAY "SPIDER-MAN"?
ENOUGH WITH THE CLICHÉS!
KTAM
"THERE'S A REASON HE WAS SPEAKING THAT WAY..."

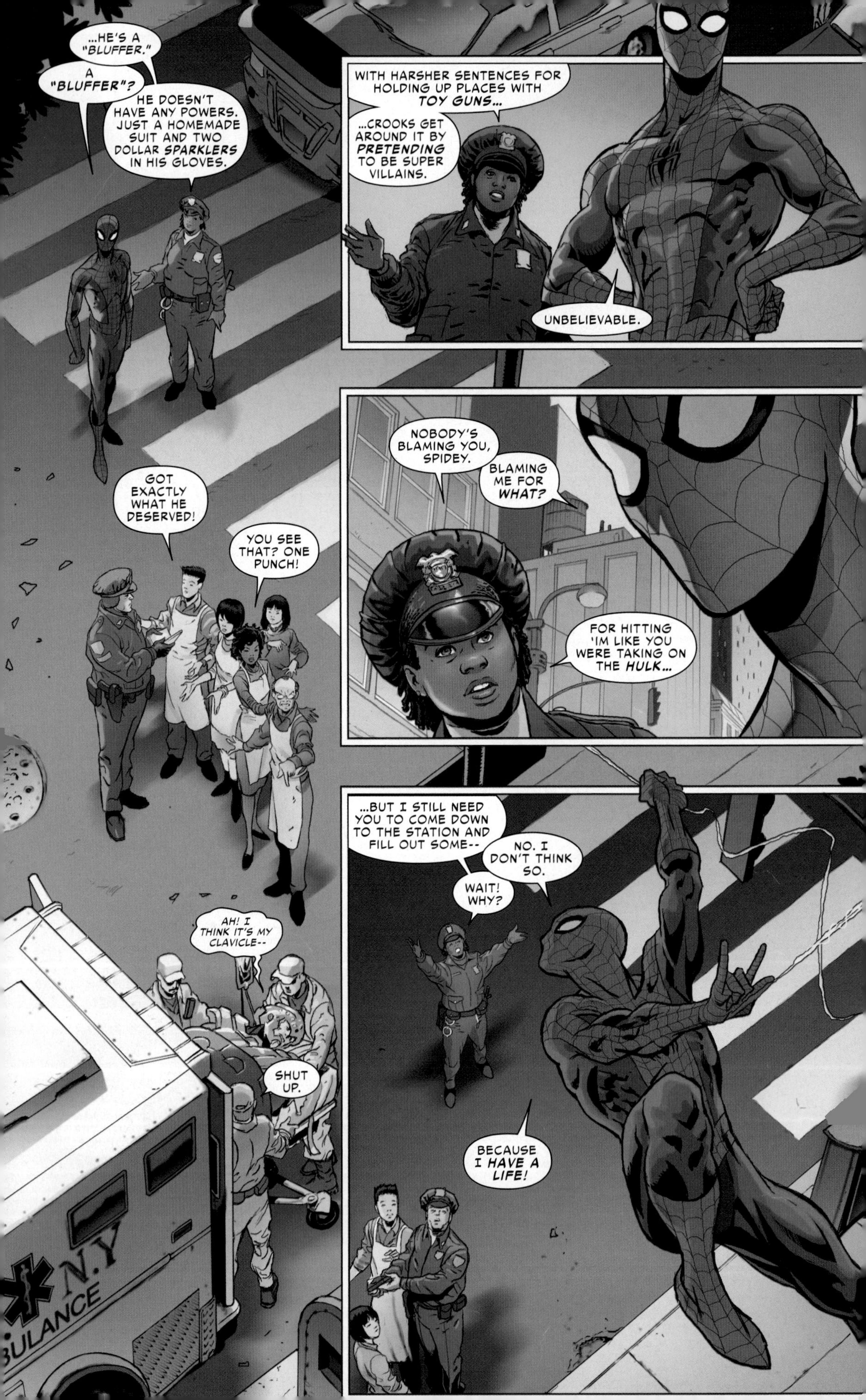
...HE'S A "BLUFFER."
A "BLUFFER"?
HE DOESN'T HAVE ANY POWERS. JUST A HOMEMADE SUIT AND TWO DOLLAR SPARKLERS IN HIS GLOVES.
WITH HARSHER SENTENCES FOR HOLDING UP PLACES WITH TOY GUNS...
...CROOKS GET AROUND IT BY PRETENDING TO BE SUPER VILLAINS.
UNBELIEVABLE.
GOT EXACTLY WHAT HE DESERVED!
YOU SEE THAT? ONE PUNCH!
NOBODY'S BLAMING YOU, SPIDEY.
BLAMING ME FOR WHAT?
FOR HITTING 'IM LIKE YOU WERE TAKING ON THE HULK...
AH! I THINK IT'S MY CLAVICLE--
SHUT UP.
...BUT I STILL NEED YOU TO COME DOWN TO THE STATION AND FILL OUT SOME--
NO. I DON'T THINK SO.
WAIT! WHY?
BECAUSE I HAVE A LIFE!
N.Y
BULANCE

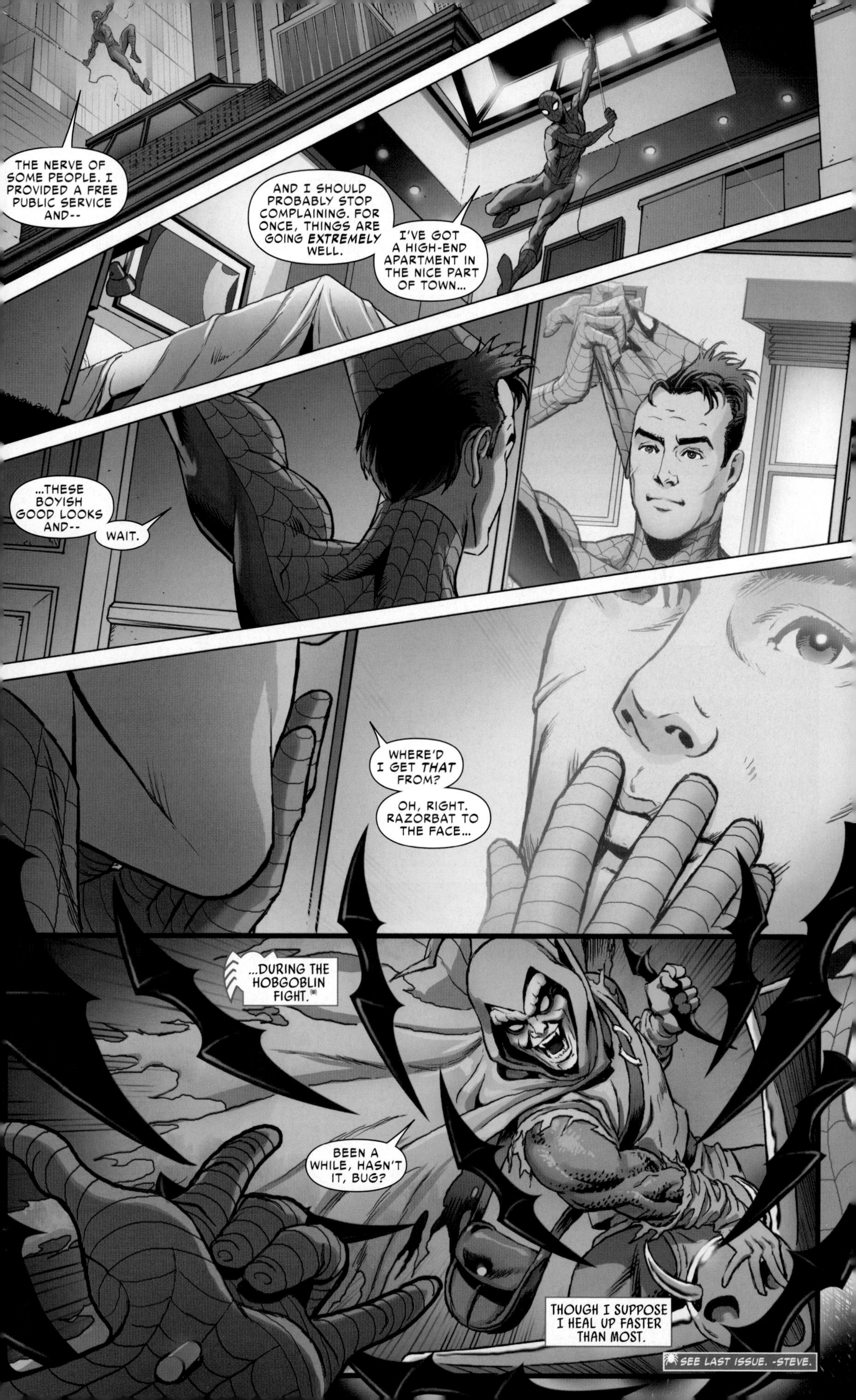
THE NERVE OF SOME PEOPLE. I PROVIDED A FREE PUBLIC SERVICE AND--
AND I SHOULD PROBABLY STOP COMPLAINING. FOR ONCE, THINGS ARE GOING EXTREMELY WELL.
I'VE GOT A HIGH-END APARTMENT IN THE NICE PART OF TOWN...
...THESE BOYISH GOOD LOOKS AND--
WAIT.
WHERE'D I GET THAT FROM?
OH, RIGHT. RAZORBAT TO THE FACE...
...DURING THE HOBGOBLIN FIGHT.*
BEEN A WHILE, HASN'T IT, BUG?
THOUGH I SUPPOSE I HEAL UP FASTER THAN MOST.
*SEE LAST ISSUE. -STEVE.

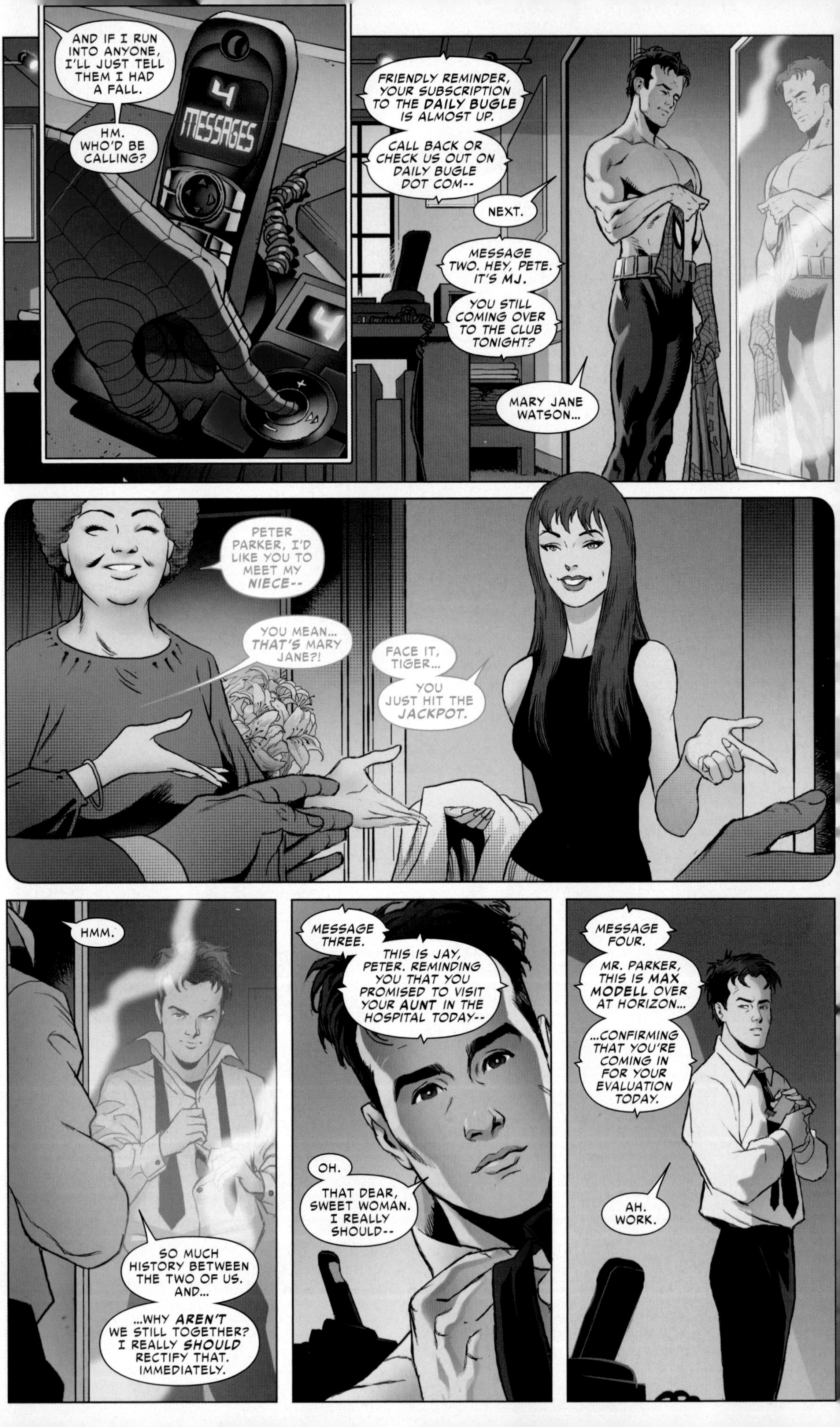
AND IF I RUN INTO ANYONE, I'LL JUST TELL THEM I HAD A FALL.
HM. WHO'D BE CALLING?
4 MESSAGES
FRIENDLY REMINDER, YOUR SUBSCRIPTION TO THE DAILY BUGLE IS ALMOST UP.
CALL BACK OR CHECK US OUT ON DAILY BUGLE DOT COM--
NEXT.
MESSAGE TWO. HEY, PETE. IT'S MJ.
YOU STILL COMING OVER TO THE CLUB TONIGHT?
MARY JANE WATSON...
PETER PARKER, I'D LIKE YOU TO MEET MY NIECE--
YOU MEAN... THAT'S MARY JANE?!
FACE IT, TIGER...
YOU JUST HIT THE JACKPOT.
HMM.
SO MUCH HISTORY BETWEEN THE TWO OF US. AND...
...WHY AREN'T WE STILL TOGETHER? I REALLY SHOULD RECTIFY THAT. IMMEDIATELY.
MESSAGE THREE.
THIS IS JAY, PETER. REMINDING YOU THAT YOU PROMISED TO VISIT YOUR AUNT IN THE HOSPITAL TODAY--
OH.
THAT DEAR, SWEET WOMAN. I REALLY SHOULD--
MESSAGE FOUR.
MR. PARKER, THIS IS MAX MODELL OVER AT HORIZON...
...CONFIRMING THAT YOU'RE COMING IN FOR YOUR EVALUATION TODAY.
AH. WORK.

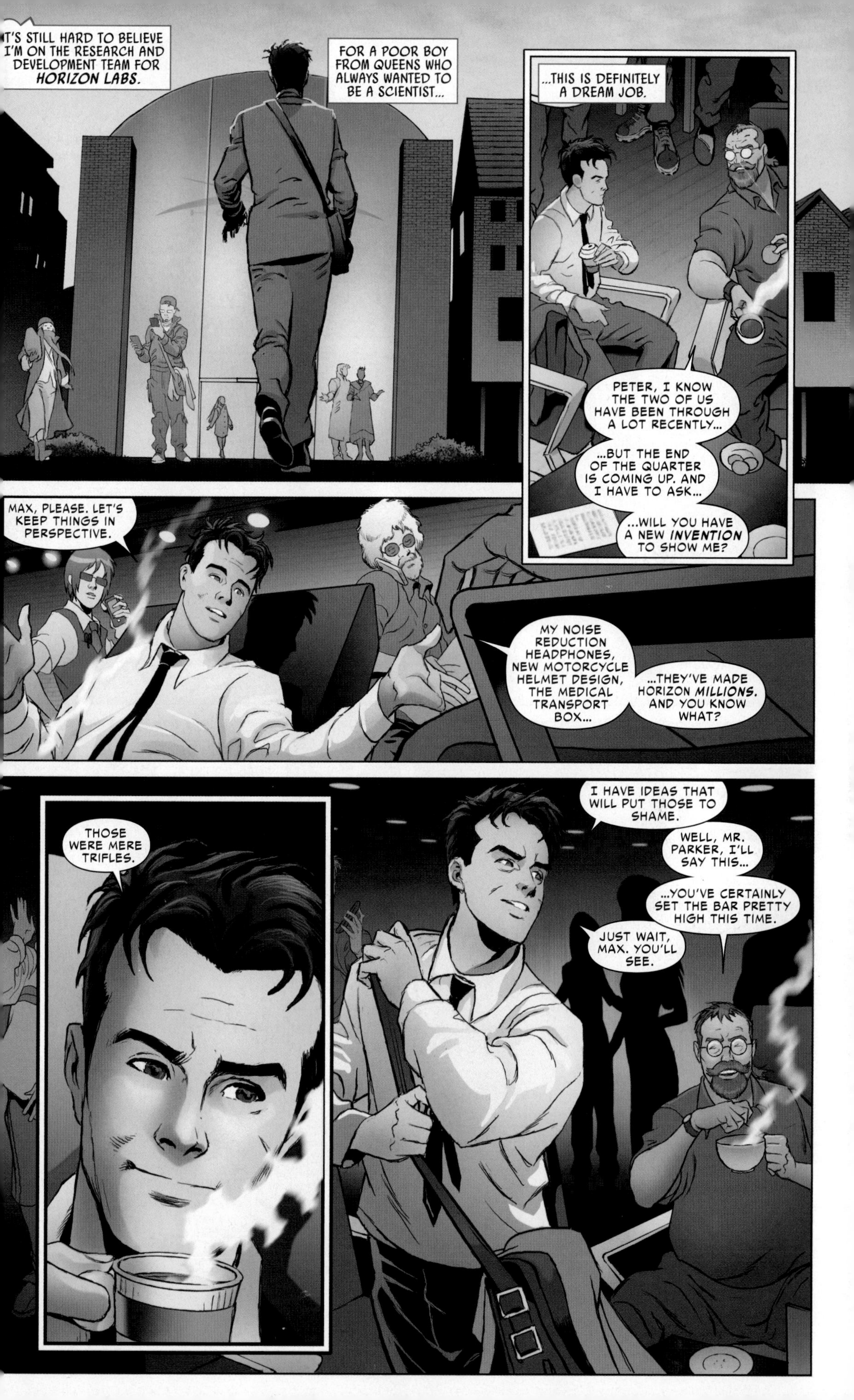
IT'S STILL HARD TO BELIEVE I'M ON THE RESEARCH AND DEVELOPMENT TEAM FOR HORIZON LABS.
FOR A POOR BOY FROM QUEENS WHO ALWAYS WANTED TO BE A SCIENTIST...
...THIS IS DEFINITELY A DREAM JOB.
PETER, I KNOW THE TWO OF US HAVE BEEN THROUGH A LOT RECENTLY...
...BUT THE END OF THE QUARTER IS COMING UP. AND I HAVE TO ASK...
...WILL YOU HAVE A NEW INVENTION TO SHOW ME?
MAX, PLEASE. LET'S KEEP THINGS IN PERSPECTIVE.
MY NOISE REDUCTION HEADPHONES, NEW MOTORCYCLE HELMET DESIGN, THE MEDICAL TRANSPORT BOX...
...THEY'VE MADE HORIZON MILLIONS. AND YOU KNOW WHAT?
THOSE WERE MERE TRIFLES.
I HAVE IDEAS THAT WILL PUT THOSE TO SHAME.
WELL, MR. PARKER, I'LL SAY THIS...
...YOU'VE CERTAINLY SET THE BAR PRETTY HIGH THIS TIME.
JUST WAIT, MAX. YOU'LL SEE.

COMING UP WITH NEW TECHNOLOGICAL MARVELS? FOR *ME*, THAT'S CHILD'S PLAY.

BUT *FIRST*, I'M RUNNING LOW ON WEB-FLUID...

THIS FORMULA IS SO BEAUTIFUL IN ITS SIMPLICITY, SO REVOLUTIONARY FOR ITS TIME...

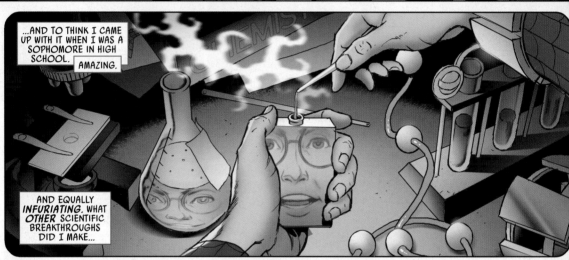

...AND TO THINK I CAME UP WITH IT WHEN I WAS A SOPHOMORE IN HIGH SCHOOL. AMAZING.

AND EQUALLY *INFURIATING*. WHAT *OTHER* SCIENTIFIC BREAKTHROUGHS DID I MAKE...

...UNTIL I CAME HERE?

ALL THOSE YEARS IN THE INTERIM-- WASTED.

WELL, NO MORE. I REFUSE TO LOSE A SINGLE MOMENT TO STAGNATION.

IT'S TIME I STARTED LIVING UP TO MY *FULL* POTENTIAL.

AS A MAN OF *SCIENCE* AND-- WELL--AS A *MAN*.

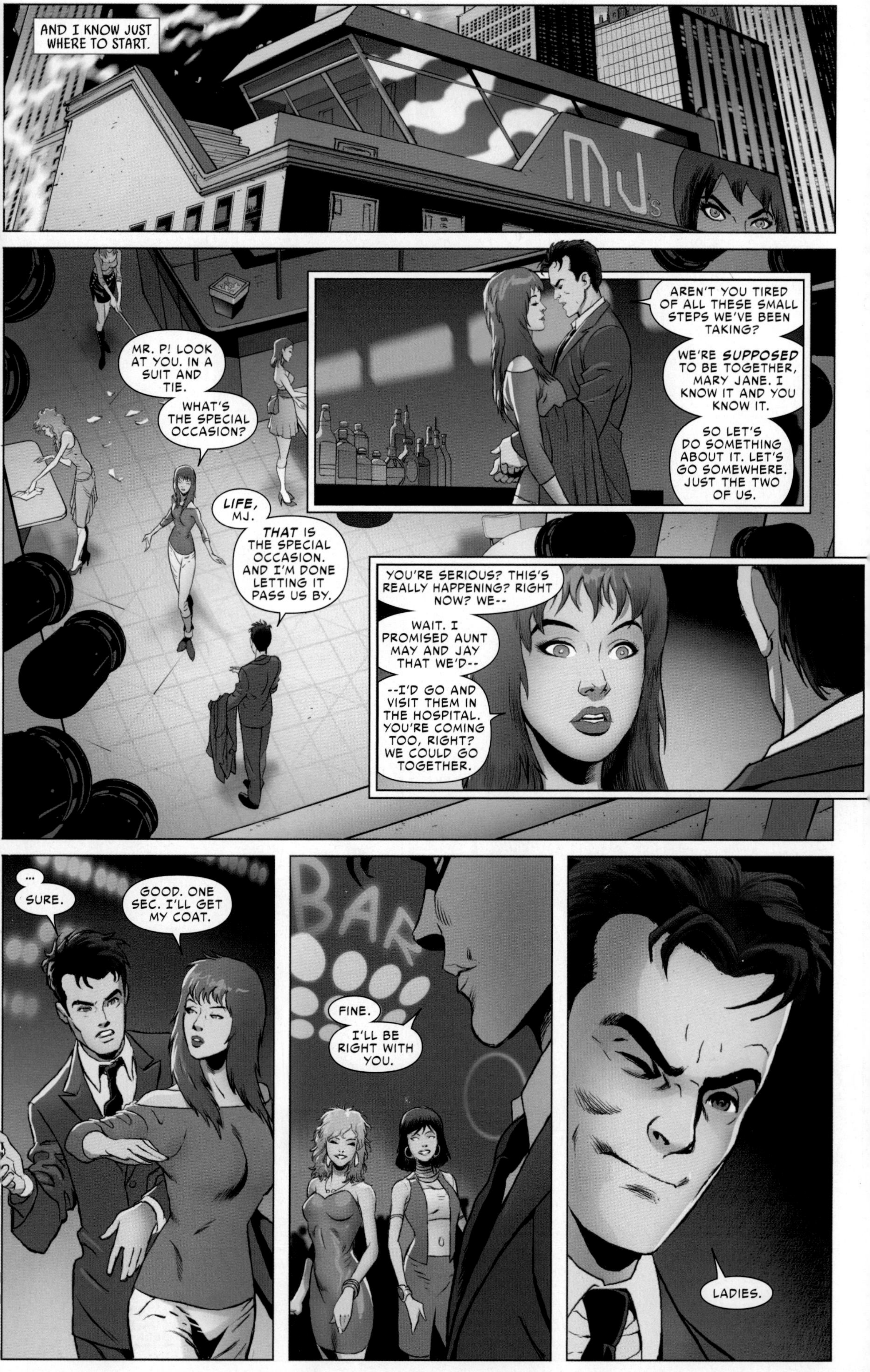
AND I KNOW JUST WHERE TO START.
MJ's
MR. P! LOOK AT YOU. IN A SUIT AND TIE.
WHAT'S THE SPECIAL OCCASION?
LIFE, MJ.
THAT IS THE SPECIAL OCCASION. AND I'M DONE LETTING IT PASS US BY.
AREN'T YOU TIRED OF ALL THESE SMALL STEPS WE'VE BEEN TAKING?
WE'RE SUPPOSED TO BE TOGETHER, MARY JANE. I KNOW IT AND YOU KNOW IT.
SO LET'S DO SOMETHING ABOUT IT. LET'S GO SOMEWHERE. JUST THE TWO OF US.
YOU'RE SERIOUS? THIS'S REALLY HAPPENING? RIGHT NOW? WE--
WAIT. I PROMISED AUNT MAY AND JAY THAT WE'D--
--I'D GO AND VISIT THEM IN THE HOSPITAL. YOU'RE COMING TOO, RIGHT? WE COULD GO TOGETHER.
... SURE.
GOOD. ONE SEC. I'LL GET MY COAT.
BAR
FINE.
I'LL BE RIGHT WITH YOU.
LADIES.

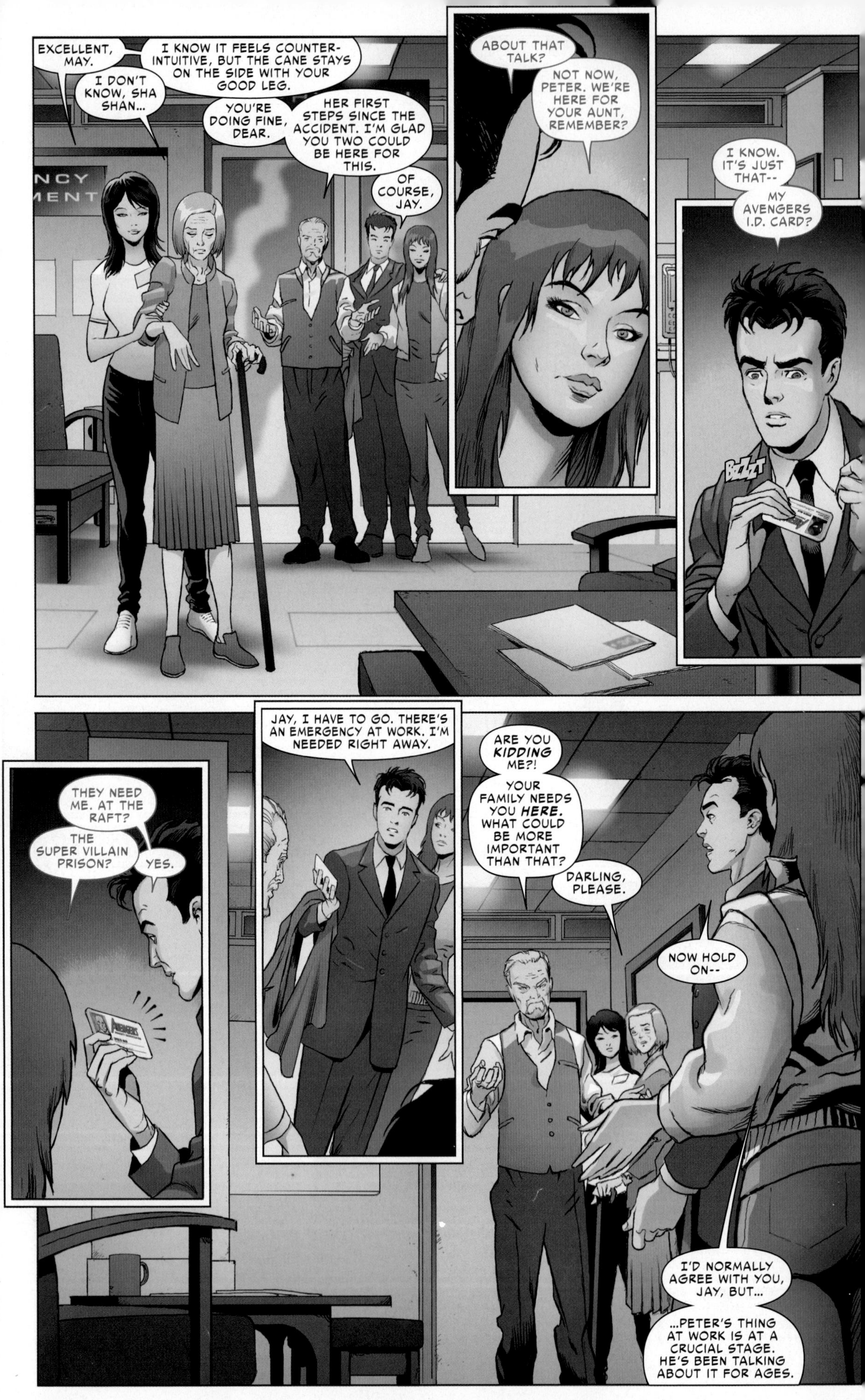
EXCELLENT, MAY.
I KNOW IT FEELS COUNTER-INTUITIVE, BUT THE CANE STAYS ON THE SIDE WITH YOUR GOOD LEG.
I DON'T KNOW, SHA SHAN...
YOU'RE DOING FINE, DEAR.
HER FIRST STEPS SINCE THE ACCIDENT. I'M GLAD YOU TWO COULD BE HERE FOR THIS.
OF COURSE, JAY.
ABOUT THAT TALK?
NOT NOW, PETER. WE'RE HERE FOR YOUR AUNT, REMEMBER?
I KNOW. IT'S JUST THAT--
MY AVENGERS I.D. CARD?
BZZZT
THEY NEED ME. AT THE RAFT?
THE SUPER VILLAIN PRISON?
YES.
JAY, I HAVE TO GO. THERE'S AN EMERGENCY AT WORK. I'M NEEDED RIGHT AWAY.
ARE YOU *KIDDING* ME?!
YOUR FAMILY NEEDS YOU *HERE*. WHAT COULD BE MORE IMPORTANT THAN THAT?
DARLING, PLEASE.
NOW HOLD ON--
I'D NORMALLY AGREE WITH YOU, JAY, BUT...
...PETER'S THING AT WORK IS AT A CRUCIAL STAGE. HE'S BEEN TALKING ABOUT IT FOR AGES.

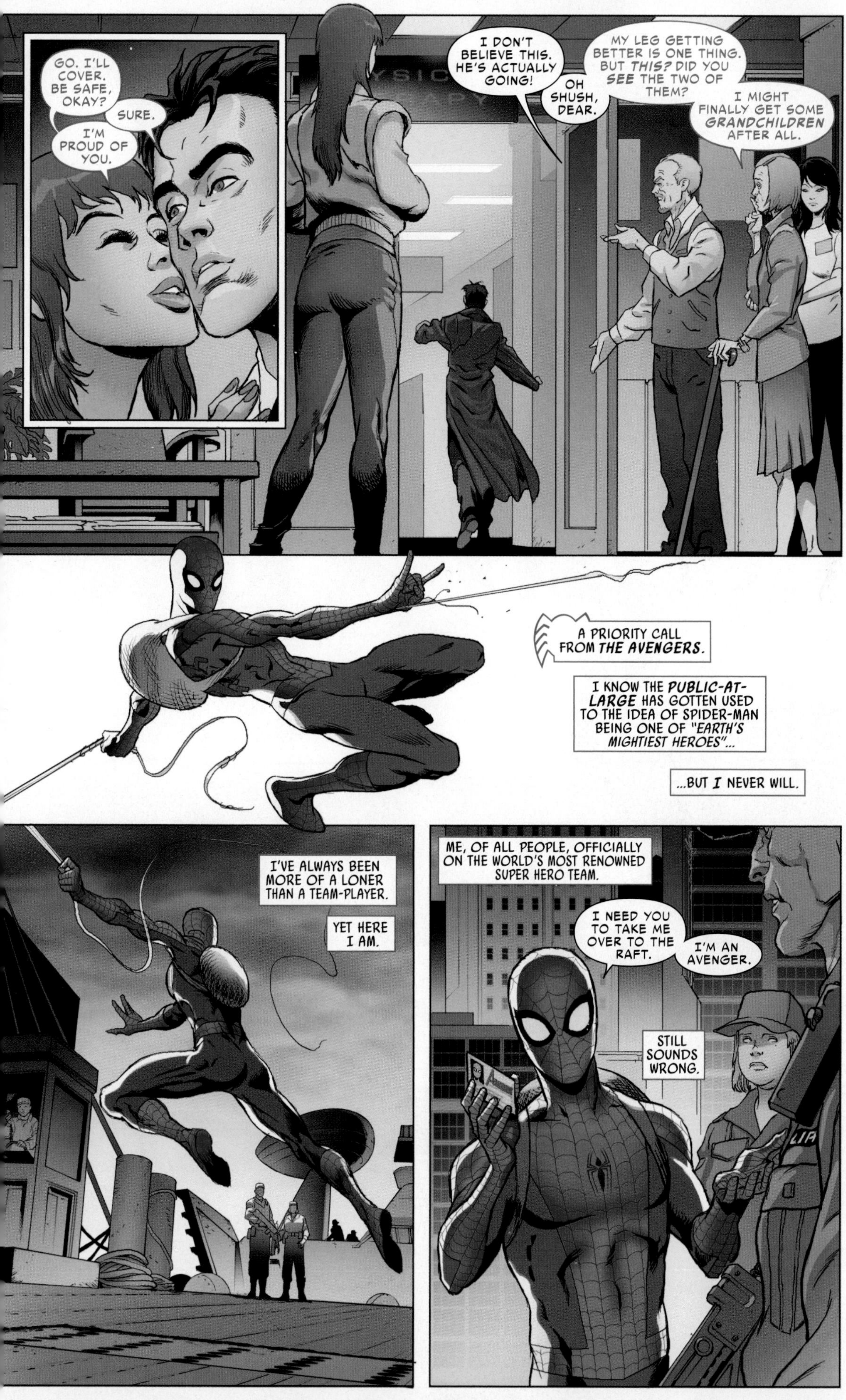
GO. I'LL COVER. BE SAFE, OKAY?
SURE.
I'M PROUD OF YOU.
I DON'T BELIEVE THIS. HE'S ACTUALLY GOING!
OH SHUSH, DEAR.
MY LEG GETTING BETTER IS ONE THING. BUT THIS? DID YOU SEE THE TWO OF THEM?
I MIGHT FINALLY GET SOME GRANDCHILDREN AFTER ALL.
A PRIORITY CALL FROM THE AVENGERS.
I KNOW THE PUBLIC-AT-LARGE HAS GOTTEN USED TO THE IDEA OF SPIDER-MAN BEING ONE OF "EARTH'S MIGHTIEST HEROES"...
...BUT I NEVER WILL.
I'VE ALWAYS BEEN MORE OF A LONER THAN A TEAM-PLAYER.
YET HERE I AM.
ME, OF ALL PEOPLE, OFFICIALLY ON THE WORLD'S MOST RENOWNED SUPER HERO TEAM.
I NEED YOU TO TAKE ME OVER TO THE RAFT.
I'M AN AVENGER.
STILL SOUNDS WRONG.

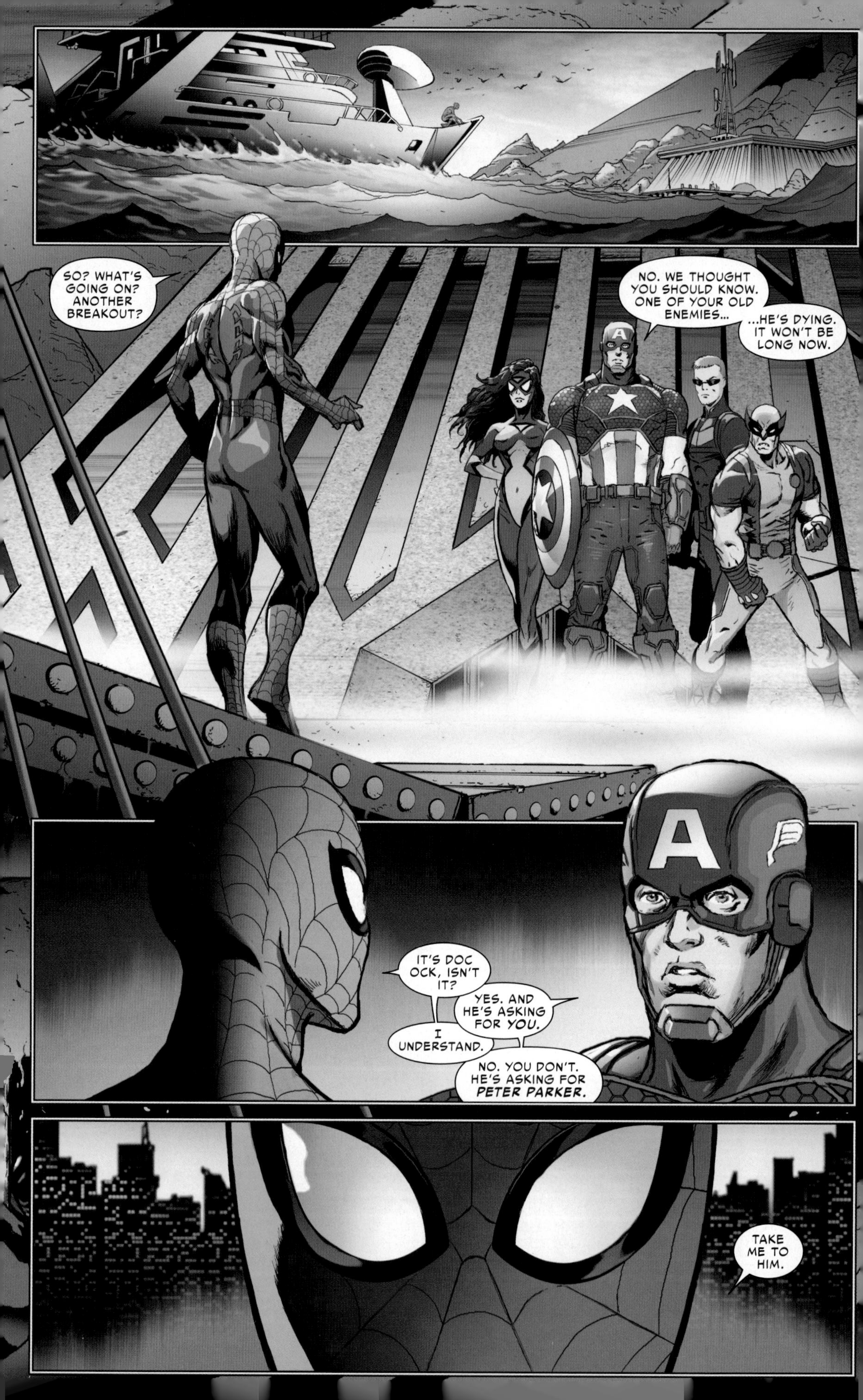
SO? WHAT'S GOING ON? ANOTHER BREAKOUT?
NO. WE THOUGHT YOU SHOULD KNOW. ONE OF YOUR OLD ENEMIES...
...HE'S DYING. IT WON'T BE LONG NOW.
IT'S DOC OCK, ISN'T IT?
YES. AND HE'S ASKING FOR *YOU*.
I UNDERSTAND.
NO. YOU DON'T. HE'S ASKING FOR **PETER PARKER**.
TAKE ME TO HIM.

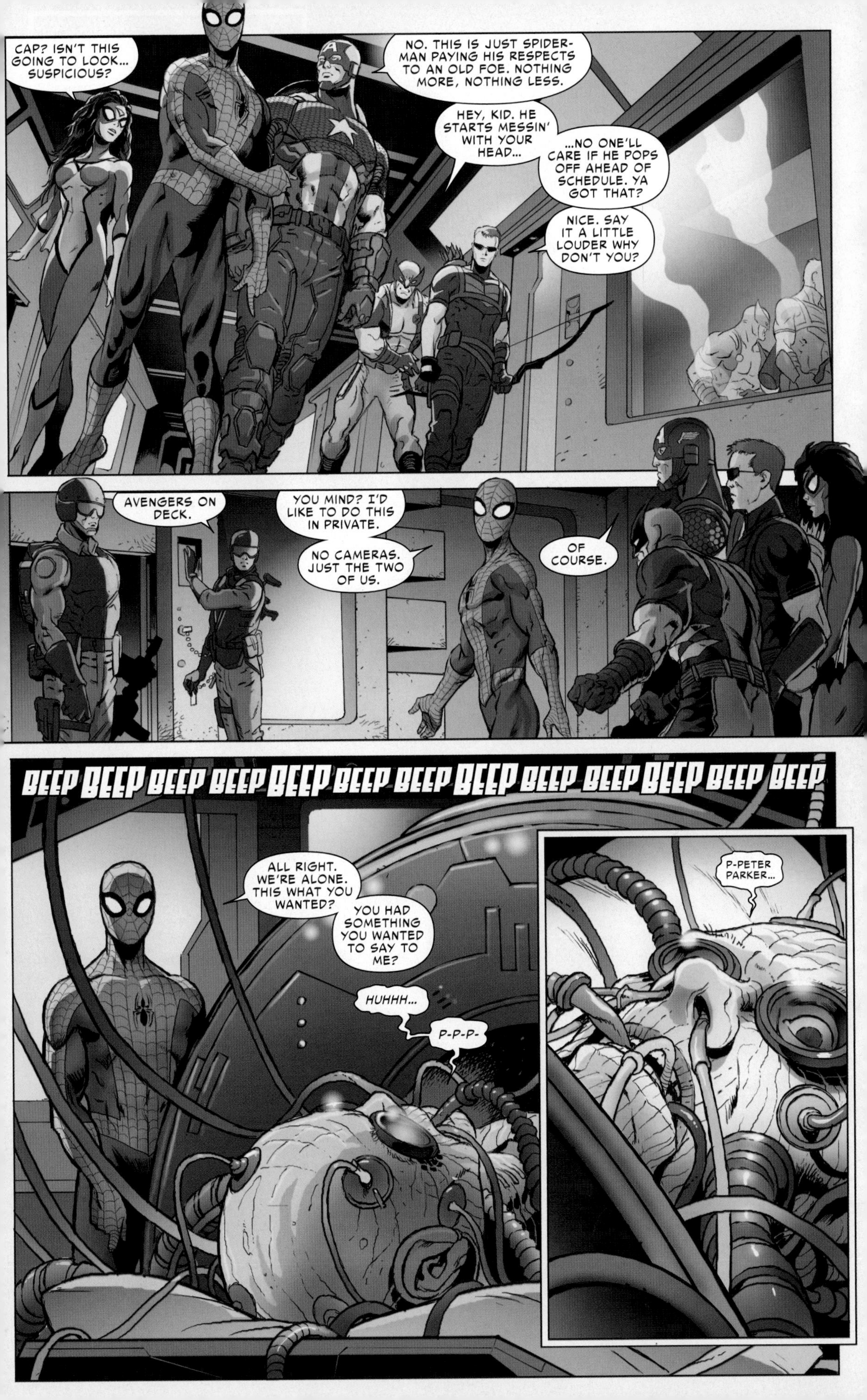
CAP? ISN'T THIS GOING TO LOOK... SUSPICIOUS?
NO. THIS IS JUST SPIDER-MAN PAYING HIS RESPECTS TO AN OLD FOE. NOTHING MORE, NOTHING LESS.
HEY, KID. HE STARTS MESSIN' WITH YOUR HEAD...
...NO ONE'LL CARE IF HE POPS OFF AHEAD OF SCHEDULE. YA GOT THAT?
NICE. SAY IT A LITTLE LOUDER WHY DON'T YOU?
AVENGERS ON DECK.
YOU MIND? I'D LIKE TO DO THIS IN PRIVATE.
NO CAMERAS. JUST THE TWO OF US.
OF COURSE.
BEEP BEEP BEEP BEEP BEEP BEEP BEEP BEEP BEEP BEEP BEEP BEEP BEEP
ALL RIGHT. WE'RE ALONE. THIS WHAT YOU WANTED?
YOU HAD SOMETHING YOU WANTED TO SAY TO ME?
HUHHH...
P-P-P-
P-PETER PARKER...

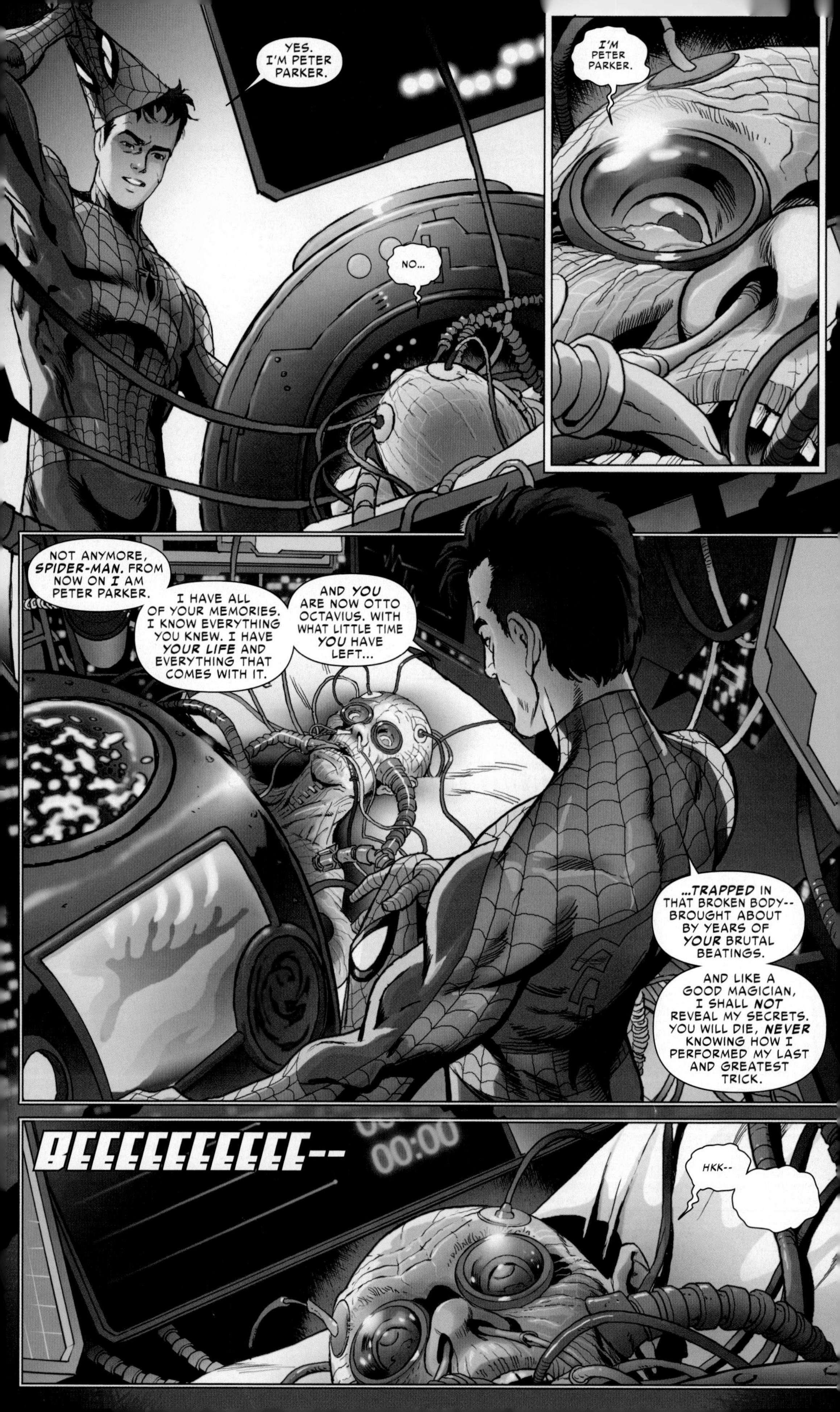
YES. I'M PETER PARKER.
I'M PETER PARKER.
NO...
NOT ANYMORE, SPIDER-MAN. FROM NOW ON I AM PETER PARKER.
I HAVE ALL OF YOUR MEMORIES. I KNOW EVERYTHING YOU KNEW. I HAVE YOUR LIFE AND EVERYTHING THAT COMES WITH IT.
AND YOU ARE NOW OTTO OCTAVIUS. WITH WHAT LITTLE TIME YOU HAVE LEFT...
...TRAPPED IN THAT BROKEN BODY-- BROUGHT ABOUT BY YEARS OF YOUR BRUTAL BEATINGS.
AND LIKE A GOOD MAGICIAN, I SHALL NOT REVEAL MY SECRETS. YOU WILL DIE, NEVER KNOWING HOW I PERFORMED MY LAST AND GREATEST TRICK.
BEEEEEEEEEE--
00:00
HKK--

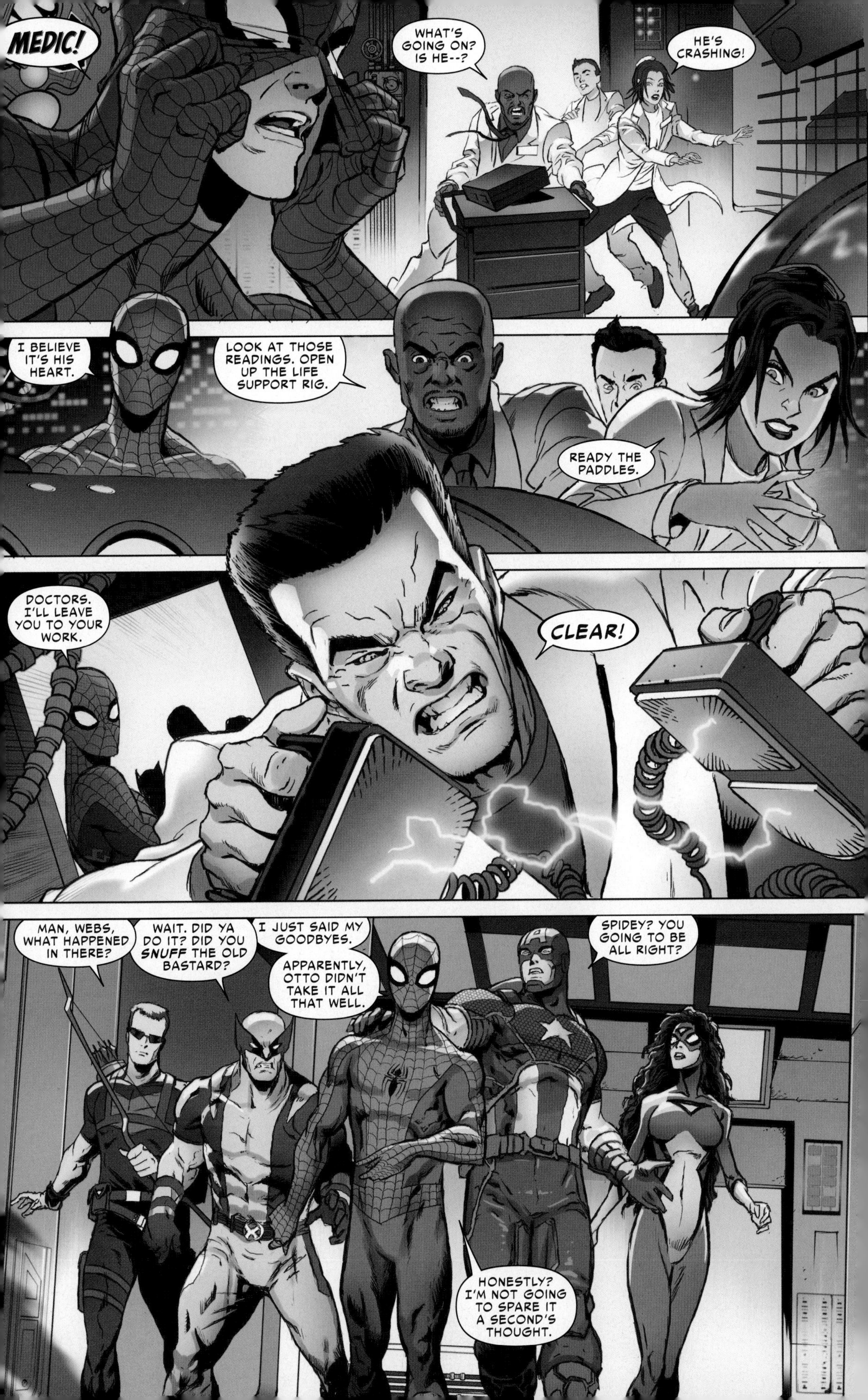
MEDIC!
WHAT'S GOING ON? IS HE--?
HE'S CRASHING!
I BELIEVE IT'S HIS HEART.
LOOK AT THOSE READINGS. OPEN UP THE LIFE SUPPORT RIG.
READY THE PADDLES.
DOCTORS. I'LL LEAVE YOU TO YOUR WORK.
CLEAR!
MAN, WEBS, WHAT HAPPENED IN THERE?
WAIT. DID YA DO IT? DID YOU SNUFF THE OLD BASTARD?
I JUST SAID MY GOODBYES.
APPARENTLY, OTTO DIDN'T TAKE IT ALL THAT WELL.
SPIDEY? YOU GOING TO BE ALL RIGHT?
HONESTLY? I'M NOT GOING TO SPARE IT A SECOND'S THOUGHT.

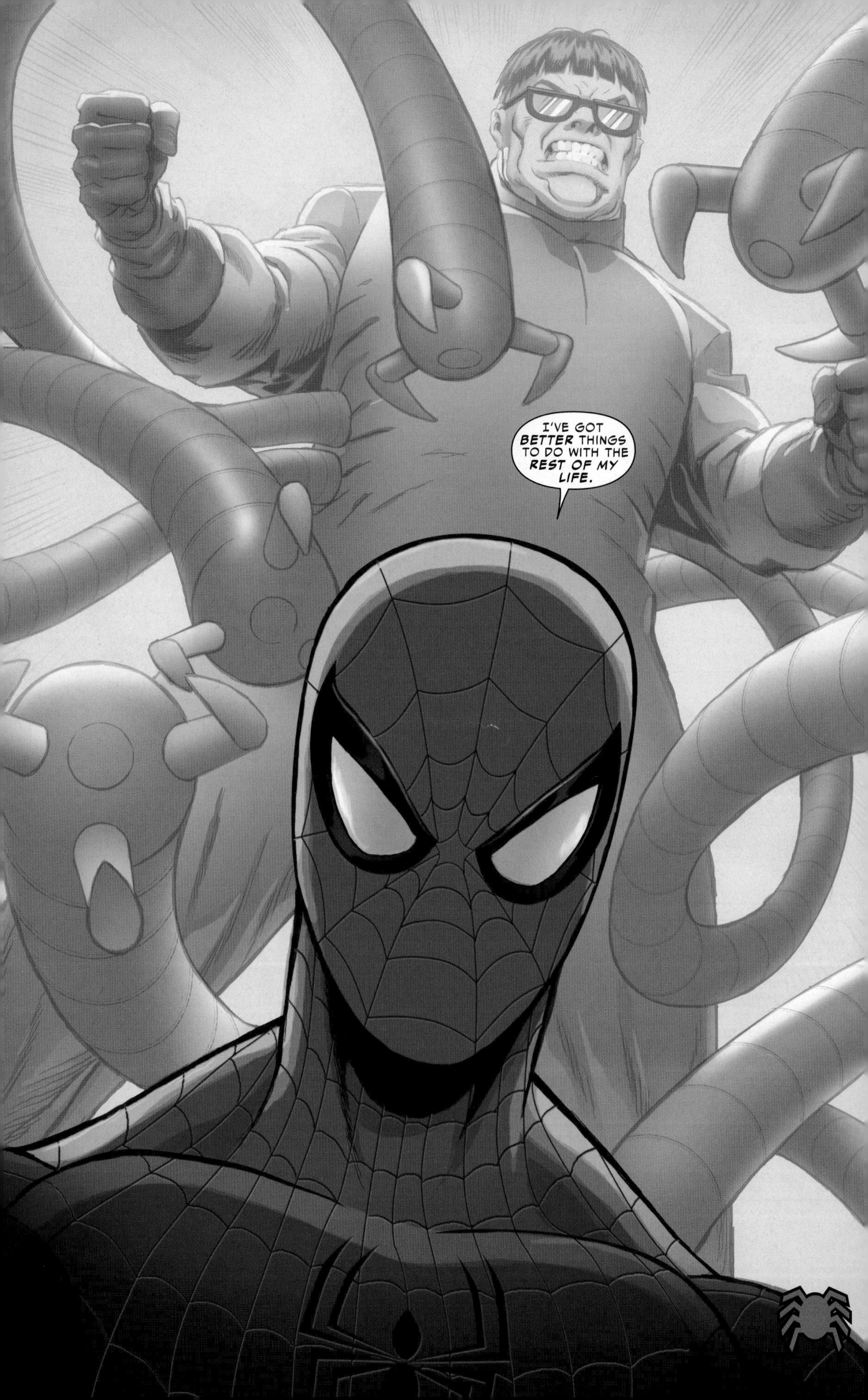
I'VE GOT **BETTER** THINGS TO DO WITH THE ***REST OF MY*** ***LIFE.***

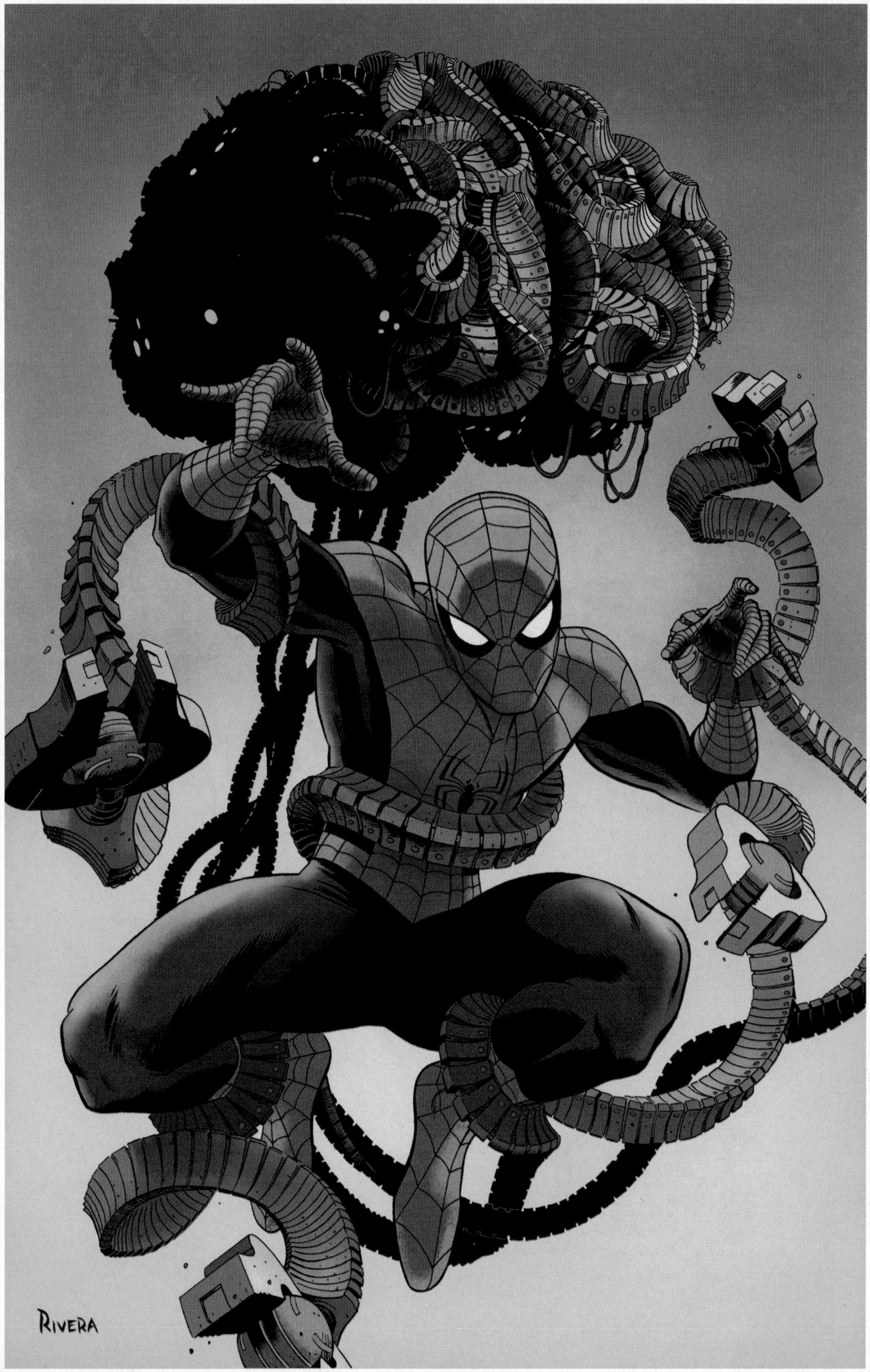
RIVERA

AMAZING SPIDER-MAN #699
COVER BY PAOLO RIVERA

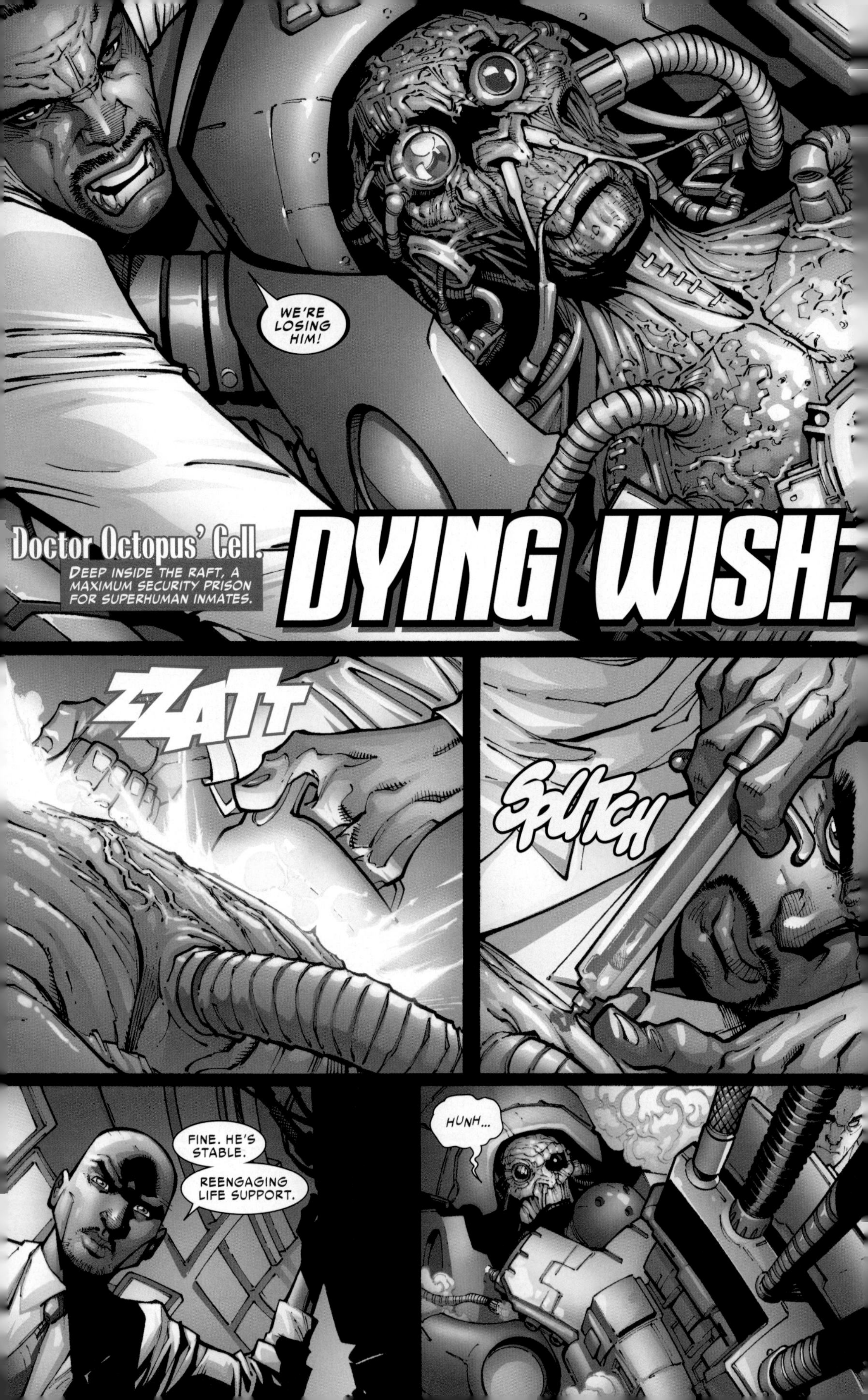
WE'RE LOSING HIM!
Doctor Octopus' Cell.
DEEP INSIDE THE RAFT, A MAXIMUM SECURITY PRISON FOR SUPERHUMAN INMATES.
DYING WISH:
ZZATT
SPLTCH
FINE. HE'S STABLE.
REENGAGING LIFE SUPPORT.
HUNH...

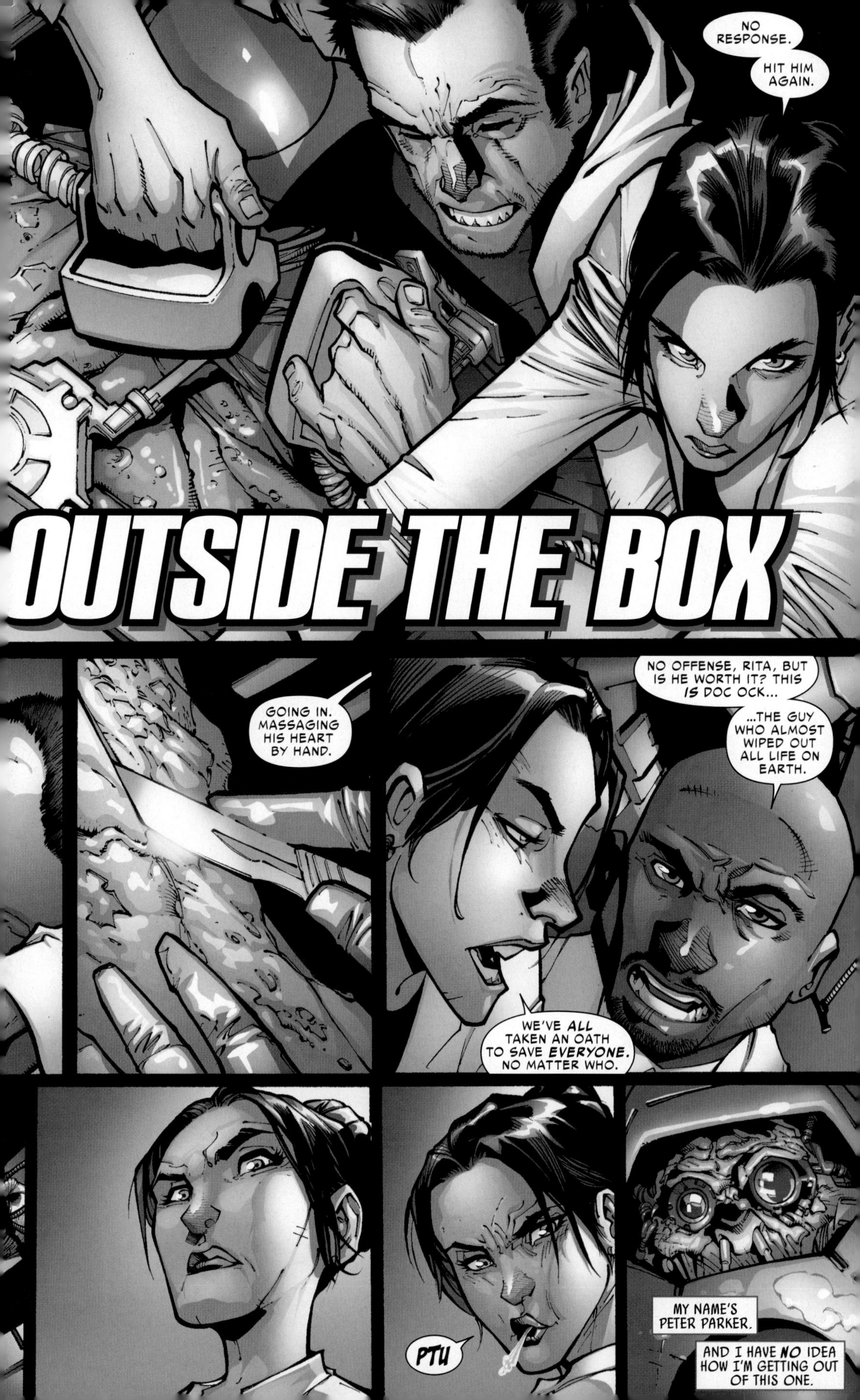
NO RESPONSE.
HIT HIM AGAIN.
OUTSIDE THE BOX
GOING IN. MASSAGING HIS HEART BY HAND.
NO OFFENSE, RITA, BUT IS HE WORTH IT? THIS IS DOC OCK...
...THE GUY WHO ALMOST WIPED OUT ALL LIFE ON EARTH.
WE'VE ALL TAKEN AN OATH TO SAVE EVERYONE. NO MATTER WHO.
PTU
MY NAME'S PETER PARKER.
AND I HAVE NO IDEA HOW I'M GETTING OUT OF THIS ONE.

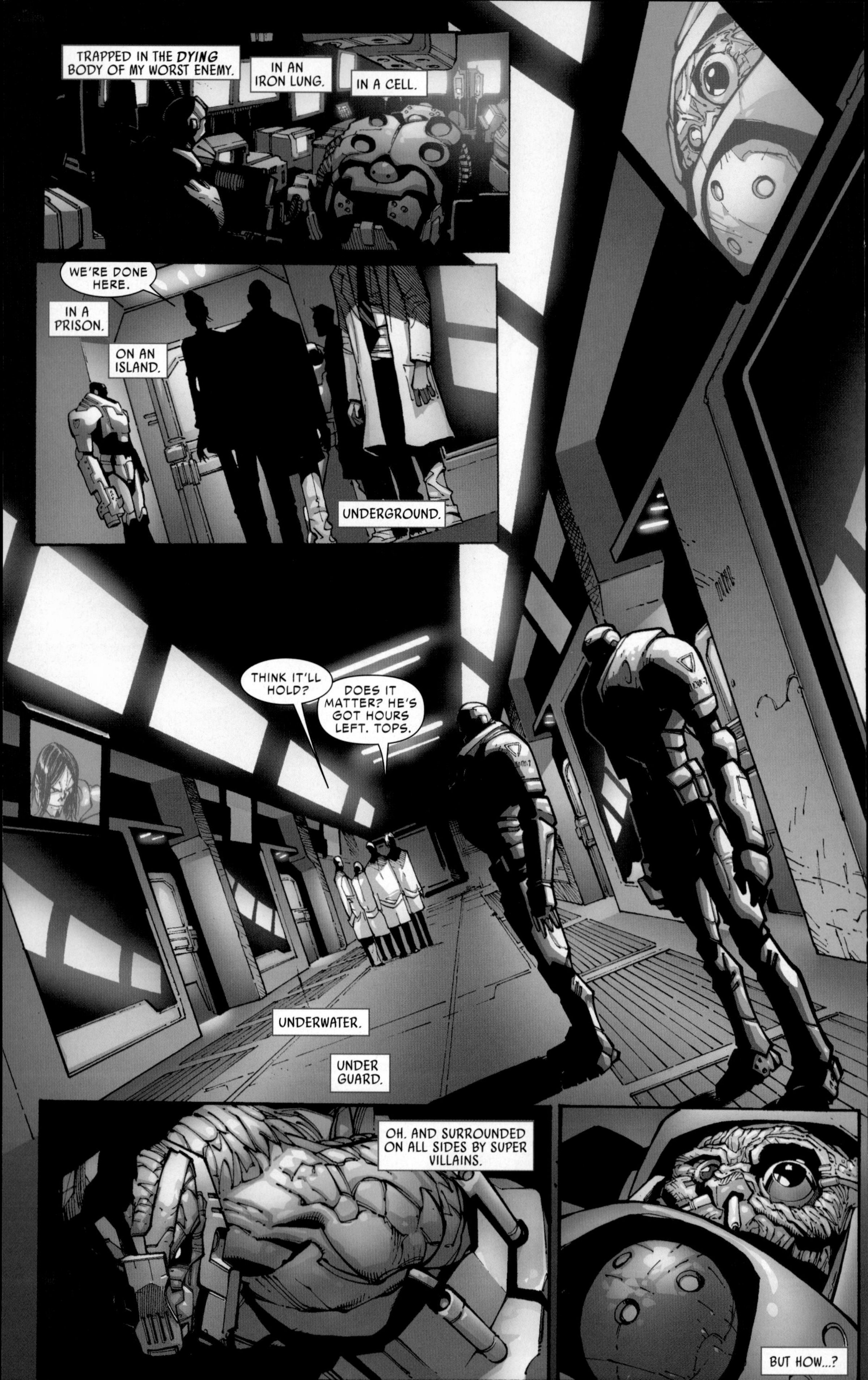
TRAPPED IN THE *DYING* BODY OF MY WORST ENEMY.
IN AN IRON LUNG.
IN A CELL.
WE'RE DONE HERE.
IN A PRISON.
ON AN ISLAND.
UNDERGROUND.
THINK IT'LL HOLD?
DOES IT MATTER? HE'S GOT HOURS LEFT. TOPS.
UNDERWATER.
UNDER GUARD.
OH. AND SURROUNDED ON ALL SIDES BY SUPER VILLAINS.
BUT HOW...?

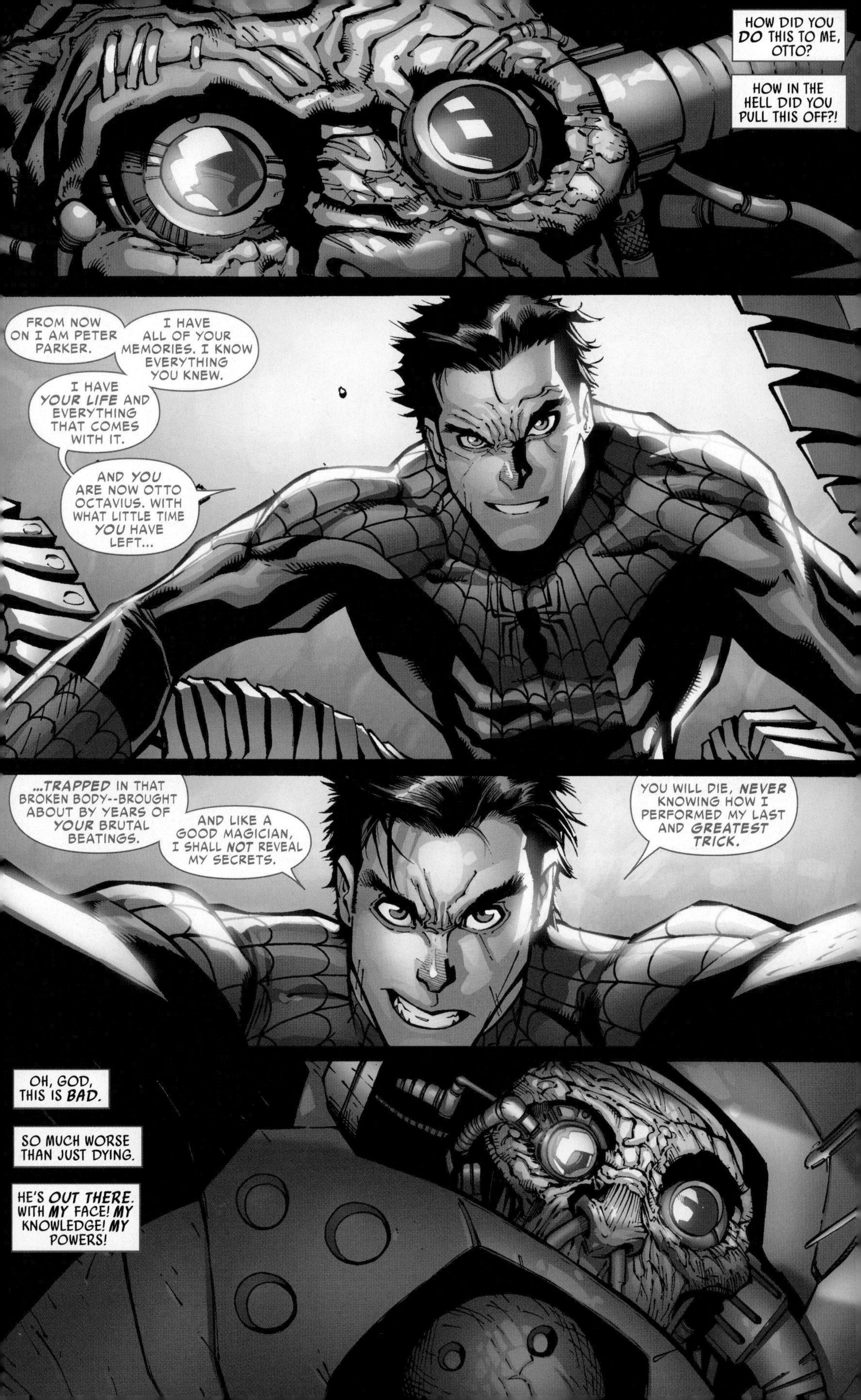
HOW DID YOU DO THIS TO ME, OTTO?
HOW IN THE HELL DID YOU PULL THIS OFF?!
FROM NOW ON I AM PETER PARKER.
I HAVE ALL OF YOUR MEMORIES. I KNOW EVERYTHING YOU KNEW.
I HAVE YOUR LIFE AND EVERYTHING THAT COMES WITH IT.
AND YOU ARE NOW OTTO OCTAVIUS. WITH WHAT LITTLE TIME YOU HAVE LEFT...
...TRAPPED IN THAT BROKEN BODY--BROUGHT ABOUT BY YEARS OF YOUR BRUTAL BEATINGS.
AND LIKE A GOOD MAGICIAN, I SHALL NOT REVEAL MY SECRETS.
YOU WILL DIE, NEVER KNOWING HOW I PERFORMED MY LAST AND GREATEST TRICK.
OH, GOD, THIS IS BAD.
SO MUCH WORSE THAN JUST DYING.
HE'S OUT THERE. WITH MY FACE! MY KNOWLEDGE! MY POWERS!

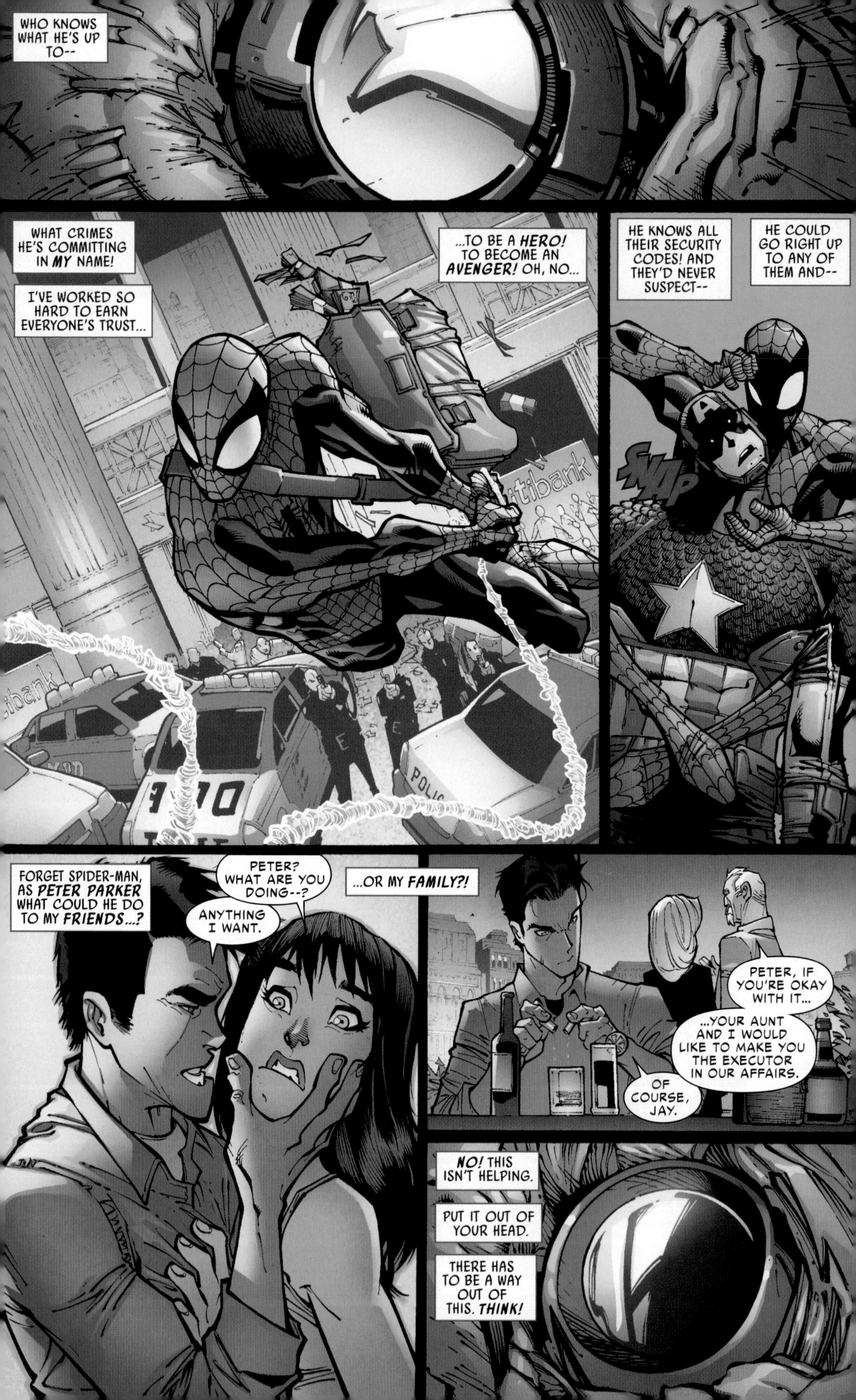
WHO KNOWS WHAT HE'S UP TO--
WHAT CRIMES HE'S COMMITTING IN MY NAME!
I'VE WORKED SO HARD TO EARN EVERYONE'S TRUST...
...TO BE A HERO! TO BECOME AN AVENGER! OH, NO...
HE KNOWS ALL THEIR SECURITY CODES! AND THEY'D NEVER SUSPECT--
HE COULD GO RIGHT UP TO ANY OF THEM AND--
SNAP
FORGET SPIDER-MAN, AS PETER PARKER WHAT COULD HE DO TO MY FRIENDS...?
PETER? WHAT ARE YOU DOING--?
ANYTHING I WANT.
...OR MY FAMILY?!
PETER, IF YOU'RE OKAY WITH IT...
...YOUR AUNT AND I WOULD LIKE TO MAKE YOU THE EXECUTOR IN OUR AFFAIRS.
OF COURSE, JAY.
NO! THIS ISN'T HELPING.
PUT IT OUT OF YOUR HEAD.
THERE HAS TO BE A WAY OUT OF THIS. THINK!

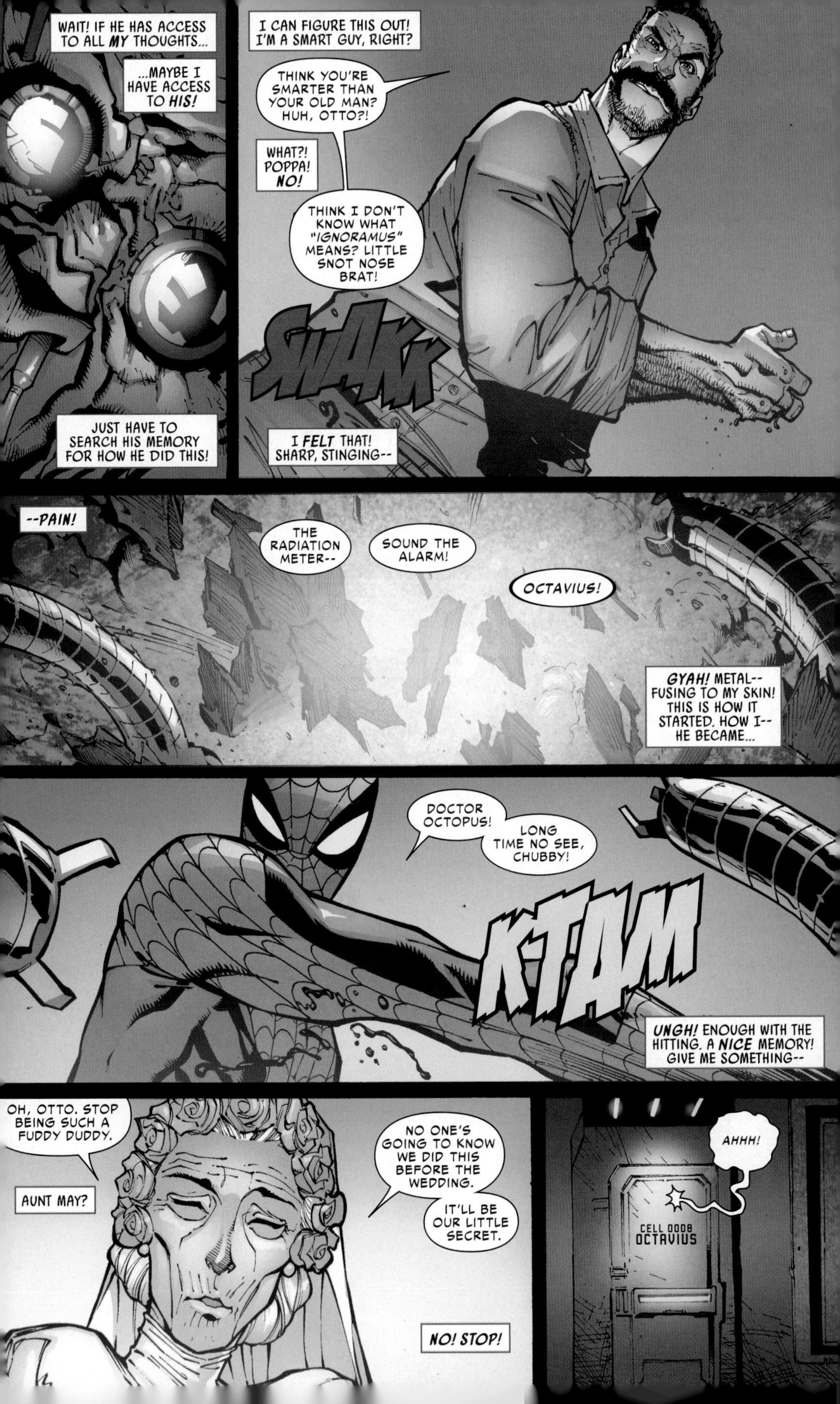
WAIT! IF HE HAS ACCESS TO ALL MY THOUGHTS...
...MAYBE I HAVE ACCESS TO HIS!
JUST HAVE TO SEARCH HIS MEMORY FOR HOW HE DID THIS!
I CAN FIGURE THIS OUT! I'M A SMART GUY, RIGHT?
THINK YOU'RE SMARTER THAN YOUR OLD MAN? HUH, OTTO?!
WHAT?! POPPA! NO!
THINK I DON'T KNOW WHAT "IGNORAMUS" MEANS? LITTLE SNOT NOSE BRAT!
SWAKK
I FELT THAT! SHARP, STINGING--
--PAIN!
THE RADIATION METER--
SOUND THE ALARM!
OCTAVIUS!
GYAH! METAL--FUSING TO MY SKIN! THIS IS HOW IT STARTED. HOW I--HE BECAME...
DOCTOR OCTOPUS!
LONG TIME NO SEE, CHUBBY!
K-TAM
UNGH! ENOUGH WITH THE HITTING. A NICE MEMORY! GIVE ME SOMETHING--
OH, OTTO. STOP BEING SUCH A FUDDY DUDDY.
AUNT MAY?
NO ONE'S GOING TO KNOW WE DID THIS BEFORE THE WEDDING.
IT'LL BE OUR LITTLE SECRET.
NO! STOP!
AHHH!
CELL 0008 OCTAVIUS

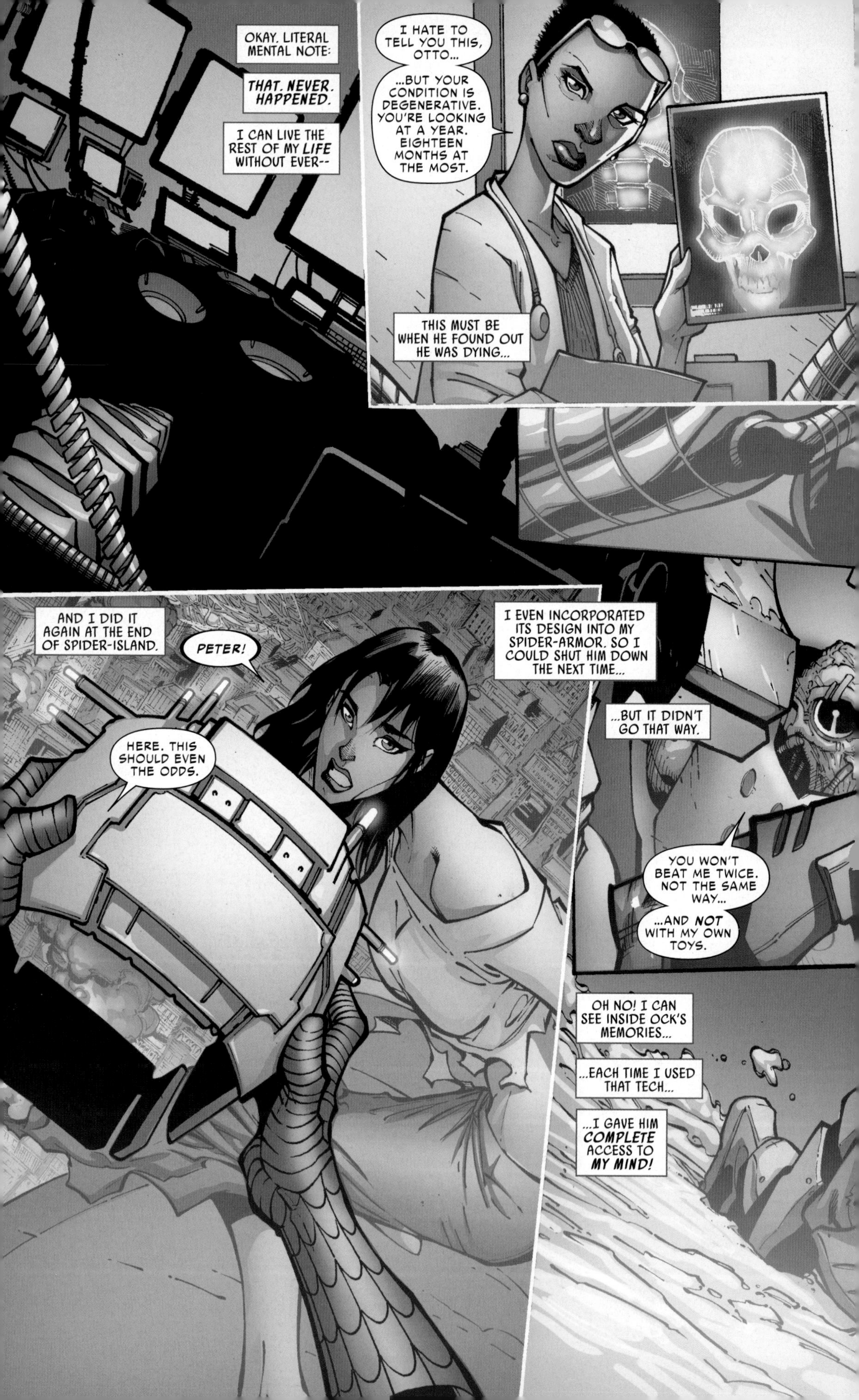

OKAY. LITERAL MENTAL NOTE:
THAT. NEVER. HAPPENED.
I CAN LIVE THE REST OF MY LIFE WITHOUT EVER--
I HATE TO TELL YOU THIS, OTTO...
...BUT YOUR CONDITION IS DEGENERATIVE. YOU'RE LOOKING AT A YEAR. EIGHTEEN MONTHS AT THE MOST.
THIS MUST BE WHEN HE FOUND OUT HE WAS DYING...
AND I DID IT AGAIN AT THE END OF SPIDER-ISLAND.
PETER!
HERE. THIS SHOULD EVEN THE ODDS.
I EVEN INCORPORATED ITS DESIGN INTO MY SPIDER-ARMOR. SO I COULD SHUT HIM DOWN THE NEXT TIME...
...BUT IT DIDN'T GO THAT WAY.
YOU WON'T BEAT ME TWICE. NOT THE SAME WAY...
...AND NOT WITH MY OWN TOYS.
OH NO! I CAN SEE INSIDE OCK'S MEMORIES...
...EACH TIME I USED THAT TECH...
...I GAVE HIM COMPLETE ACCESS TO MY MIND!

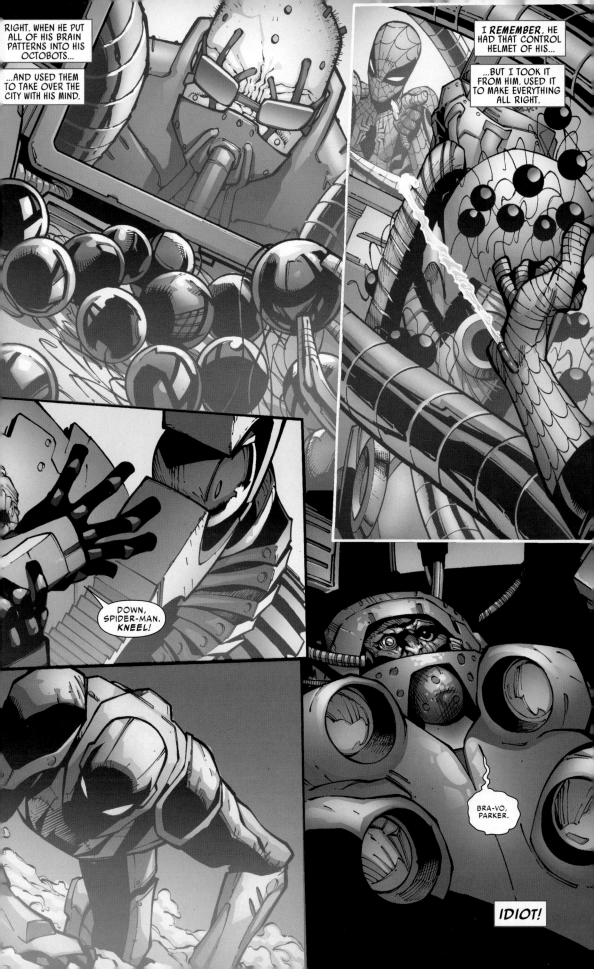

RIGHT. WHEN HE PUT ALL OF HIS BRAIN PATTERNS INTO HIS OCTOBOTS...

...AND USED THEM TO TAKE OVER THE CITY WITH HIS MIND.

I *REMEMBER*. HE HAD THAT CONTROL HELMET OF HIS...

...BUT I TOOK IT FROM HIM. USED IT TO MAKE EVERYTHING ALL RIGHT.

DOWN, SPIDER-MAN. *KNEEL!*

BRA-VO, PARKER.

IDIOT!

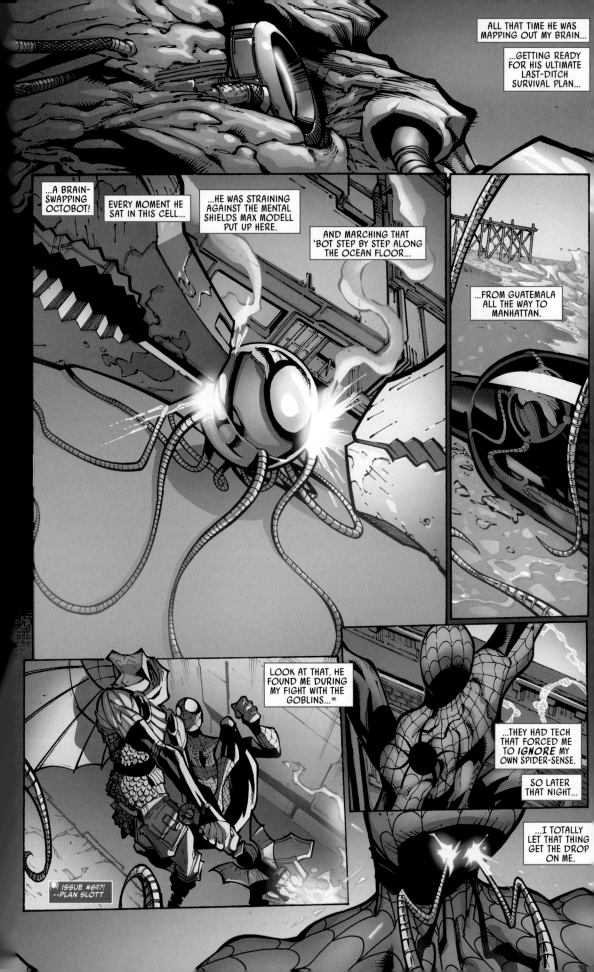

ALL THAT TIME HE WAS MAPPING OUT MY BRAIN...

...GETTING READY FOR HIS ULTIMATE LAST-DITCH SURVIVAL PLAN...

...A BRAIN-SWAPPING OCTOBOT!

EVERY MOMENT HE SAT IN THIS CELL...

...HE WAS STRAINING AGAINST THE MENTAL SHIELDS MAX MODELL PUT UP HERE.

AND MARCHING THAT 'BOT STEP BY STEP ALONG THE OCEAN FLOOR...

...FROM GUATEMALA ALL THE WAY TO MANHATTAN.

LOOK AT THAT. HE FOUND ME DURING MY FIGHT WITH THE GOBLINS...*

...THEY HAD TECH THAT FORCED ME TO *IGNORE* MY OWN SPIDER-SENSE.

SO LATER THAT NIGHT...

...I TOTALLY LET THAT THING GET THE DROP ON ME.

*ISSUE #697!
--PLAN SLOTT

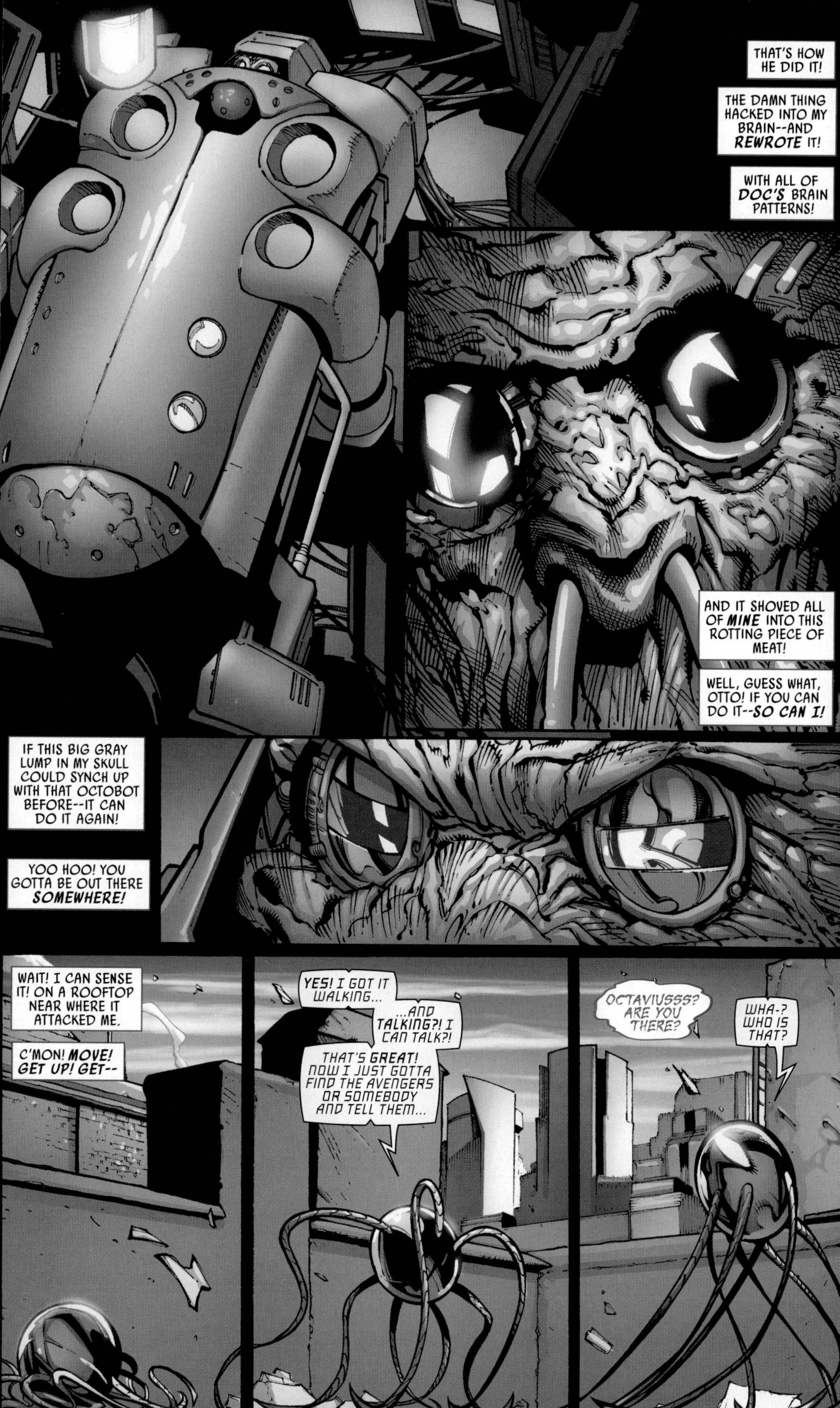
THAT'S HOW HE DID IT!
THE DAMN THING HACKED INTO MY BRAIN--AND *REWROTE* IT!
WITH ALL OF *DOC'S* BRAIN PATTERNS!
AND IT SHOVED ALL OF *MINE* INTO THIS ROTTING PIECE OF MEAT!
WELL, GUESS WHAT, OTTO! IF YOU CAN DO IT--*SO CAN I!*
IF THIS BIG GRAY LUMP IN MY SKULL COULD SYNCH UP WITH THAT OCTOBOT BEFORE--IT CAN DO IT AGAIN!
YOO HOO! YOU GOTTA BE OUT THERE *SOMEWHERE!*
WAIT! I CAN SENSE IT! ON A ROOFTOP NEAR WHERE IT ATTACKED ME.
C'MON! *MOVE! GET UP! GET--*
YES! I GOT IT WALKING...
...AND *TALKING?!* I CAN TALK?!
THAT'S *GREAT!* NOW I JUST GOTTA FIND THE AVENGERS OR SOMEBODY AND TELL THEM...
OCTAVIUSSS? ARE YOU THERE?
WHA-? WHO IS THAT?

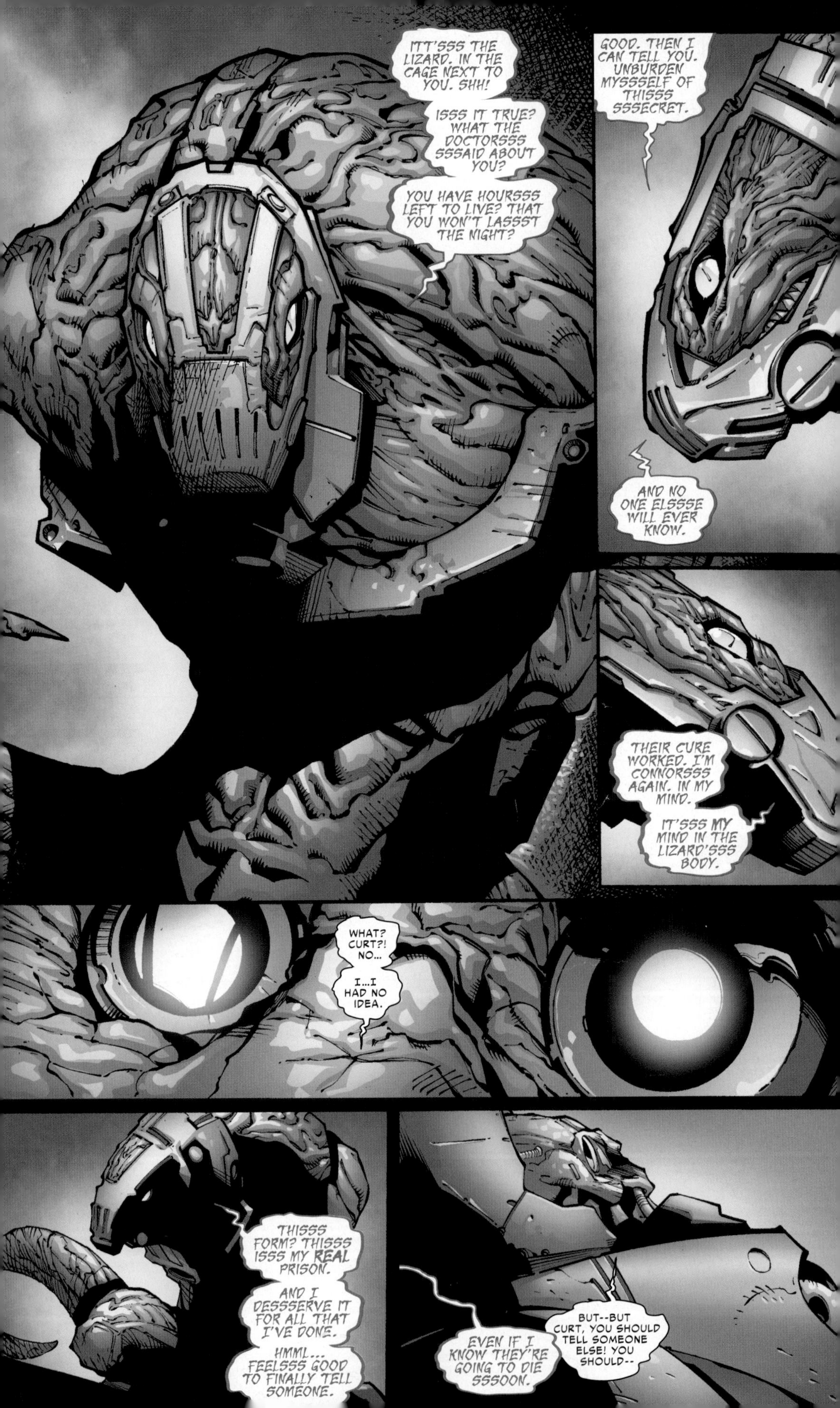

ITT'SSS THE LIZARD. IN THE CAGE NEXT TO YOU. SHH!
ISSS IT TRUE? WHAT THE DOCTORSSS SSSAID ABOUT YOU?
YOU HAVE HOURSSS LEFT TO LIVE? THAT YOU WON'T LASSST THE NIGHT?
GOOD. THEN I CAN TELL YOU. UNBURDEN MYSSSELF OF THISSS SSSECRET.
AND NO ONE ELSSSE WILL EVER KNOW.
THEIR CURE WORKED. I'M CONNORSSS AGAIN. IN MY MIND.
IT'SSS MY MIND IN THE LIZARD'SSS BODY.
WHAT? CURT?! NO...
I...I HAD NO IDEA.
THISSS FORM? THISSS ISSS MY **REAL** PRISON.
AND I DESSSERVE IT FOR ALL THAT I'VE DONE.
HMML... FEELSSS GOOD TO FINALLY TELL SOMEONE.
EVEN IF I KNOW THEY'RE GOING TO DIE SSSOON.
BUT--BUT CURT, YOU SHOULD TELL SOMEONE ELSE! YOU SHOULD--

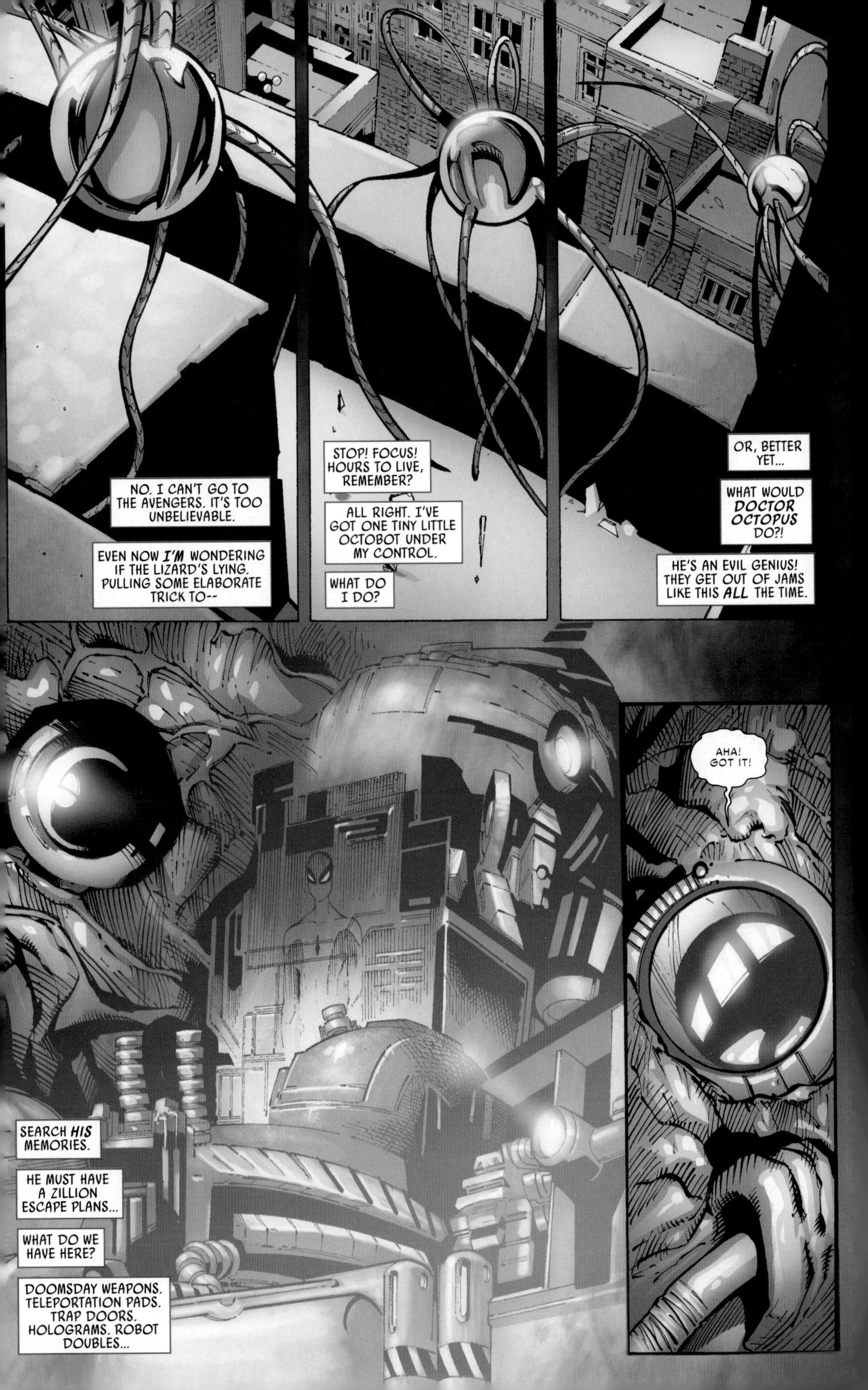
NO. I CAN'T GO TO THE AVENGERS. IT'S TOO UNBELIEVABLE.
EVEN NOW I'M WONDERING IF THE LIZARD'S LYING. PULLING SOME ELABORATE TRICK TO--
STOP! FOCUS! HOURS TO LIVE, REMEMBER?
ALL RIGHT. I'VE GOT ONE TINY LITTLE OCTOBOT UNDER MY CONTROL.
WHAT DO I DO?
OR, BETTER YET...
WHAT WOULD DOCTOR OCTOPUS DO?!
HE'S AN EVIL GENIUS! THEY GET OUT OF JAMS LIKE THIS ALL THE TIME.
SEARCH HIS MEMORIES.
HE MUST HAVE A ZILLION ESCAPE PLANS...
WHAT DO WE HAVE HERE?
DOOMSDAY WEAPONS. TELEPORTATION PADS. TRAP DOORS. HOLOGRAMS. ROBOT DOUBLES...
AHA! GOT IT!

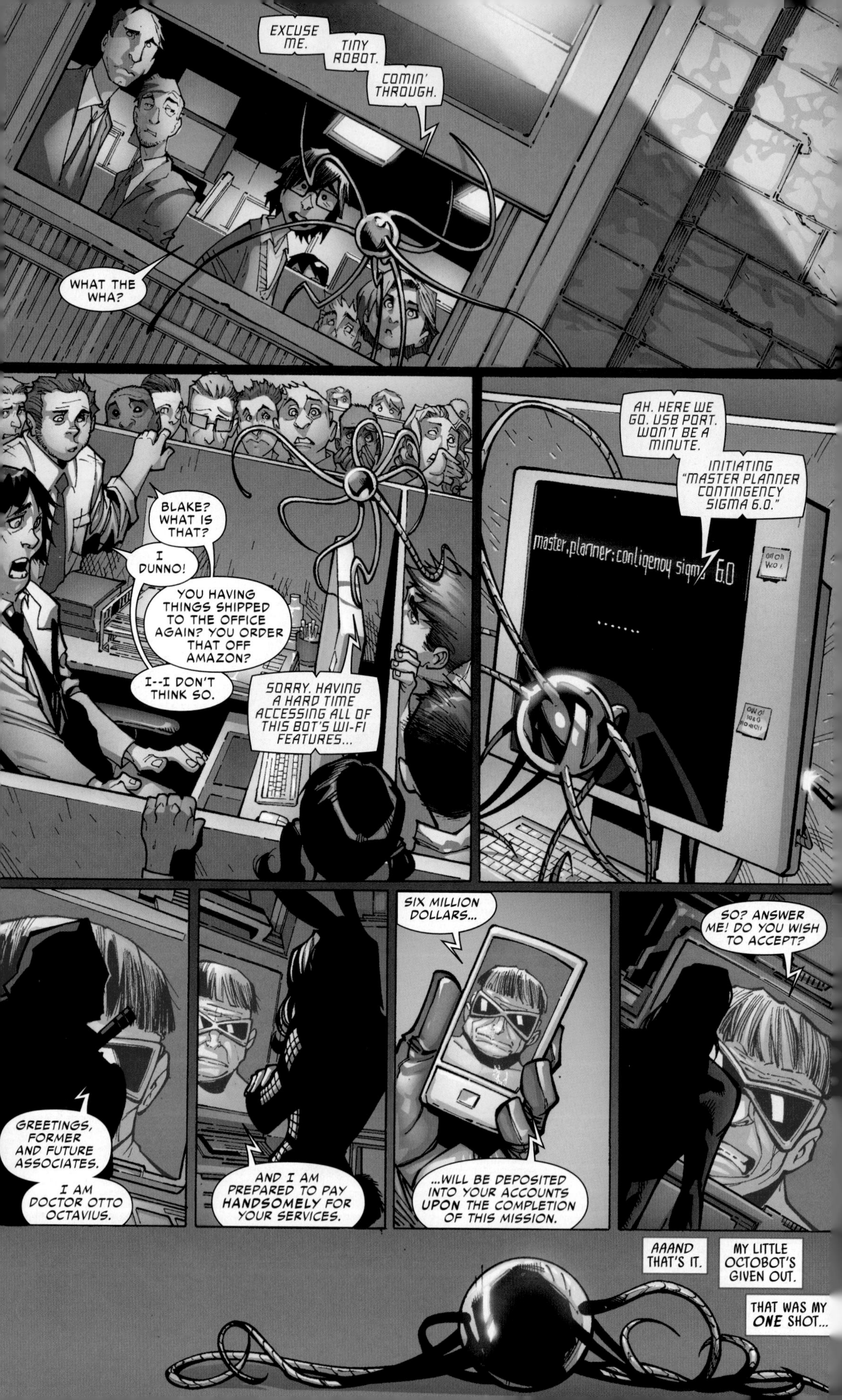

EXCUSE ME.
TINY ROBOT.
COMIN' THROUGH.
WHAT THE WHA?
BLAKE? WHAT IS THAT?
I DUNNO!
YOU HAVING THINGS SHIPPED TO THE OFFICE AGAIN? YOU ORDER THAT OFF AMAZON?
I--I DON'T THINK SO.
SORRY. HAVING A HARD TIME ACCESSING ALL OF THIS BOT'S WI-FI FEATURES...
AH. HERE WE GO. USB PORT. WON'T BE A MINUTE.
INITIATING "MASTER PLANNER CONTINGENCY SIGMA 6.0."
master.planner:contigenoy sigma 6.0
GREETINGS, FORMER AND FUTURE ASSOCIATES.
I AM DOCTOR OTTO OCTAVIUS.
AND I AM PREPARED TO PAY HANDSOMELY FOR YOUR SERVICES.
SIX MILLION DOLLARS...
...WILL BE DEPOSITED INTO YOUR ACCOUNTS UPON THE COMPLETION OF THIS MISSION.
SO? ANSWER ME! DO YOU WISH TO ACCEPT?
AAAND THAT'S IT.
MY LITTLE OCTOBOT'S GIVEN OUT.
THAT WAS MY ONE SHOT...

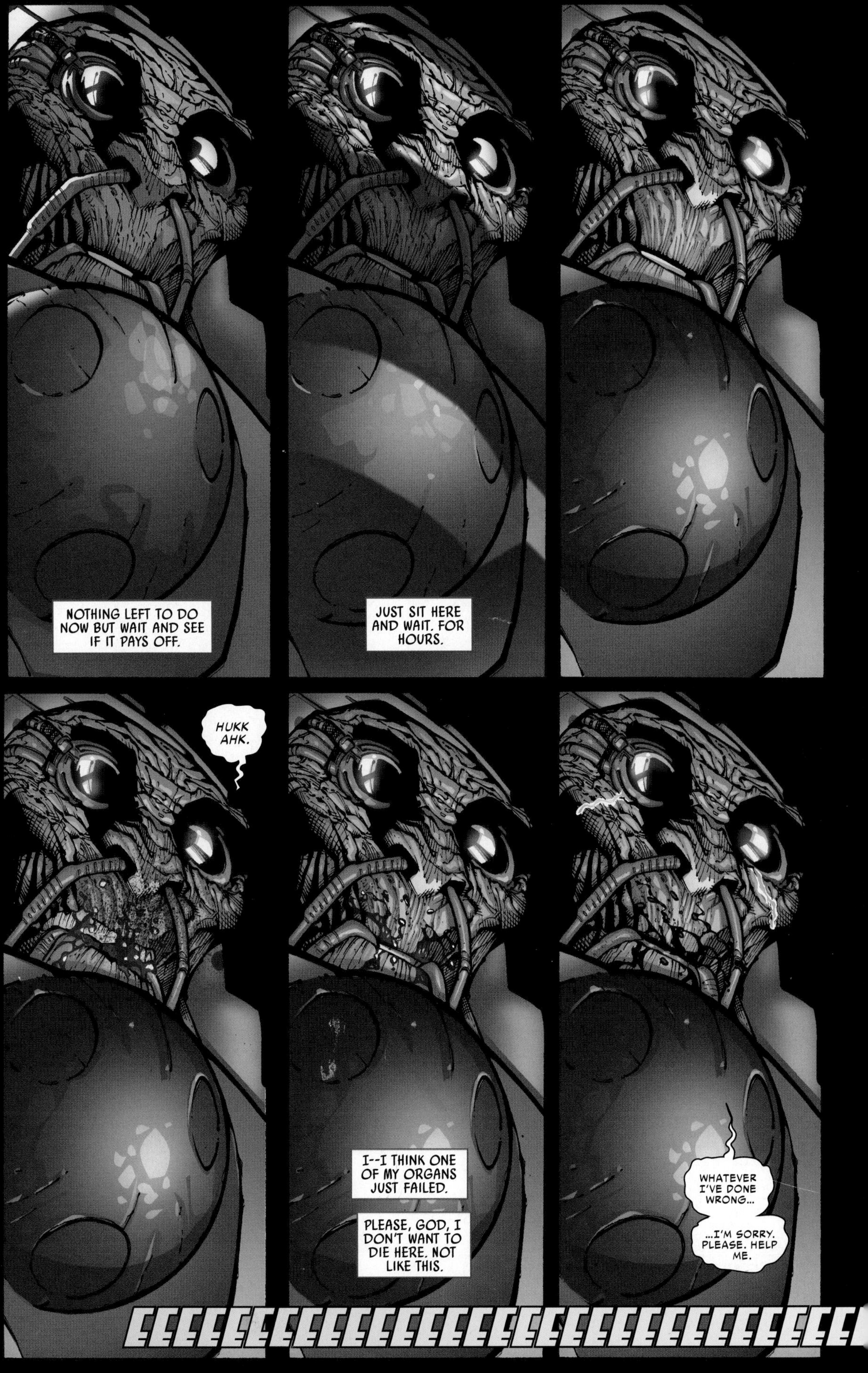
NOTHING LEFT TO DO NOW BUT WAIT AND SEE IF IT PAYS OFF.
JUST SIT HERE AND WAIT. FOR HOURS.
HUKK AHK.
I--I THINK ONE OF MY ORGANS JUST FAILED.
PLEASE, GOD, I DON'T WANT TO DIE HERE. NOT LIKE THIS.
WHATEVER I'VE DONE WRONG...
...I'M SORRY. PLEASE. HELP ME.
EEEEEEEEEEEEEEEEEEEEEEEEEEEEEEEEEEEEEEEEEEEEEE

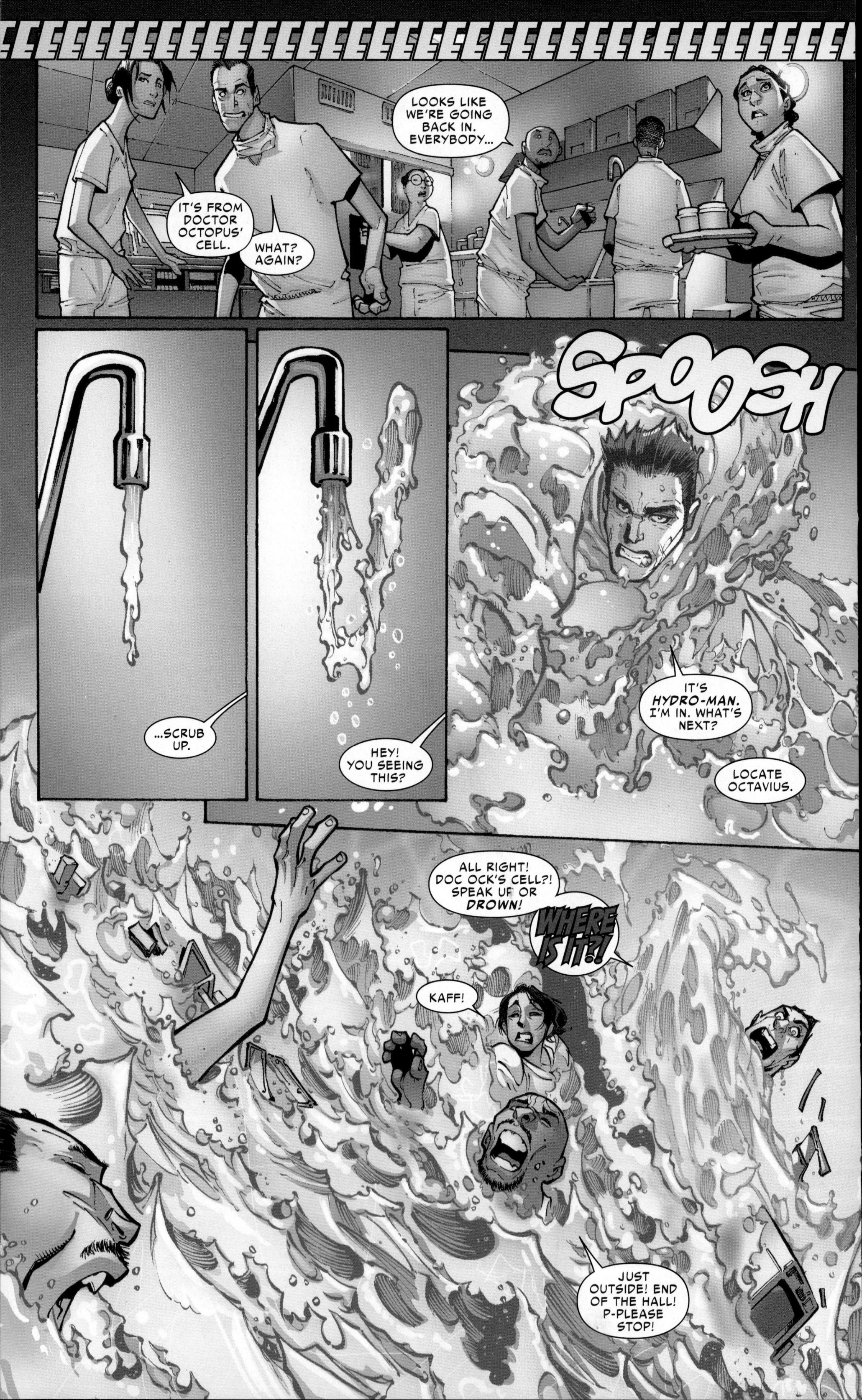
EEEEEEEEEEEEEEEEEEEEEEEEEEEEEEEEEEE
LOOKS LIKE WE'RE GOING BACK IN. EVERYBODY...
IT'S FROM DOCTOR OCTOPUS' CELL.
WHAT? AGAIN?
...SCRUB UP.
HEY! YOU SEEING THIS?
SPOOSH
IT'S HYDRO-MAN. I'M IN. WHAT'S NEXT?
LOCATE OCTAVIUS.
ALL RIGHT! DOC OCK'S CELL?! SPEAK UP OR DROWN!
WHERE IS IT?!
KAFF!
JUST OUTSIDE! END OF THE HALL! P-PLEASE STOP!

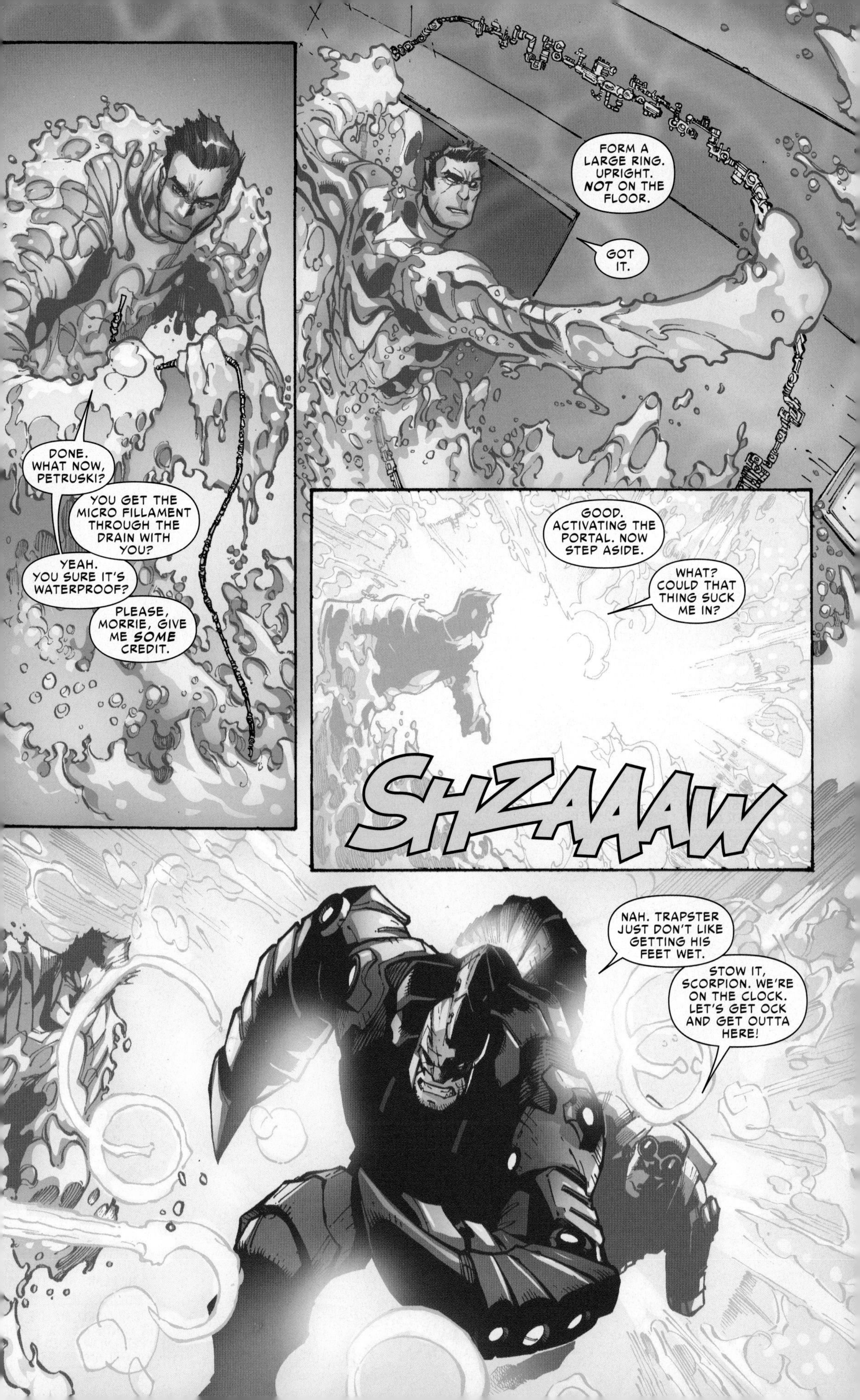
DONE. WHAT NOW, PETRUSKI?
YOU GET THE MICRO FILLAMENT THROUGH THE DRAIN WITH YOU?
YEAH. YOU SURE IT'S WATERPROOF?
PLEASE, MORRIE, GIVE ME SOME CREDIT.
FORM A LARGE RING. UPRIGHT. NOT ON THE FLOOR.
GOT IT.
GOOD. ACTIVATING THE PORTAL. NOW STEP ASIDE.
WHAT? COULD THAT THING SUCK ME IN?
SHZAAAW
NAH. TRAPSTER JUST DON'T LIKE GETTING HIS FEET WET.
STOW IT, SCORPION. WE'RE ON THE CLOCK. LET'S GET OCK AND GET OUTTA HERE!

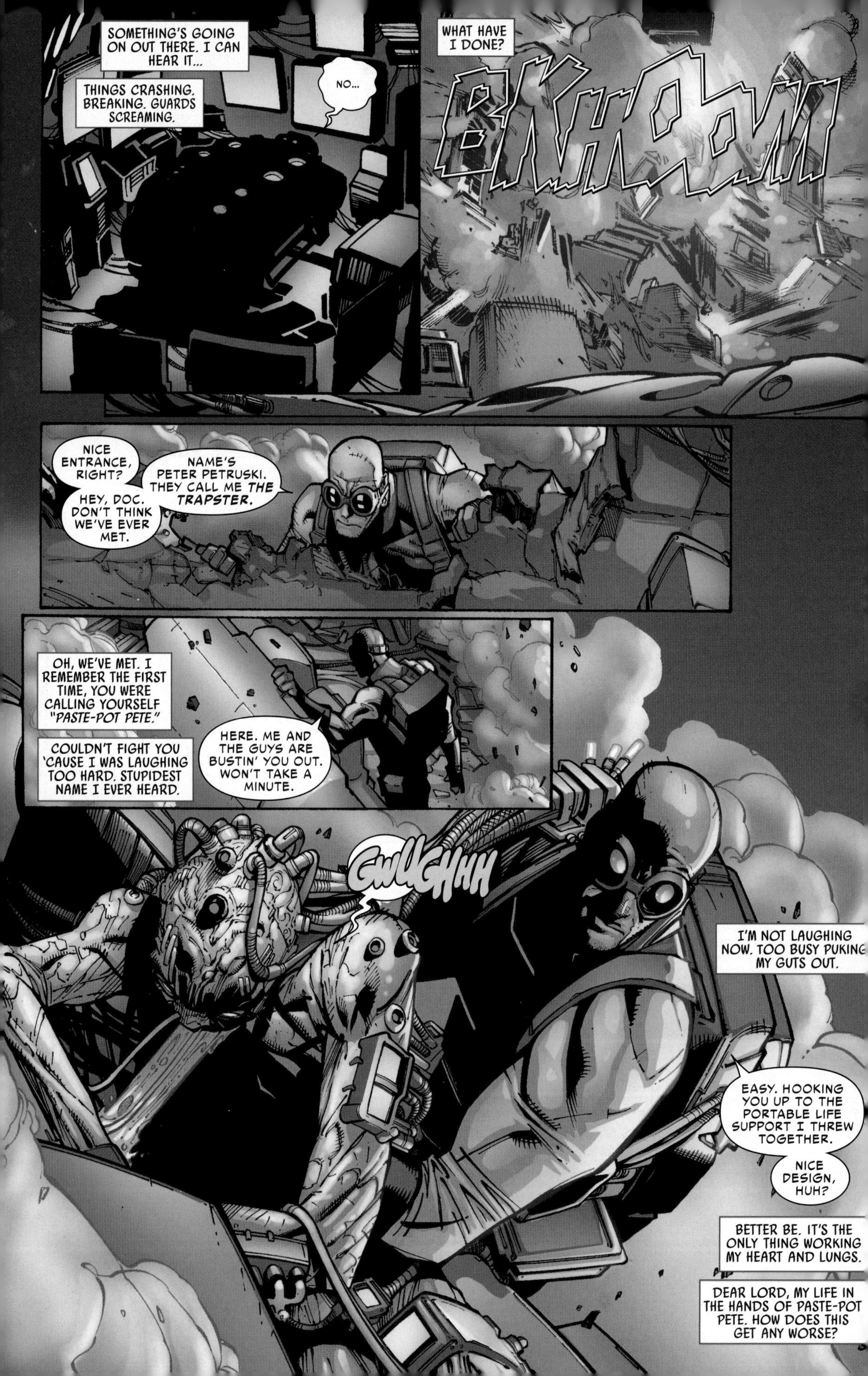
SOMETHING'S GOING ON OUT THERE. I CAN HEAR IT...
THINGS CRASHING. BREAKING. GUARDS SCREAMING.
NO...
WHAT HAVE I DONE?
BKHOOM
NICE ENTRANCE, RIGHT?
HEY, DOC. DON'T THINK WE'VE EVER MET.
NAME'S PETER PETRUSKI. THEY CALL ME *THE TRAPSTER.*
OH, WE'VE MET. I REMEMBER THE FIRST TIME, YOU WERE CALLING YOURSELF *"PASTE-POT PETE."*
COULDN'T FIGHT YOU 'CAUSE I WAS LAUGHING TOO HARD. STUPIDEST NAME I EVER HEARD.
HERE. ME AND THE GUYS ARE BUSTIN' YOU OUT. WON'T TAKE A MINUTE.
GWUUGHHH
I'M NOT LAUGHING NOW. TOO BUSY PUKING MY GUTS OUT.
EASY. HOOKING YOU UP TO THE PORTABLE LIFE SUPPORT I THREW TOGETHER.
NICE DESIGN, HUH?
BETTER BE. IT'S THE ONLY THING WORKING MY HEART AND LUNGS.
DEAR LORD, MY LIFE IN THE HANDS OF PASTE-POT PETE. HOW DOES THIS GET ANY WORSE?

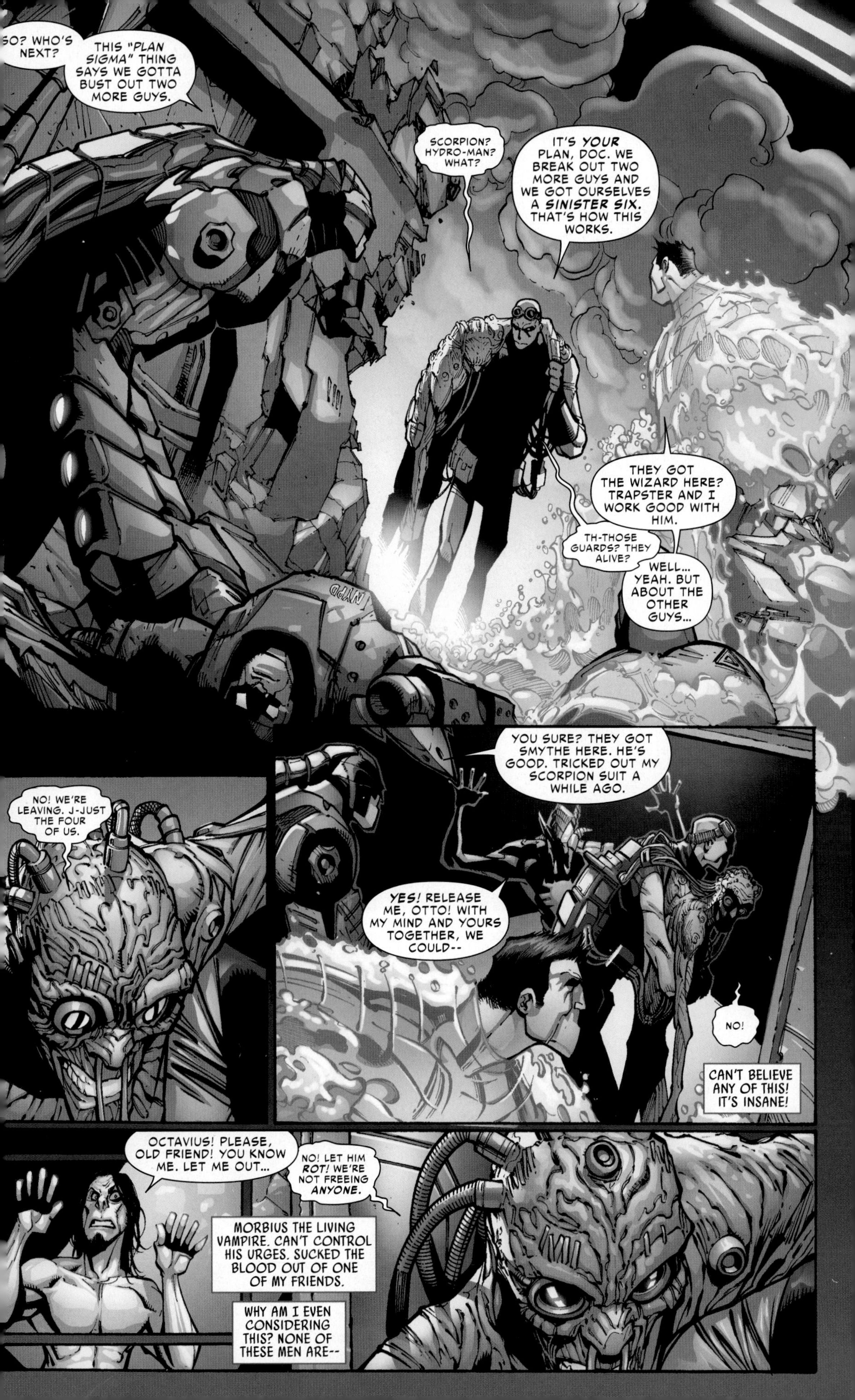
SO? WHO'S NEXT?
THIS "PLAN SIGMA" THING SAYS WE GOTTA BUST OUT TWO MORE GUYS.
SCORPION? HYDRO-MAN? WHAT?
IT'S YOUR PLAN, DOC. WE BREAK OUT TWO MORE GUYS AND WE GOT OURSELVES A SINISTER SIX. THAT'S HOW THIS WORKS.
THEY GOT THE WIZARD HERE? TRAPSTER AND I WORK GOOD WITH HIM.
TH-THOSE GUARDS? THEY ALIVE?
WELL... YEAH. BUT ABOUT THE OTHER GUYS...
NYPD
YOU SURE? THEY GOT SMYTHE HERE. HE'S GOOD. TRICKED OUT MY SCORPION SUIT A WHILE AGO.
NO! WE'RE LEAVING. J-JUST THE FOUR OF US.
YES! RELEASE ME, OTTO! WITH MY MIND AND YOURS TOGETHER, WE COULD--
NO!
CAN'T BELIEVE ANY OF THIS! IT'S INSANE!
OCTAVIUS! PLEASE, OLD FRIEND! YOU KNOW ME. LET ME OUT...
NO! LET HIM ROT! WE'RE NOT FREEING ANYONE.
MORBIUS THE LIVING VAMPIRE. CAN'T CONTROL HIS URGES. SUCKED THE BLOOD OUT OF ONE OF MY FRIENDS.
WHY AM I EVEN CONSIDERING THIS? NONE OF THESE MEN ARE--

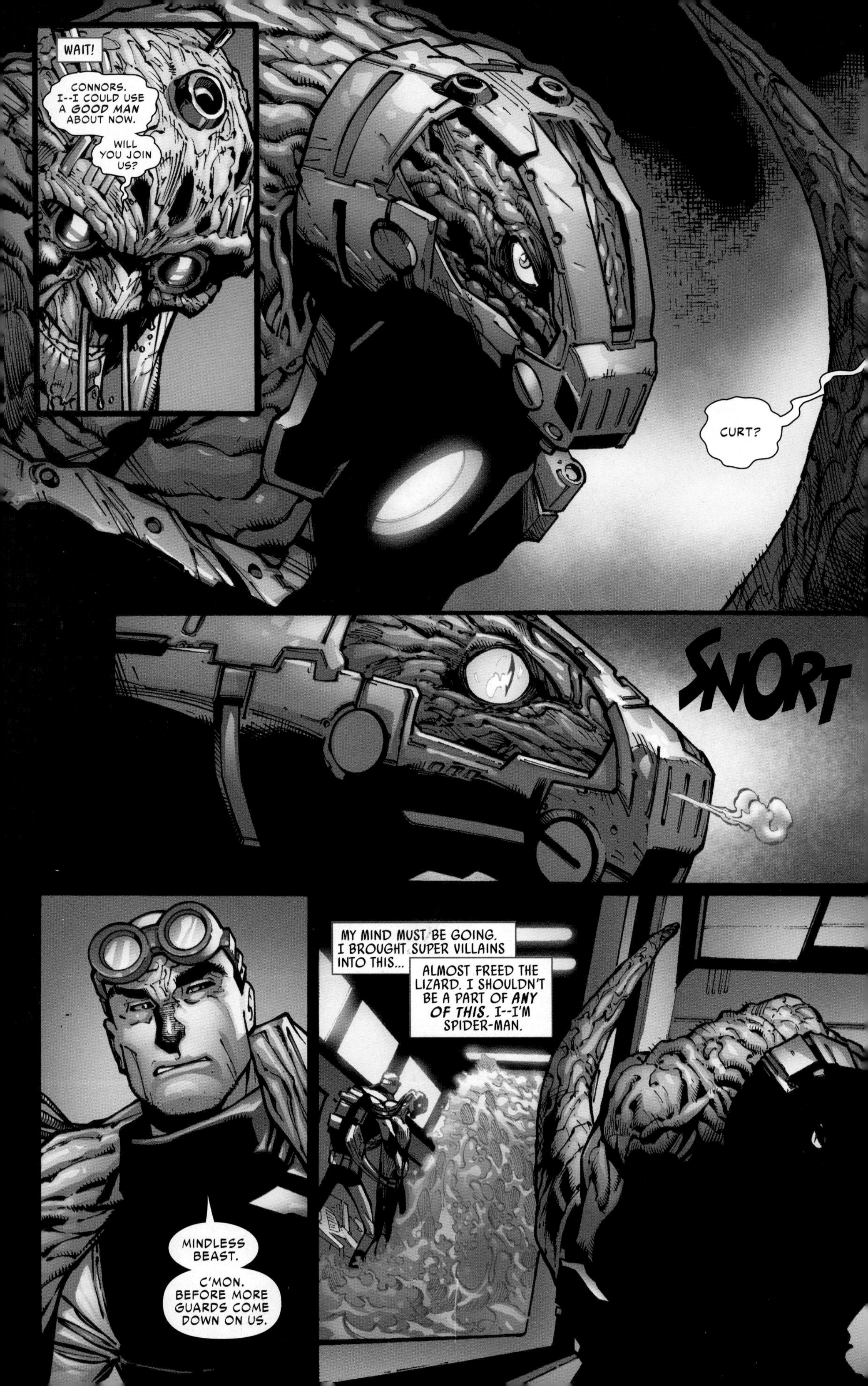
WAIT!
CONNORS. I--I COULD USE A *GOOD MAN* ABOUT NOW.
WILL YOU JOIN US?
CURT?
SNORT
MY MIND MUST BE GOING. I BROUGHT SUPER VILLAINS INTO THIS...
ALMOST FREED THE LIZARD. I SHOULDN'T BE A PART OF *ANY OF THIS*. I--I'M SPIDER-MAN.
MINDLESS BEAST.
C'MON. BEFORE MORE GUARDS COME DOWN ON US.

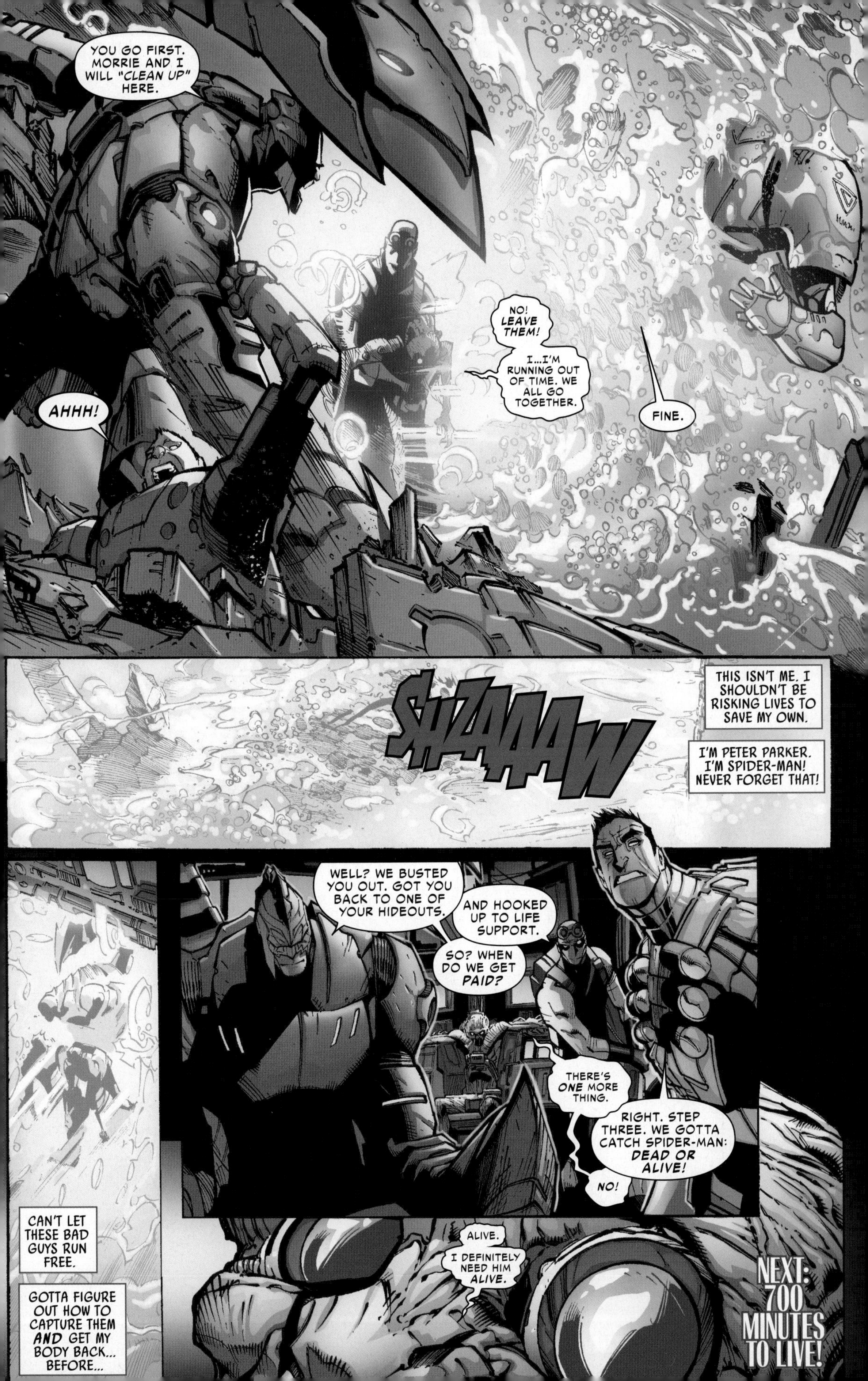
YOU GO FIRST. MORRIE AND I WILL "CLEAN UP" HERE.
AHHH!
NO! LEAVE THEM!
I...I'M RUNNING OUT OF TIME. WE ALL GO TOGETHER.
FINE.
SHZAAAW
THIS ISN'T ME. I SHOULDN'T BE RISKING LIVES TO SAVE MY OWN.
I'M PETER PARKER. I'M SPIDER-MAN! NEVER FORGET THAT!
WELL? WE BUSTED YOU OUT. GOT YOU BACK TO ONE OF YOUR HIDEOUTS.
AND HOOKED UP TO LIFE SUPPORT.
SO? WHEN DO WE GET PAID?
THERE'S ONE MORE THING.
RIGHT. STEP THREE. WE GOTTA CATCH SPIDER-MAN: DEAD OR ALIVE!
NO!
CAN'T LET THESE BAD GUYS RUN FREE.
GOTTA FIGURE OUT HOW TO CAPTURE THEM AND GET MY BODY BACK... BEFORE...
ALIVE.
I DEFINITELY NEED HIM ALIVE.
NEXT: 700 MINUTES TO LIVE!

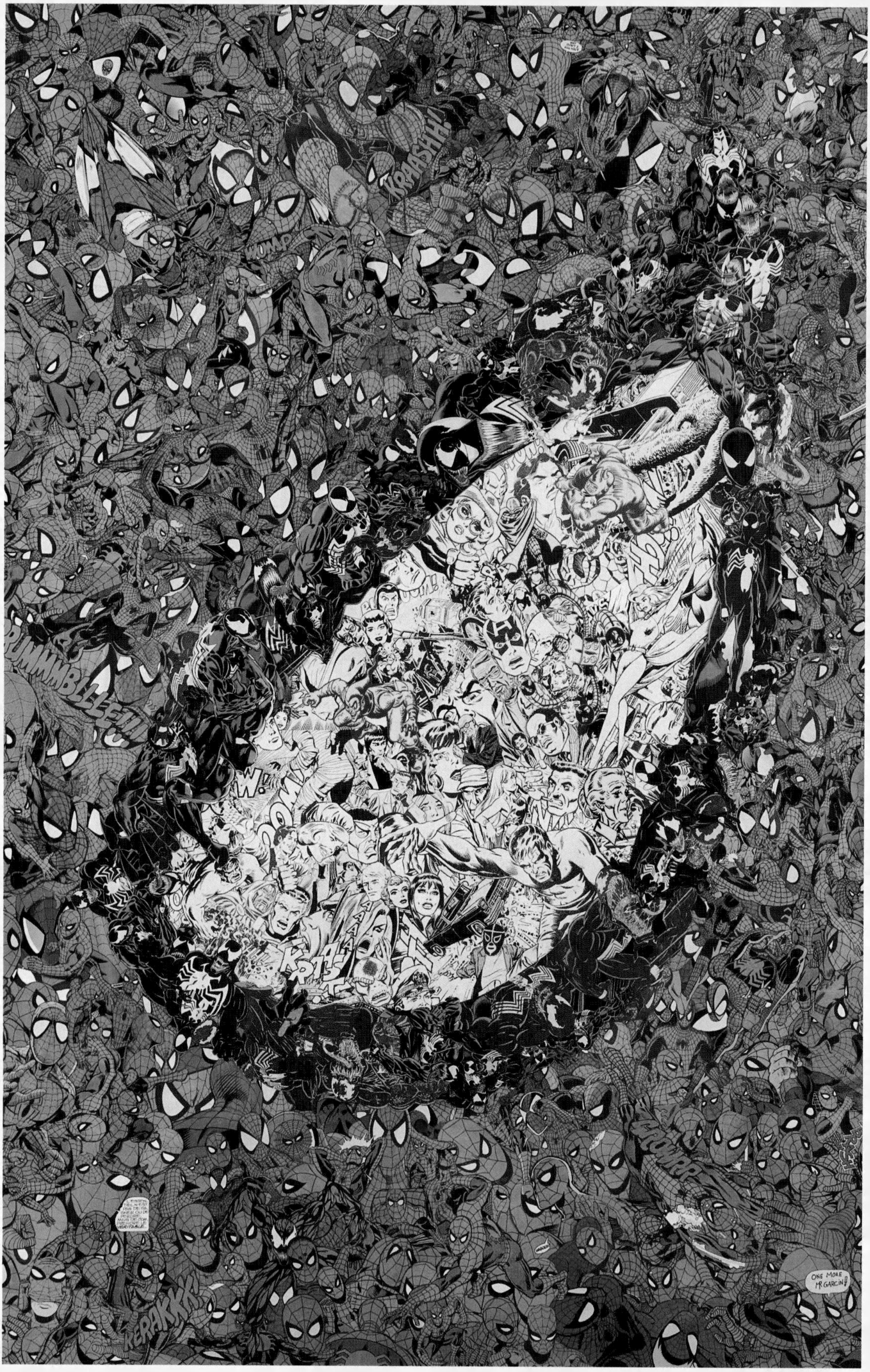
KRAASHH!
WOMP
RUMMMBLLE
KRAKKK
ONE MORE MR GARCIN!

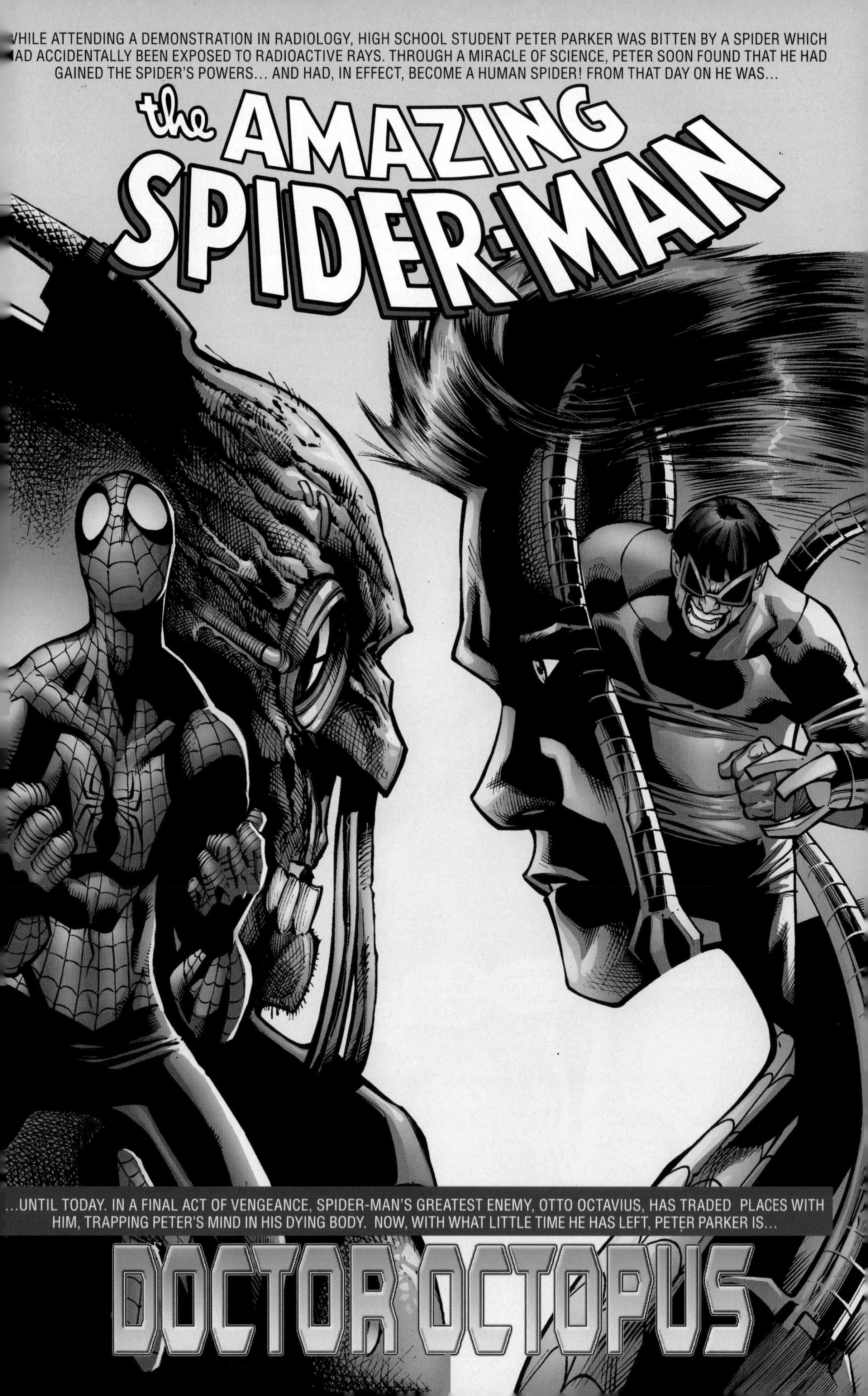
WHILE ATTENDING A DEMONSTRATION IN RADIOLOGY, HIGH SCHOOL STUDENT PETER PARKER WAS BITTEN BY A SPIDER WHICH HAD ACCIDENTALLY BEEN EXPOSED TO RADIOACTIVE RAYS. THROUGH A MIRACLE OF SCIENCE, PETER SOON FOUND THAT HE HAD GAINED THE SPIDER'S POWERS… AND HAD, IN EFFECT, BECOME A HUMAN SPIDER! FROM THAT DAY ON HE WAS…
the AMAZING SPIDER-MAN
…UNTIL TODAY. IN A FINAL ACT OF VENGEANCE, SPIDER-MAN'S GREATEST ENEMY, OTTO OCTAVIUS, HAS TRADED PLACES WITH HIM, TRAPPING PETER'S MIND IN HIS DYING BODY. NOW, WITH WHAT LITTLE TIME HE HAS LEFT, PETER PARKER IS…
DOCTOR OCTOPUS

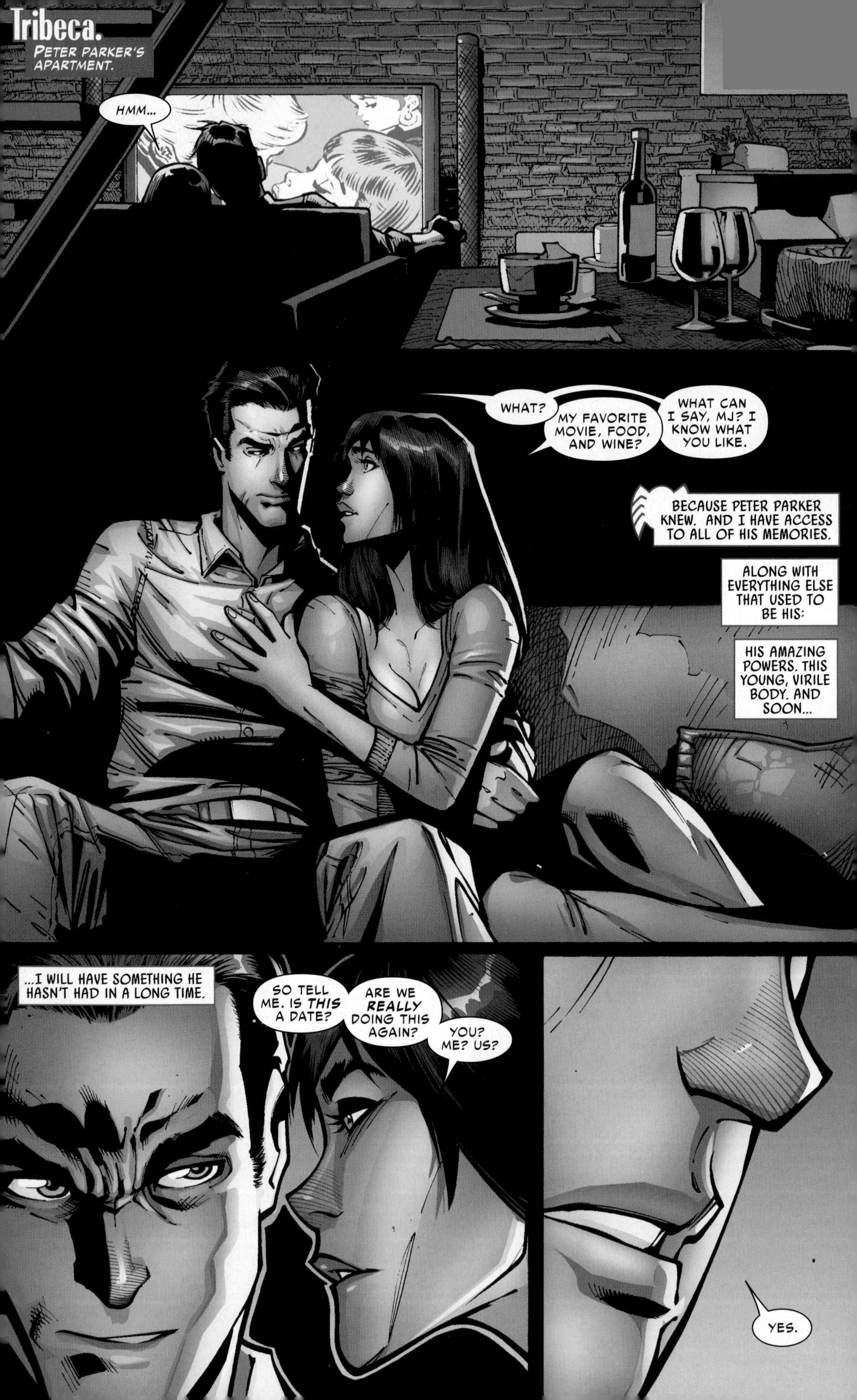
Tribeca.
PETER PARKER'S APARTMENT.
HMM...
WHAT?
MY FAVORITE MOVIE, FOOD, AND WINE?
WHAT CAN I SAY, MJ? I KNOW WHAT YOU LIKE.
BECAUSE PETER PARKER KNEW. AND I HAVE ACCESS TO ALL OF HIS MEMORIES.
ALONG WITH EVERYTHING ELSE THAT USED TO BE HIS:
HIS AMAZING POWERS. THIS YOUNG, VIRILE BODY. AND SOON...
...I WILL HAVE SOMETHING HE HASN'T HAD IN A LONG TIME.
SO TELL ME. IS THIS A DATE?
ARE WE REALLY DOING THIS AGAIN?
YOU? ME? US?
YES.

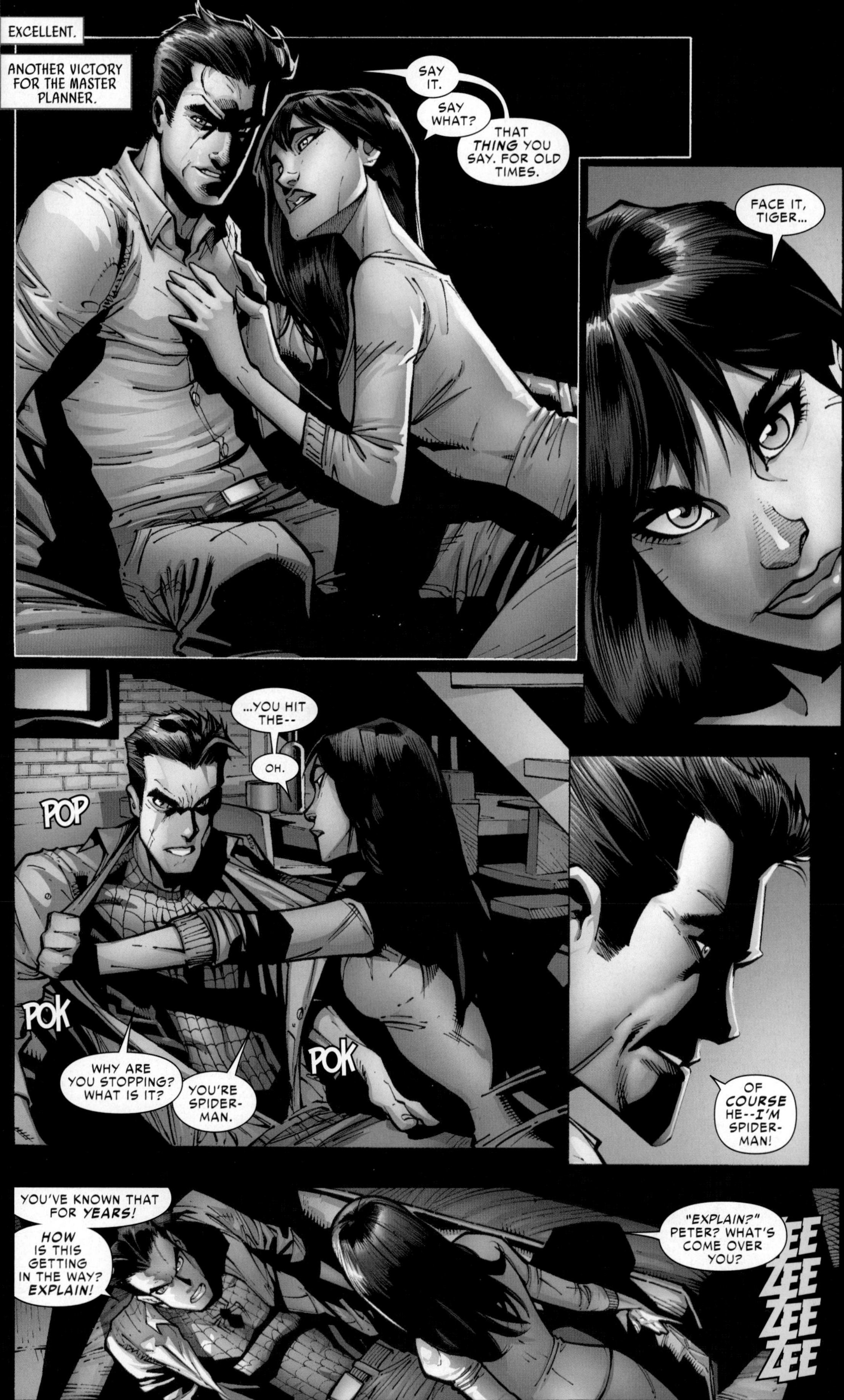
EXCELLENT.
ANOTHER VICTORY FOR THE MASTER PLANNER.
SAY IT.
SAY WHAT?
THAT THING YOU SAY. FOR OLD TIMES.
FACE IT, TIGER...
...YOU HIT THE--
OH.
POP
POK
WHY ARE YOU STOPPING? WHAT IS IT?
YOU'RE SPIDER-MAN.
POK
OF COURSE HE--I'M SPIDER-MAN!
YOU'VE KNOWN THAT FOR YEARS!
HOW IS THIS GETTING IN THE WAY? EXPLAIN!
"EXPLAIN?" PETER? WHAT'S COME OVER YOU?
ZEE ZEE ZEE ZEE

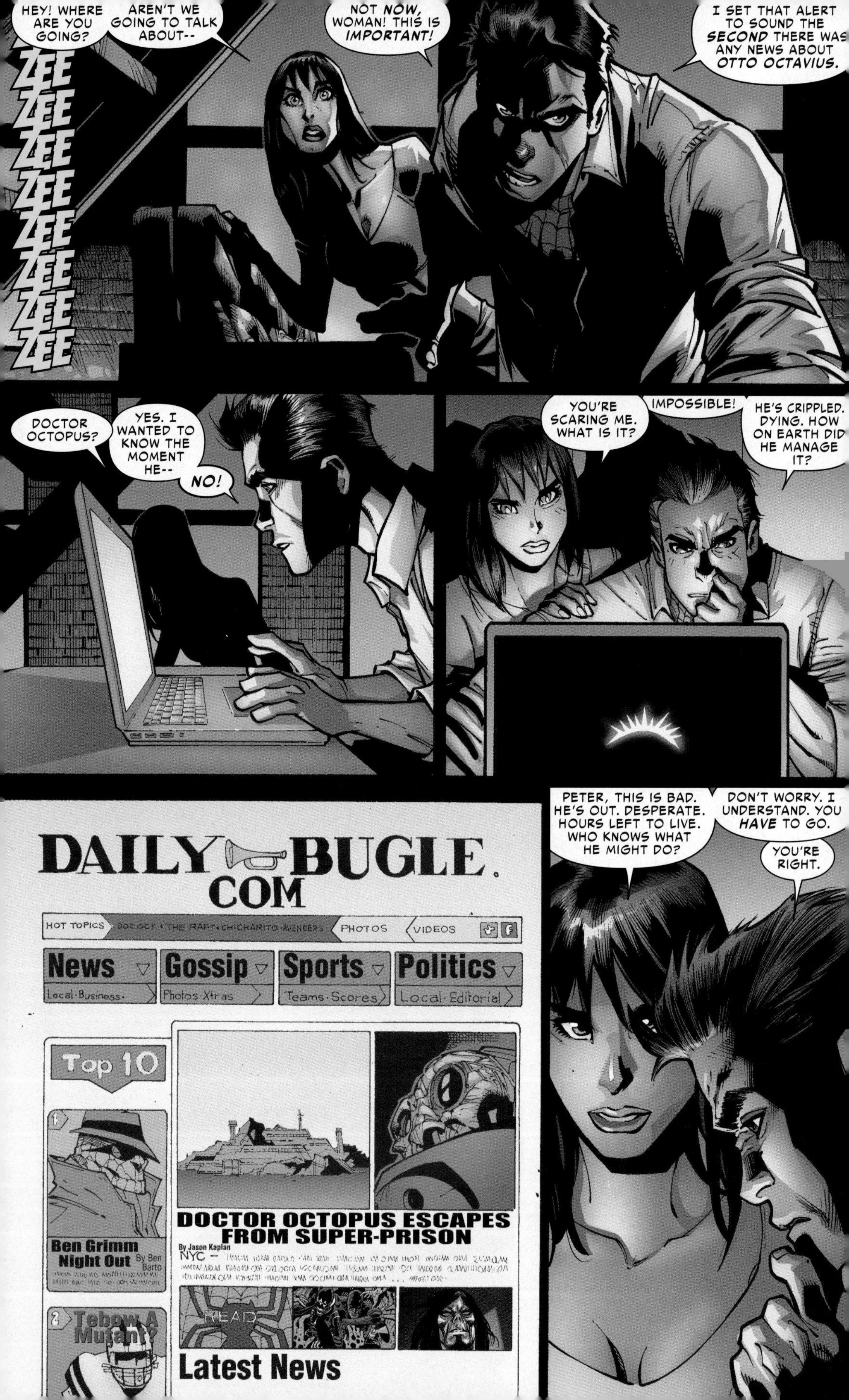

HEY! WHERE ARE YOU GOING?
AREN'T WE GOING TO TALK ABOUT--
ZEE ZEE ZEE ZEE ZEE ZEE ZEE ZEE
NOT *NOW*, WOMAN! THIS IS *IMPORTANT*!
I SET THAT ALERT TO SOUND THE *SECOND* THERE WAS ANY NEWS ABOUT *OTTO OCTAVIUS*.
DOCTOR OCTOPUS?
YES. I WANTED TO KNOW THE MOMENT HE--
NO!
YOU'RE SCARING ME. WHAT IS IT?
IMPOSSIBLE!
HE'S CRIPPLED. DYING. HOW ON EARTH DID HE MANAGE IT?
DAILY BUGLE .COM
HOT TOPICS
DOC OCK • THE RAFT • CHICHARITO • AVENGERS
PHOTOS
VIDEOS
News
Local·Business·
Gossip
Photos·Xtras
Sports
Teams·Scores
Politics
Local·Editorial
Top 10
1
Ben Grimm Night Out
By Ben Barto
2
Tebow A Mutant?
DOCTOR OCTOPUS ESCAPES FROM SUPER-PRISON
By Jason Kaplan
NYC —
READ
Latest News
PETER, THIS IS BAD. HE'S OUT. DESPERATE. HOURS LEFT TO LIVE. WHO KNOWS WHAT HE MIGHT DO?
DON'T WORRY. I UNDERSTAND. YOU *HAVE* TO GO.
YOU'RE RIGHT.

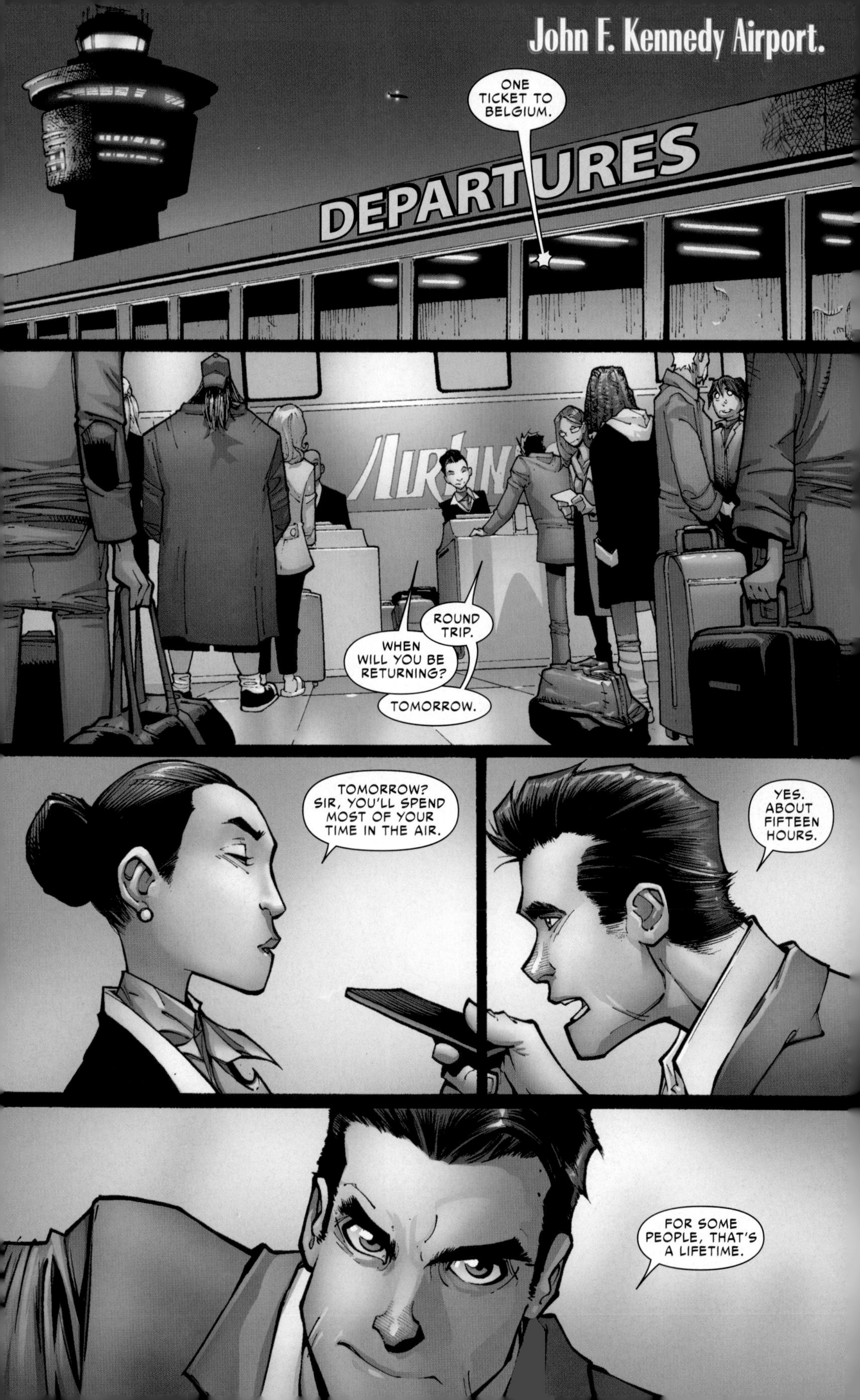
John F. Kennedy Airport.
ONE TICKET TO BELGIUM.
DEPARTURES
ROUND TRIP.
WHEN WILL YOU BE RETURNING?
TOMORROW.
TOMORROW? SIR, YOU'LL SPEND MOST OF YOUR TIME IN THE AIR.
YES. ABOUT FIFTEEN HOURS.
FOR SOME PEOPLE, THAT'S A LIFETIME.

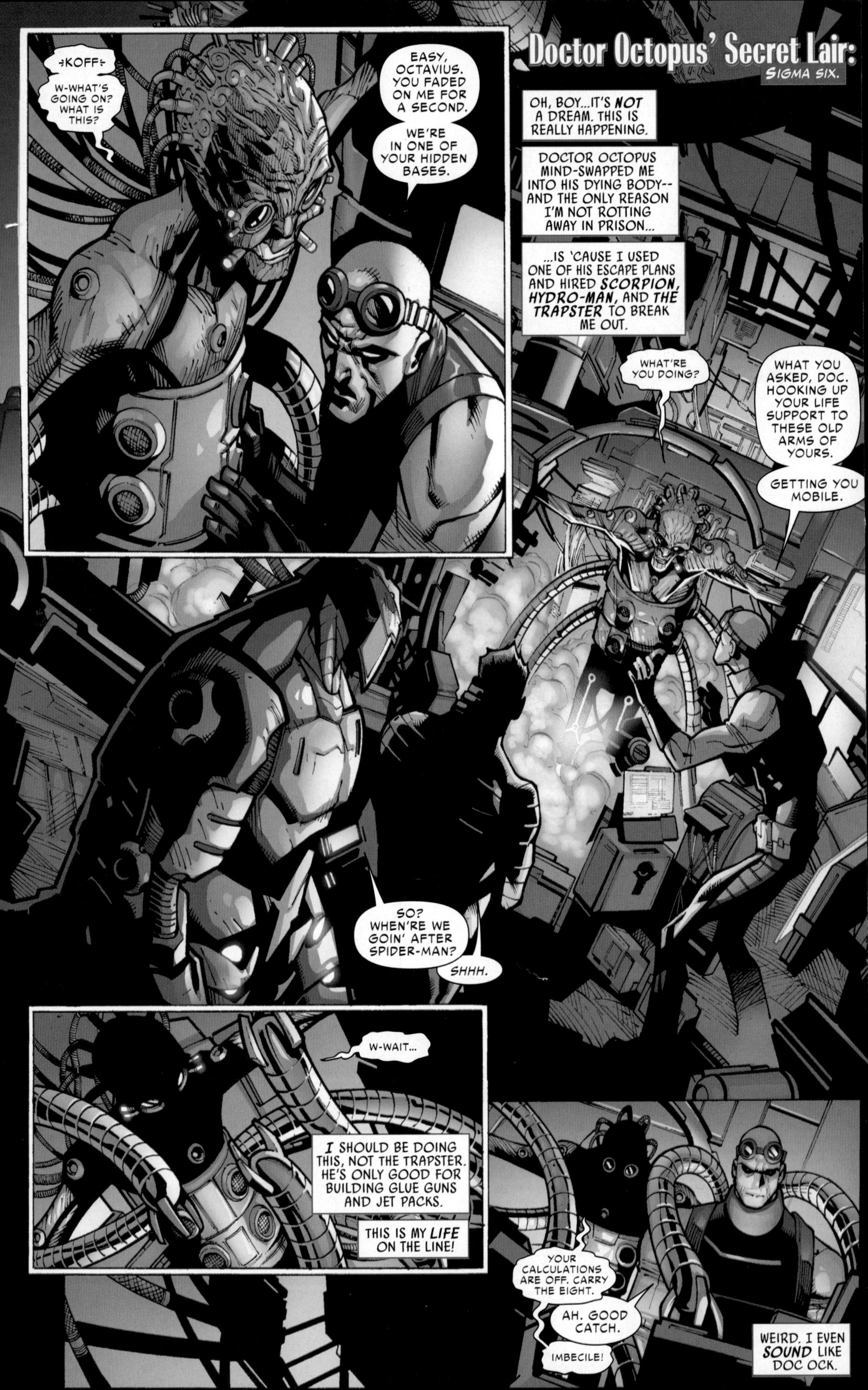

Doctor Octopus' Secret Lair: Sigma Six.
⊰KOFF⊱
W-WHAT'S GOING ON? WHAT IS THIS?
EASY, OCTAVIUS. YOU FADED ON ME FOR A SECOND.
WE'RE IN ONE OF YOUR HIDDEN BASES.
OH, BOY...IT'S NOT A DREAM. THIS IS REALLY HAPPENING.
DOCTOR OCTOPUS MIND-SWAPPED ME INTO HIS DYING BODY--AND THE ONLY REASON I'M NOT ROTTING AWAY IN PRISON...
...IS 'CAUSE I USED ONE OF HIS ESCAPE PLANS AND HIRED SCORPION, HYDRO-MAN, AND THE TRAPSTER TO BREAK ME OUT.
WHAT'RE YOU DOING?
WHAT YOU ASKED, DOC. HOOKING UP YOUR LIFE SUPPORT TO THESE OLD ARMS OF YOURS.
GETTING YOU MOBILE.
SO? WHEN'RE WE GOIN' AFTER SPIDER-MAN?
SHHH.
W-WAIT...
I SHOULD BE DOING THIS, NOT THE TRAPSTER. HE'S ONLY GOOD FOR BUILDING GLUE GUNS AND JET PACKS.
THIS IS MY LIFE ON THE LINE!
YOUR CALCULATIONS ARE OFF. CARRY THE EIGHT.
AH. GOOD CATCH.
IMBECILE!
WEIRD. I EVEN SOUND LIKE DOC OCK.

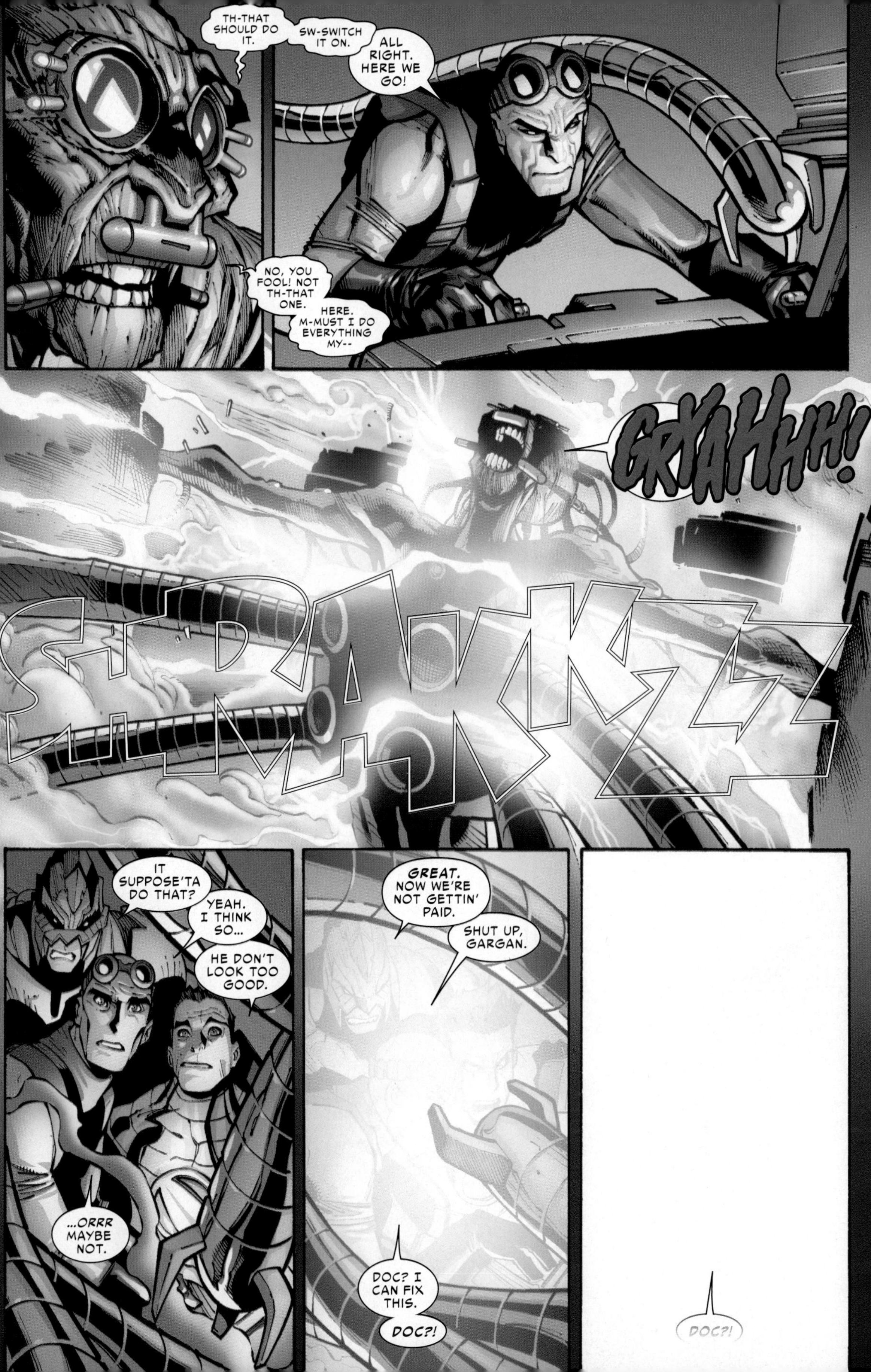
TH-THAT SHOULD DO IT.
SW-SWITCH IT ON.
ALL RIGHT. HERE WE GO!
NO, YOU FOOL! NOT TH-THAT ONE.
HERE. M-MUST I DO EVERYTHING MY--
GRYAHHH!
SHRAKKZZ
IT SUPPOSE'TA DO THAT?
YEAH. I THINK SO...
HE DON'T LOOK TOO GOOD.
...ORRR MAYBE NOT.
GREAT. NOW WE'RE NOT GETTIN' PAID.
SHUT UP, GARGAN.
DOC? I CAN FIX THIS.
DOC?!
DOC?!

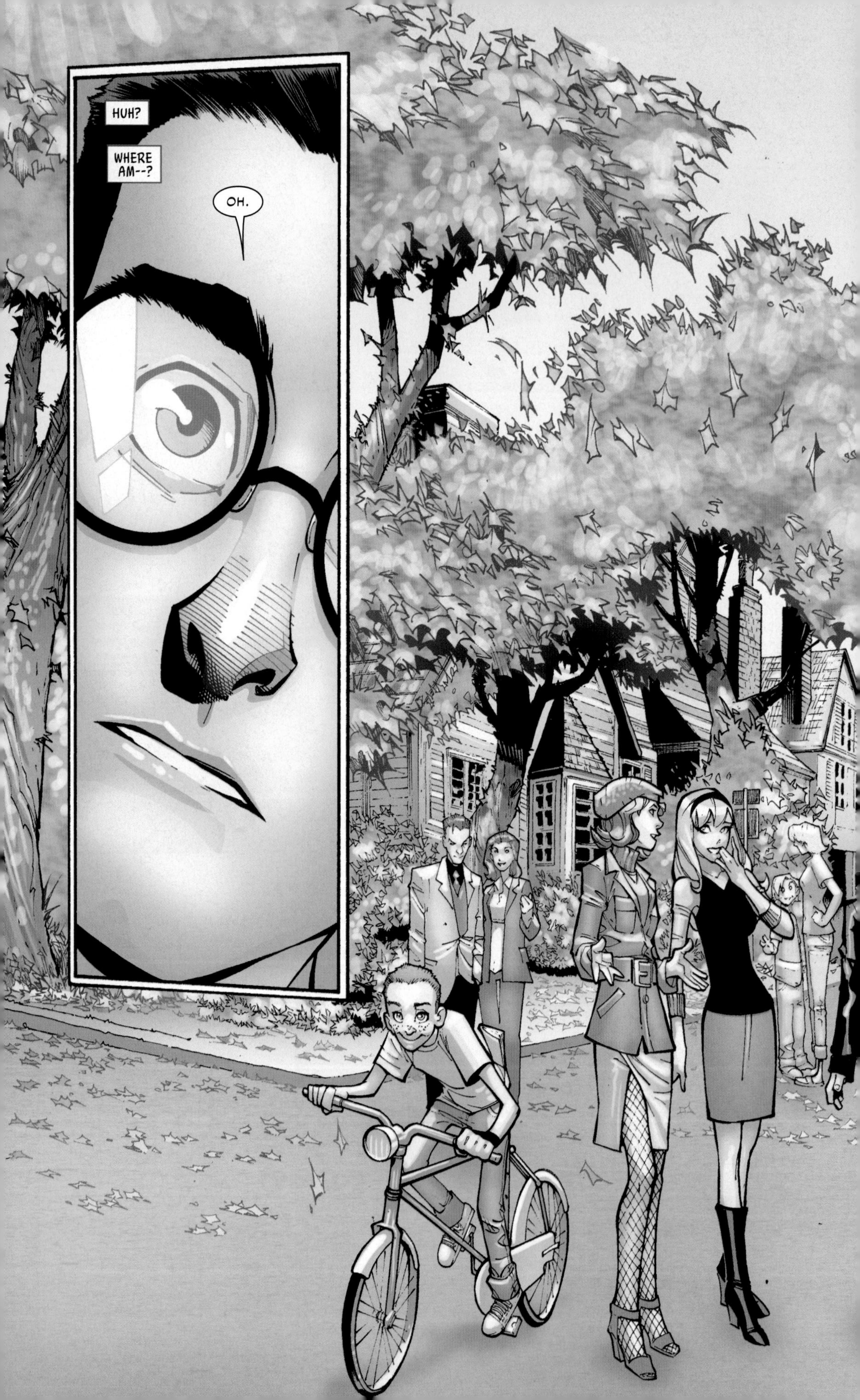
HUH?
WHERE AM--?
OH.

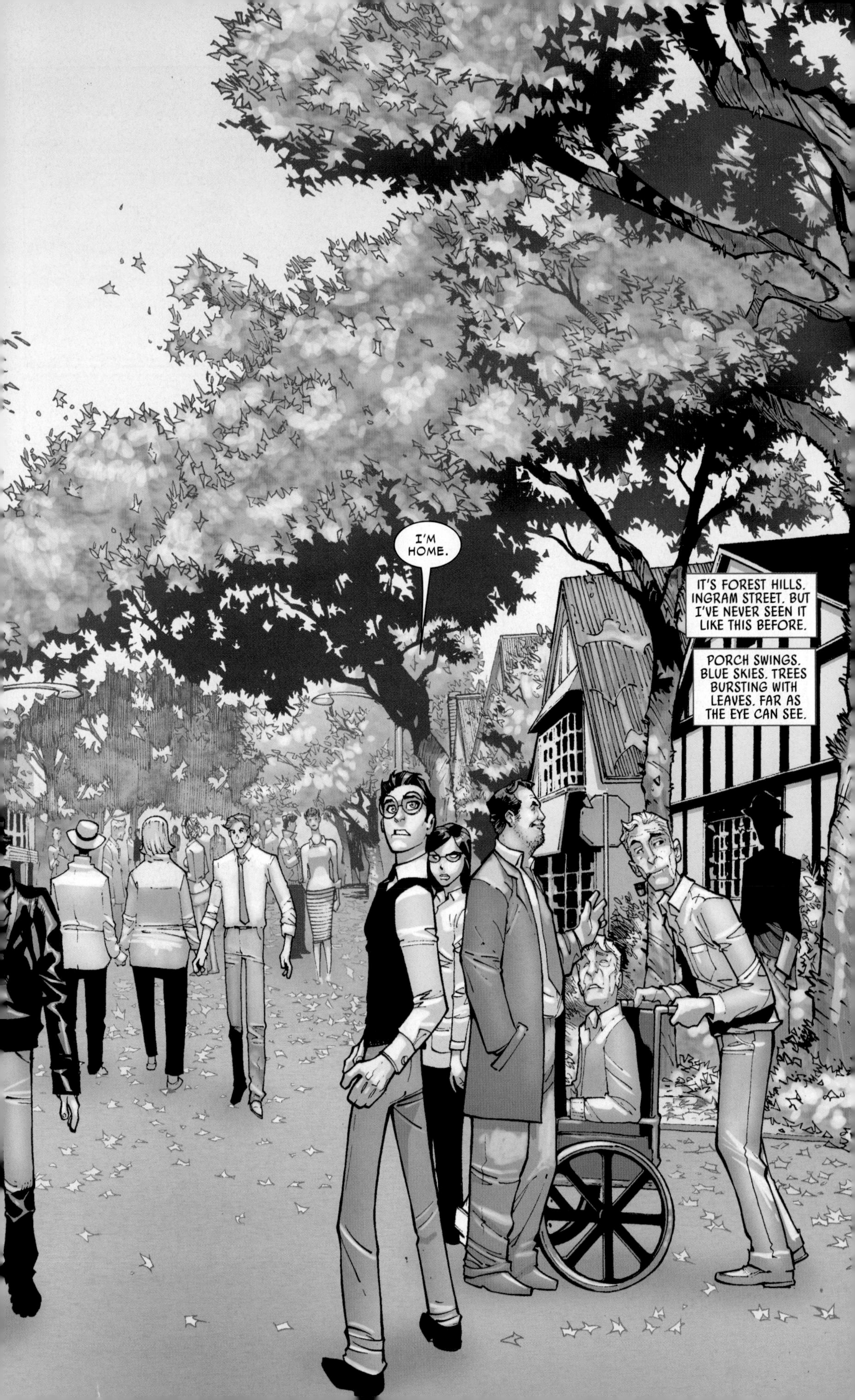
I'M HOME.
IT'S FOREST HILLS. INGRAM STREET. BUT I'VE NEVER SEEN IT LIKE THIS BEFORE.
PORCH SWINGS. BLUE SKIES. TREES BURSTING WITH LEAVES. FAR AS THE EYE CAN SEE.

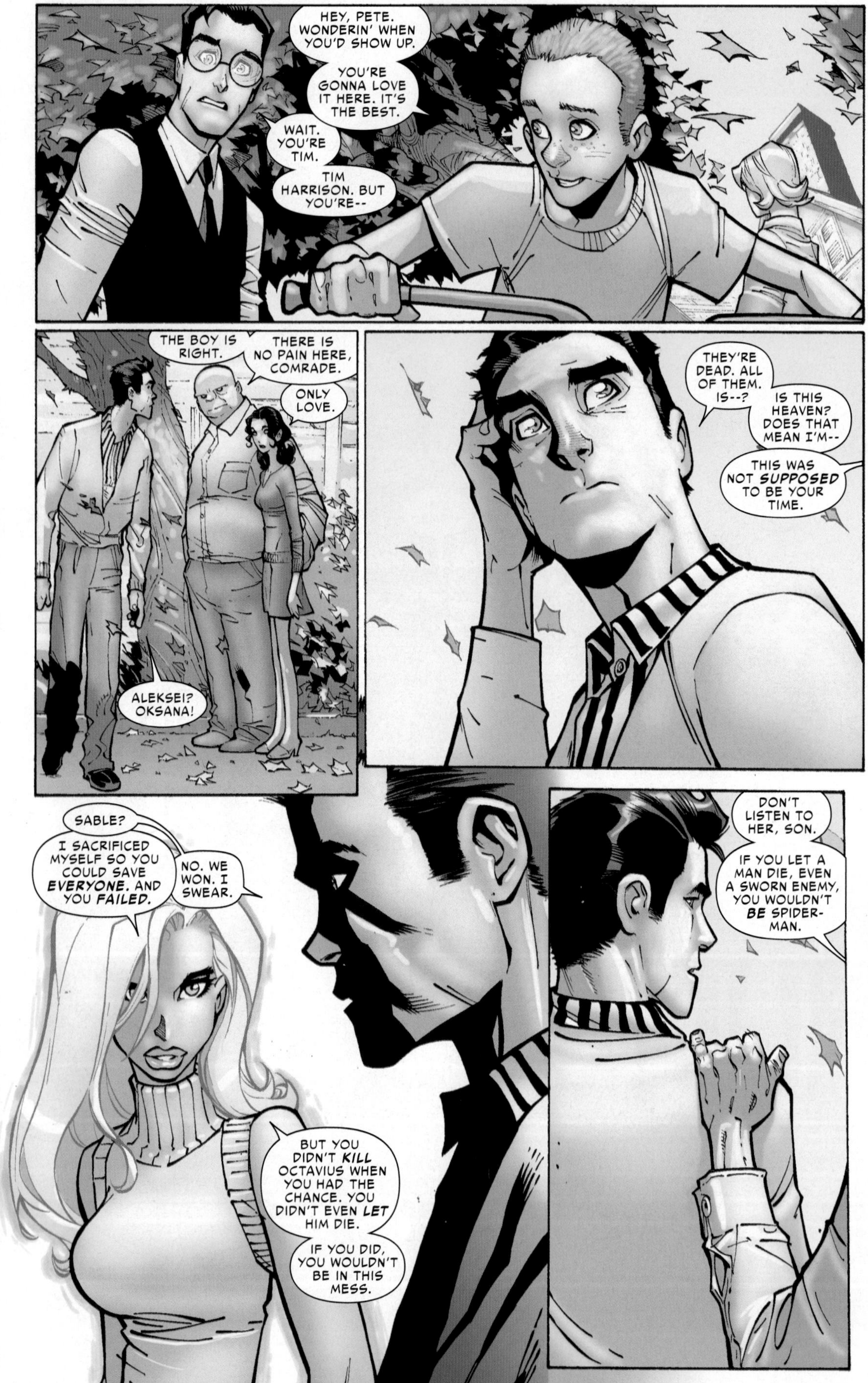

HEY, PETE. WONDERIN' WHEN YOU'D SHOW UP.
YOU'RE GONNA LOVE IT HERE. IT'S THE BEST.
WAIT. YOU'RE TIM.
TIM HARRISON. BUT YOU'RE--
THE BOY IS RIGHT.
THERE IS NO PAIN HERE, COMRADE.
ONLY LOVE.
ALEKSEI? OKSANA!
THEY'RE DEAD. ALL OF THEM. IS--?
IS THIS HEAVEN? DOES THAT MEAN I'M--
THIS WAS NOT SUPPOSED TO BE YOUR TIME.
SABLE?
I SACRIFICED MYSELF SO YOU COULD SAVE EVERYONE. AND YOU FAILED.
NO. WE WON. I SWEAR.
BUT YOU DIDN'T KILL OCTAVIUS WHEN YOU HAD THE CHANCE. YOU DIDN'T EVEN LET HIM DIE.
IF YOU DID, YOU WOULDN'T BE IN THIS MESS.
DON'T LISTEN TO HER, SON.
IF YOU LET A MAN DIE, EVEN A SWORN ENEMY, YOU WOULDN'T BE SPIDER-MAN.

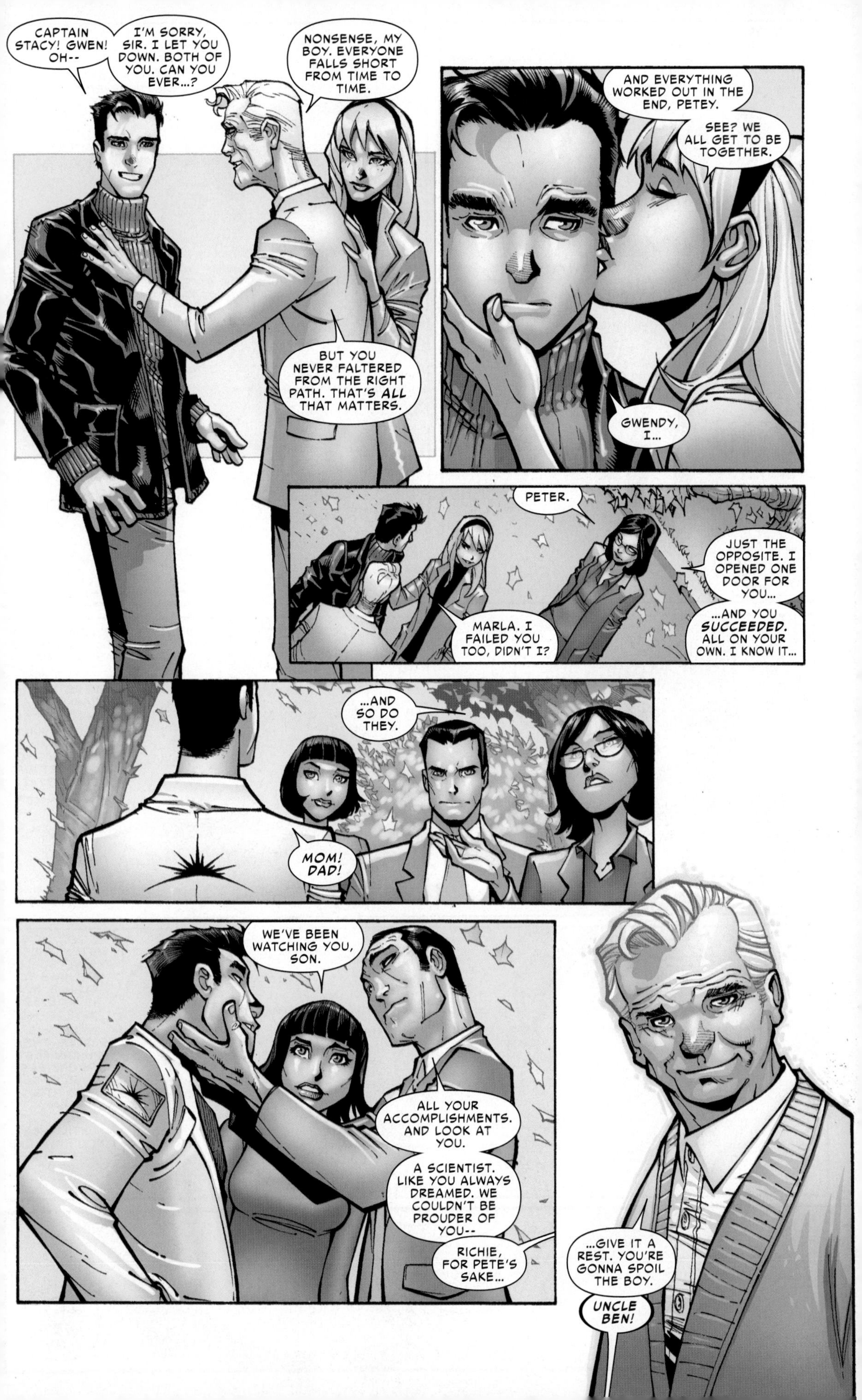
CAPTAIN STACY! GWEN! OH--
I'M SORRY, SIR. I LET YOU DOWN. BOTH OF YOU. CAN YOU EVER...?
NONSENSE, MY BOY. EVERYONE FALLS SHORT FROM TIME TO TIME.
BUT YOU NEVER FALTERED FROM THE RIGHT PATH. THAT'S ALL THAT MATTERS.
AND EVERYTHING WORKED OUT IN THE END, PETEY.
SEE? WE ALL GET TO BE TOGETHER.
GWENDY, I...
PETER.
MARLA. I FAILED YOU TOO, DIDN'T I?
JUST THE OPPOSITE. I OPENED ONE DOOR FOR YOU...
...AND YOU SUCCEEDED. ALL ON YOUR OWN. I KNOW IT...
...AND SO DO THEY.
MOM! DAD!
WE'VE BEEN WATCHING YOU, SON.
ALL YOUR ACCOMPLISHMENTS. AND LOOK AT YOU.
A SCIENTIST. LIKE YOU ALWAYS DREAMED. WE COULDN'T BE PROUDER OF YOU--
RICHIE, FOR PETE'S SAKE...
...GIVE IT A REST. YOU'RE GONNA SPOIL THE BOY.
UNCLE BEN!

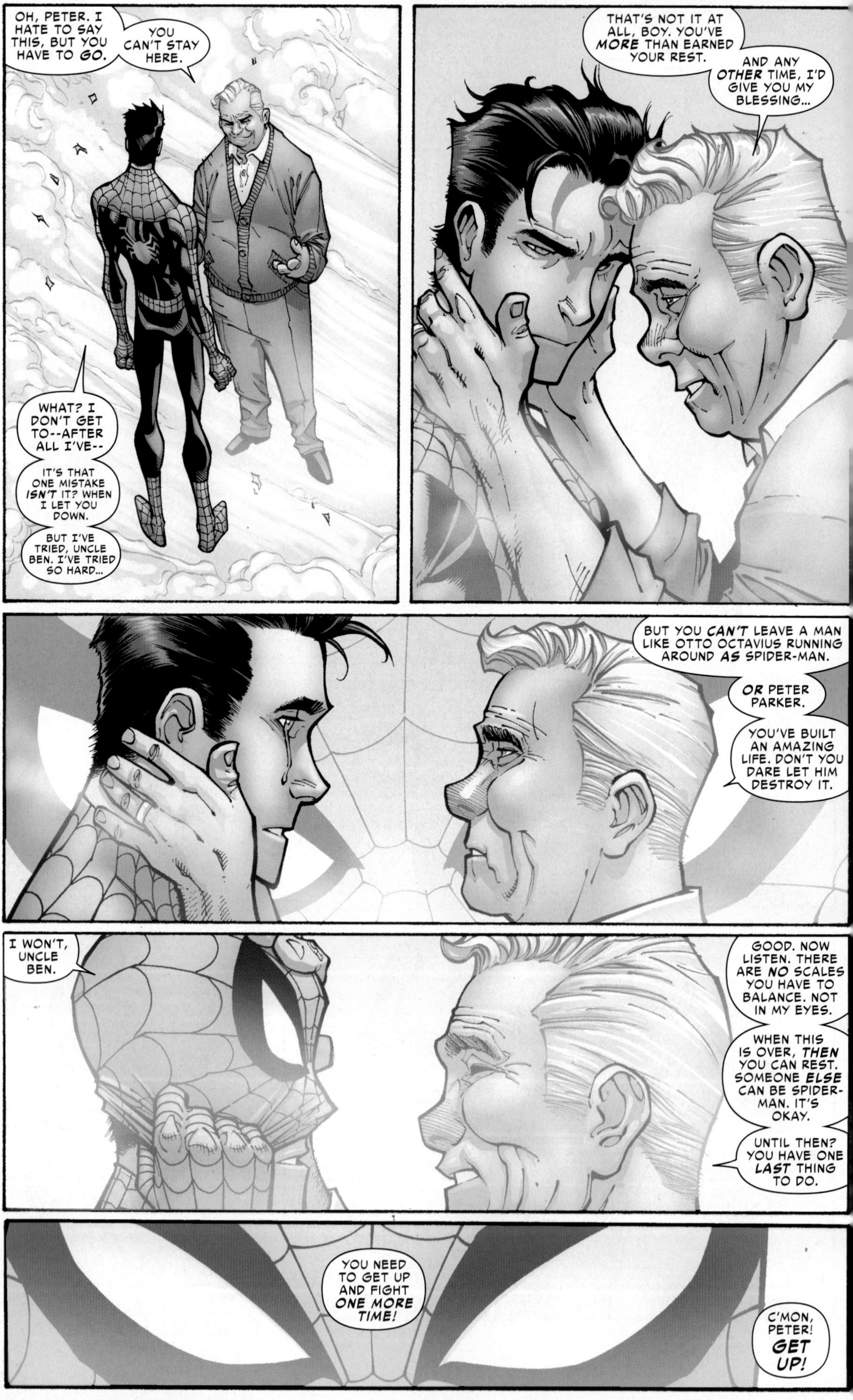
OH, PETER. I HATE TO SAY THIS, BUT YOU HAVE TO GO.
YOU CAN'T STAY HERE.
WHAT? I DON'T GET TO--AFTER ALL I'VE--
IT'S THAT ONE MISTAKE ISN'T IT? WHEN I LET YOU DOWN.
BUT I'VE TRIED, UNCLE BEN. I'VE TRIED SO HARD...
THAT'S NOT IT AT ALL, BOY. YOU'VE MORE THAN EARNED YOUR REST.
AND ANY OTHER TIME, I'D GIVE YOU MY BLESSING...
BUT YOU CAN'T LEAVE A MAN LIKE OTTO OCTAVIUS RUNNING AROUND AS SPIDER-MAN.
OR PETER PARKER.
YOU'VE BUILT AN AMAZING LIFE. DON'T YOU DARE LET HIM DESTROY IT.
I WON'T, UNCLE BEN.
GOOD. NOW LISTEN. THERE ARE NO SCALES YOU HAVE TO BALANCE. NOT IN MY EYES.
WHEN THIS IS OVER, THEN YOU CAN REST. SOMEONE ELSE CAN BE SPIDER-MAN. IT'S OKAY.
UNTIL THEN? YOU HAVE ONE LAST THING TO DO.
YOU NEED TO GET UP AND FIGHT ONE MORE TIME!
C'MON, PETER! GET UP!

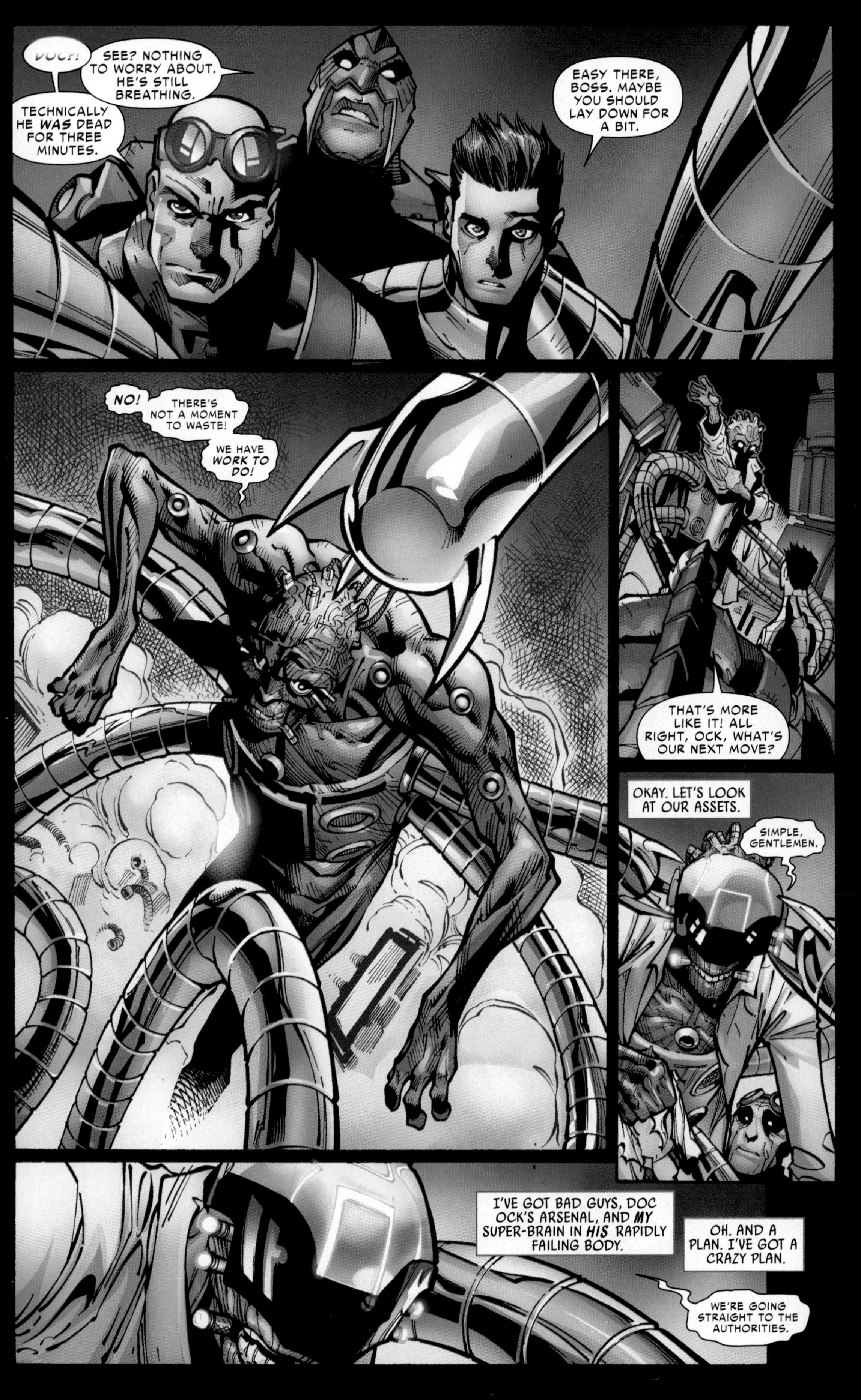

DOC?!
SEE? NOTHING TO WORRY ABOUT. HE'S STILL BREATHING.
TECHNICALLY HE WAS DEAD FOR THREE MINUTES.
EASY THERE, BOSS. MAYBE YOU SHOULD LAY DOWN FOR A BIT.
NO!
THERE'S NOT A MOMENT TO WASTE!
WE HAVE WORK TO DO!
THAT'S MORE LIKE IT! ALL RIGHT, OCK, WHAT'S OUR NEXT MOVE?
OKAY. LET'S LOOK AT OUR ASSETS.
SIMPLE, GENTLEMEN.
I'VE GOT BAD GUYS, DOC OCK'S ARSENAL, AND MY SUPER-BRAIN IN HIS RAPIDLY FAILING BODY.
OH. AND A PLAN. I'VE GOT A CRAZY PLAN.
WE'RE GOING STRAIGHT TO THE AUTHORITIES.

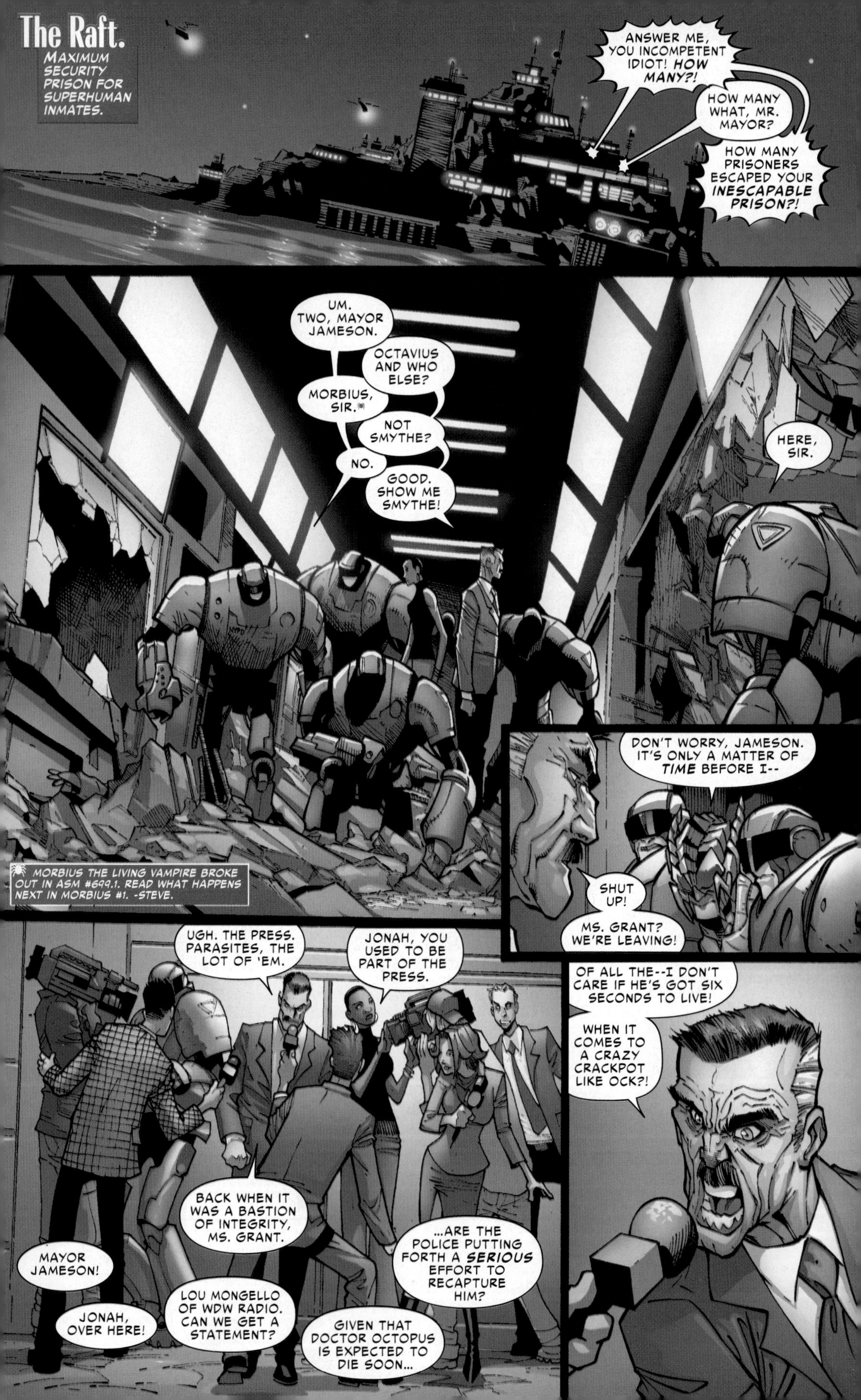
The Raft.
MAXIMUM SECURITY PRISON FOR SUPERHUMAN INMATES.
ANSWER ME, YOU INCOMPETENT IDIOT! HOW MANY?!
HOW MANY WHAT, MR. MAYOR?
HOW MANY PRISONERS ESCAPED YOUR INESCAPABLE PRISON?!
UM. TWO, MAYOR JAMESON.
OCTAVIUS AND WHO ELSE?
MORBIUS, SIR.
NOT SMYTHE?
NO.
GOOD. SHOW ME SMYTHE!
HERE, SIR.
MORBIUS THE LIVING VAMPIRE BROKE OUT IN ASM #699.1. READ WHAT HAPPENS NEXT IN MORBIUS #1. -STEVE.
DON'T WORRY, JAMESON. IT'S ONLY A MATTER OF TIME BEFORE I--
SHUT UP!
MS. GRANT? WE'RE LEAVING!
UGH. THE PRESS. PARASITES, THE LOT OF 'EM.
JONAH, YOU USED TO BE PART OF THE PRESS.
BACK WHEN IT WAS A BASTION OF INTEGRITY, MS. GRANT.
MAYOR JAMESON!
JONAH, OVER HERE!
LOU MONGELLO OF WDW RADIO. CAN WE GET A STATEMENT?
GIVEN THAT DOCTOR OCTOPUS IS EXPECTED TO DIE SOON...
...ARE THE POLICE PUTTING FORTH A SERIOUS EFFORT TO RECAPTURE HIM?
OF ALL THE--I DON'T CARE IF HE'S GOT SIX SECONDS TO LIVE!
WHEN IT COMES TO A CRAZY CRACKPOT LIKE OCK?!

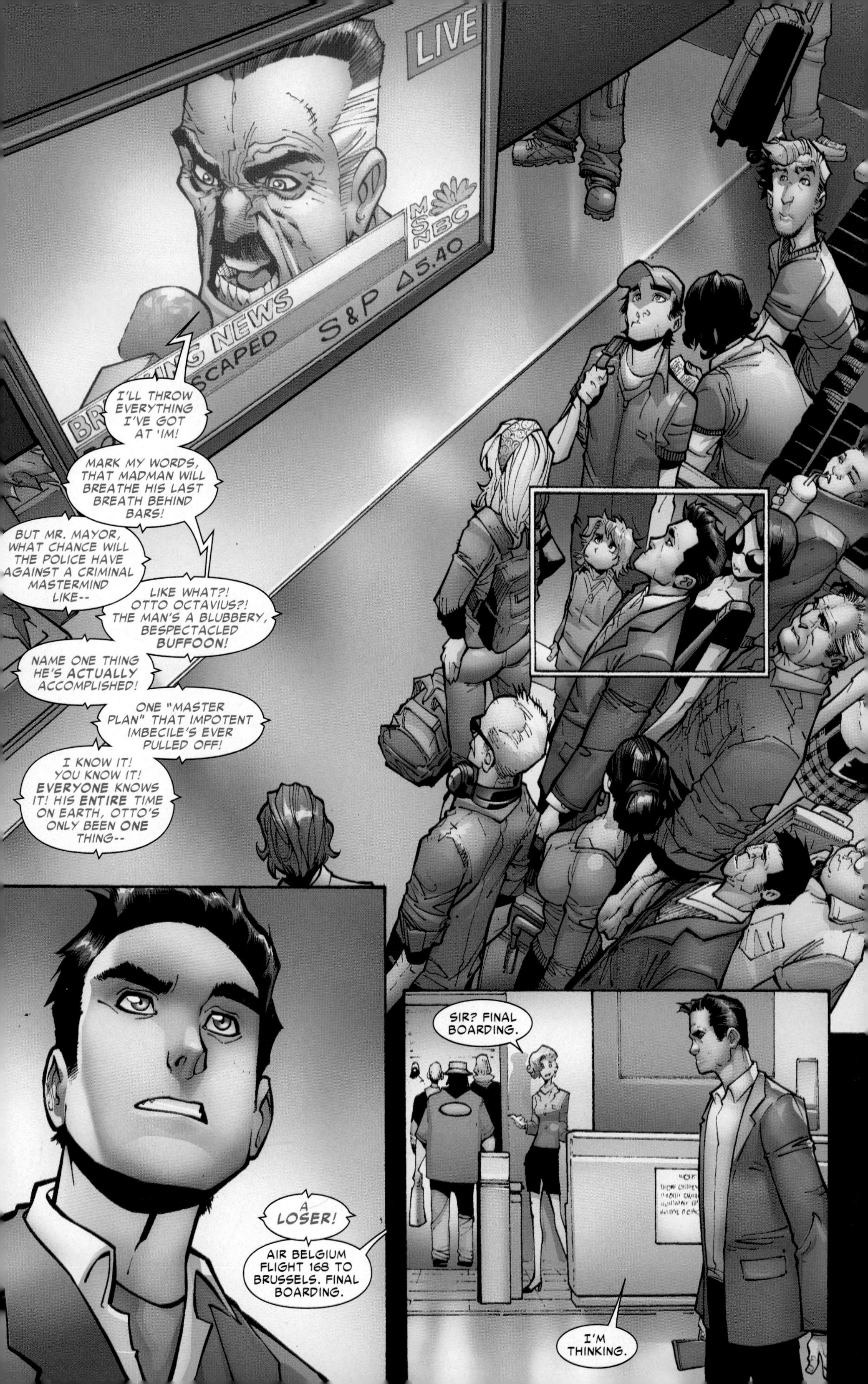
LIVE
MSNBC
BREAKING NEWS
SCAPED
S&P Δ5.40
I'LL THROW EVERYTHING I'VE GOT AT 'IM!
MARK MY WORDS, THAT MADMAN WILL BREATHE HIS LAST BREATH BEHIND BARS!
BUT MR. MAYOR, WHAT CHANCE WILL THE POLICE HAVE AGAINST A CRIMINAL MASTERMIND LIKE--
LIKE WHAT?! OTTO OCTAVIUS?! THE MAN'S A BLUBBERY, BESPECTACLED **BUFFOON!**
NAME ONE THING HE'S **ACTUALLY** ACCOMPLISHED!
ONE "MASTER PLAN" THAT IMPOTENT IMBECILE'S EVER PULLED OFF!
I KNOW IT! YOU KNOW IT! **EVERYONE** KNOWS IT! HIS **ENTIRE** TIME ON EARTH, OTTO'S ONLY BEEN **ONE** THING--
A **LOSER!**
AIR BELGIUM FLIGHT 168 TO BRUSSELS. FINAL BOARDING.
SIR? FINAL BOARDING.
I'M THINKING.

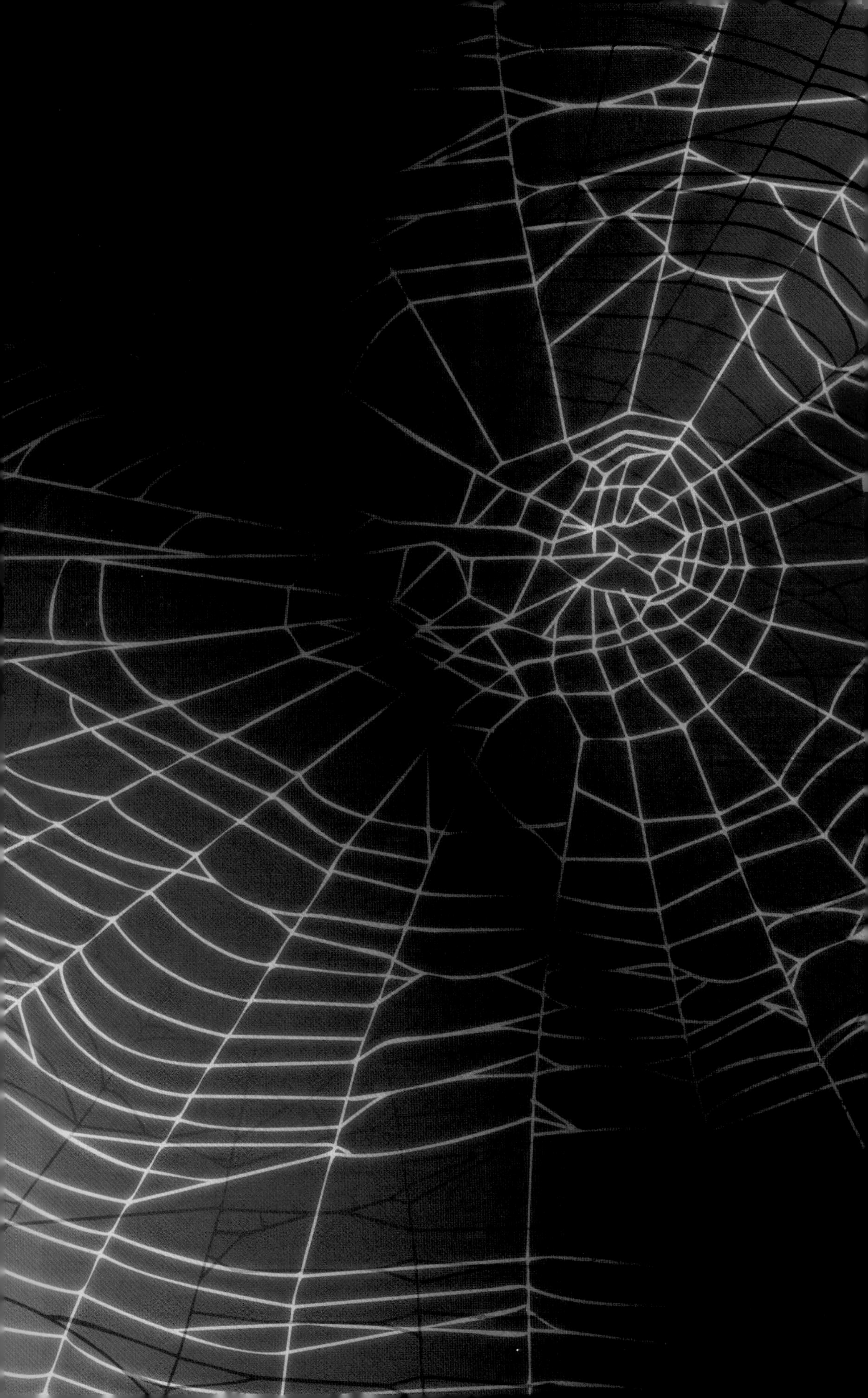

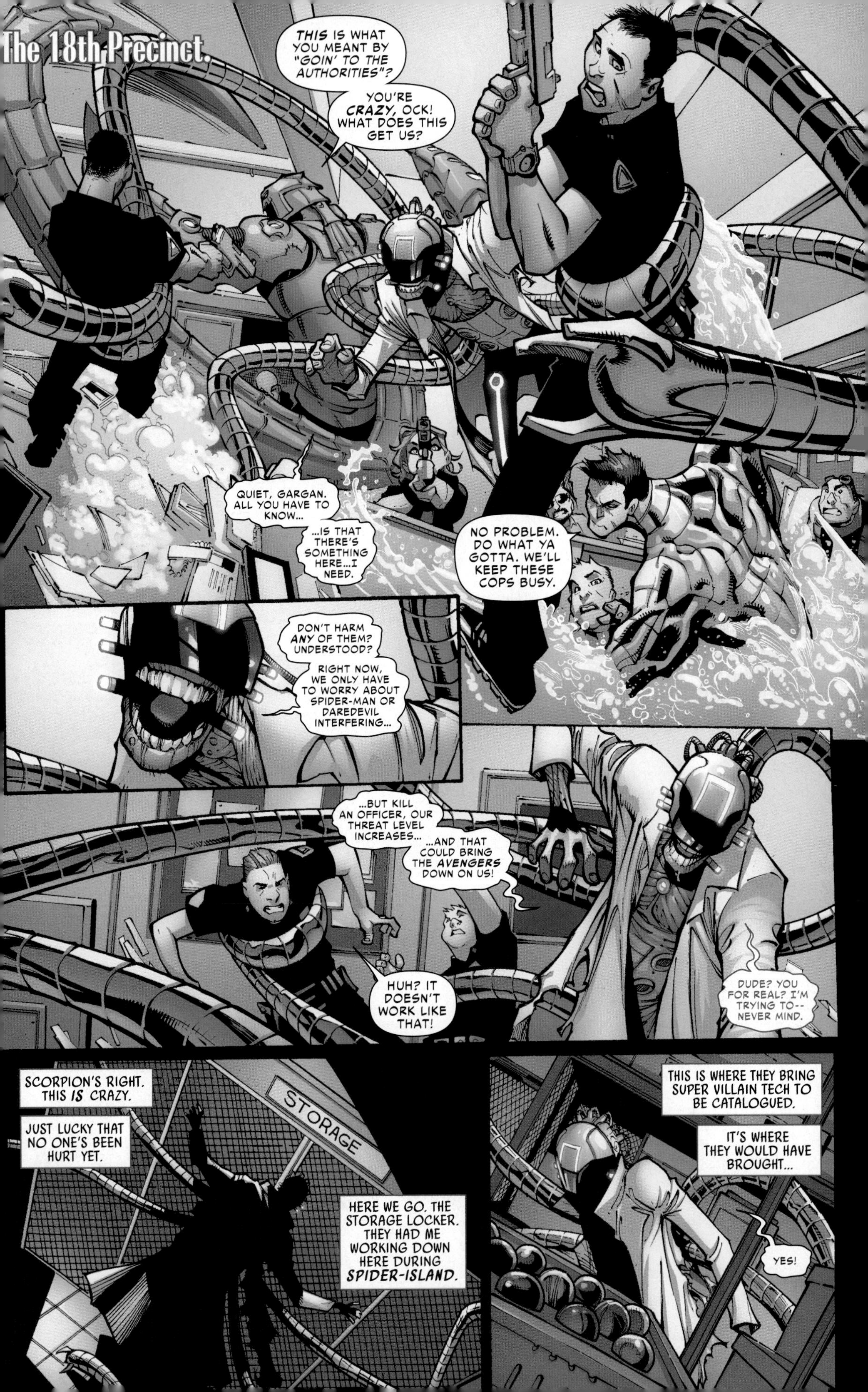
The 18th Precinct.
THIS IS WHAT YOU MEANT BY "GOIN' TO THE AUTHORITIES"?
YOU'RE CRAZY, OCK! WHAT DOES THIS GET US?
QUIET, GARGAN. ALL YOU HAVE TO KNOW...
...IS THAT THERE'S SOMETHING HERE...I NEED.
NO PROBLEM. DO WHAT YA GOTTA. WE'LL KEEP THESE COPS BUSY.
DON'T HARM ANY OF THEM? UNDERSTOOD?
RIGHT NOW, WE ONLY HAVE TO WORRY ABOUT SPIDER-MAN OR DAREDEVIL INTERFERING...
...BUT KILL AN OFFICER, OUR THREAT LEVEL INCREASES...
...AND THAT COULD BRING THE AVENGERS DOWN ON US!
HUH? IT DOESN'T WORK LIKE THAT!
DUDE? YOU FOR REAL? I'M TRYING TO-- NEVER MIND.
SCORPION'S RIGHT. THIS IS CRAZY.
JUST LUCKY THAT NO ONE'S BEEN HURT YET.
STORAGE
HERE WE GO. THE STORAGE LOCKER. THEY HAD ME WORKING DOWN HERE DURING SPIDER-ISLAND.
THIS IS WHERE THEY BRING SUPER VILLAIN TECH TO BE CATALOGUED.
IT'S WHERE THEY WOULD HAVE BROUGHT...
YES!

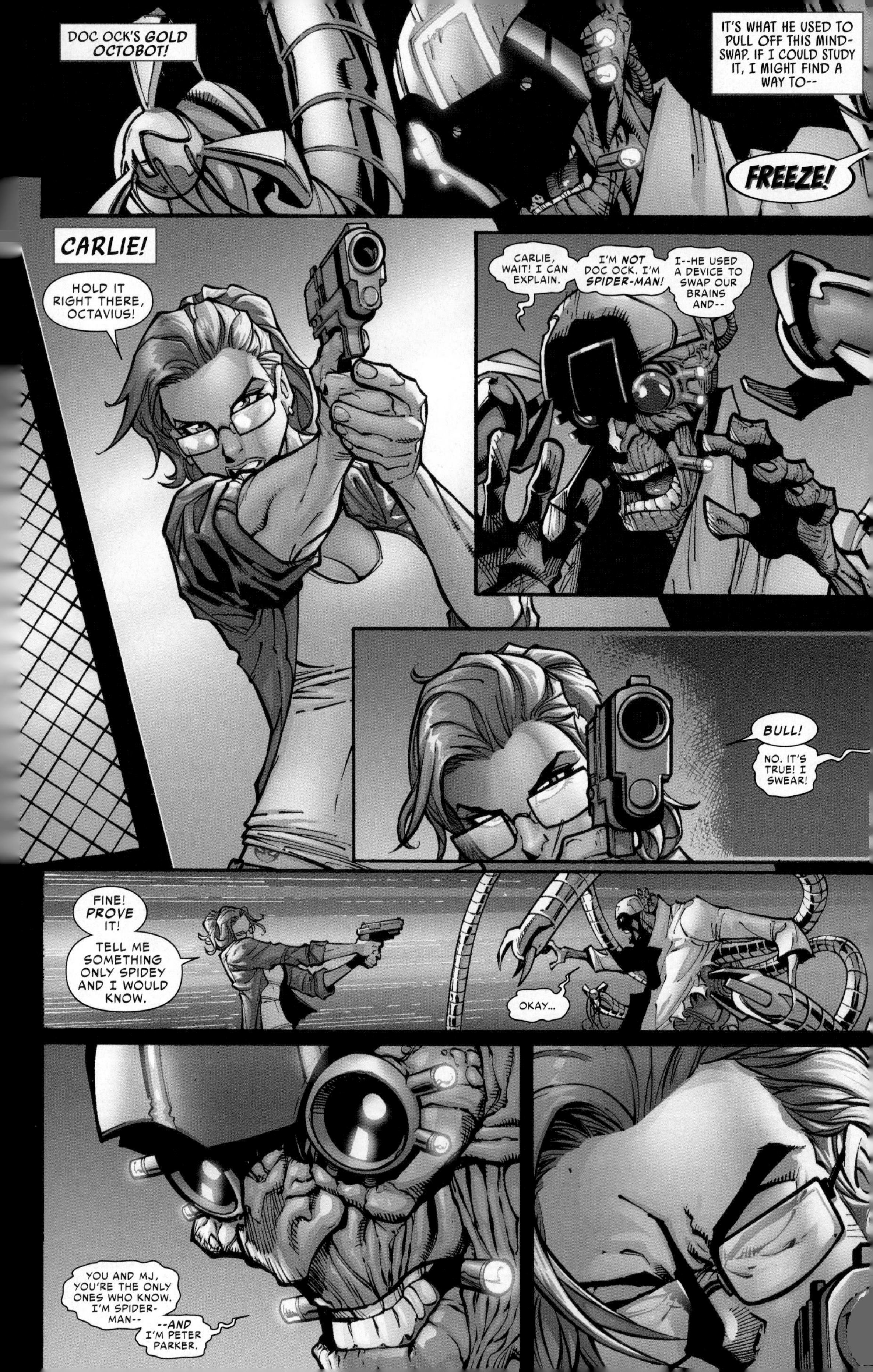

DOC OCK'S GOLD OCTOBOT!
IT'S WHAT HE USED TO PULL OFF THIS MIND-SWAP. IF I COULD STUDY IT, I MIGHT FIND A WAY TO--
FREEZE!
CARLIE!
HOLD IT RIGHT THERE, OCTAVIUS!
CARLIE, WAIT! I CAN EXPLAIN.
I'M NOT DOC OCK. I'M SPIDER-MAN!
I--HE USED A DEVICE TO SWAP OUR BRAINS AND--
BULL!
NO. IT'S TRUE! I SWEAR!
FINE! PROVE IT!
TELL ME SOMETHING ONLY SPIDEY AND I WOULD KNOW.
OKAY...
YOU AND MJ, YOU'RE THE ONLY ONES WHO KNOW. I'M SPIDER-MAN--
--AND I'M PETER PARKER.

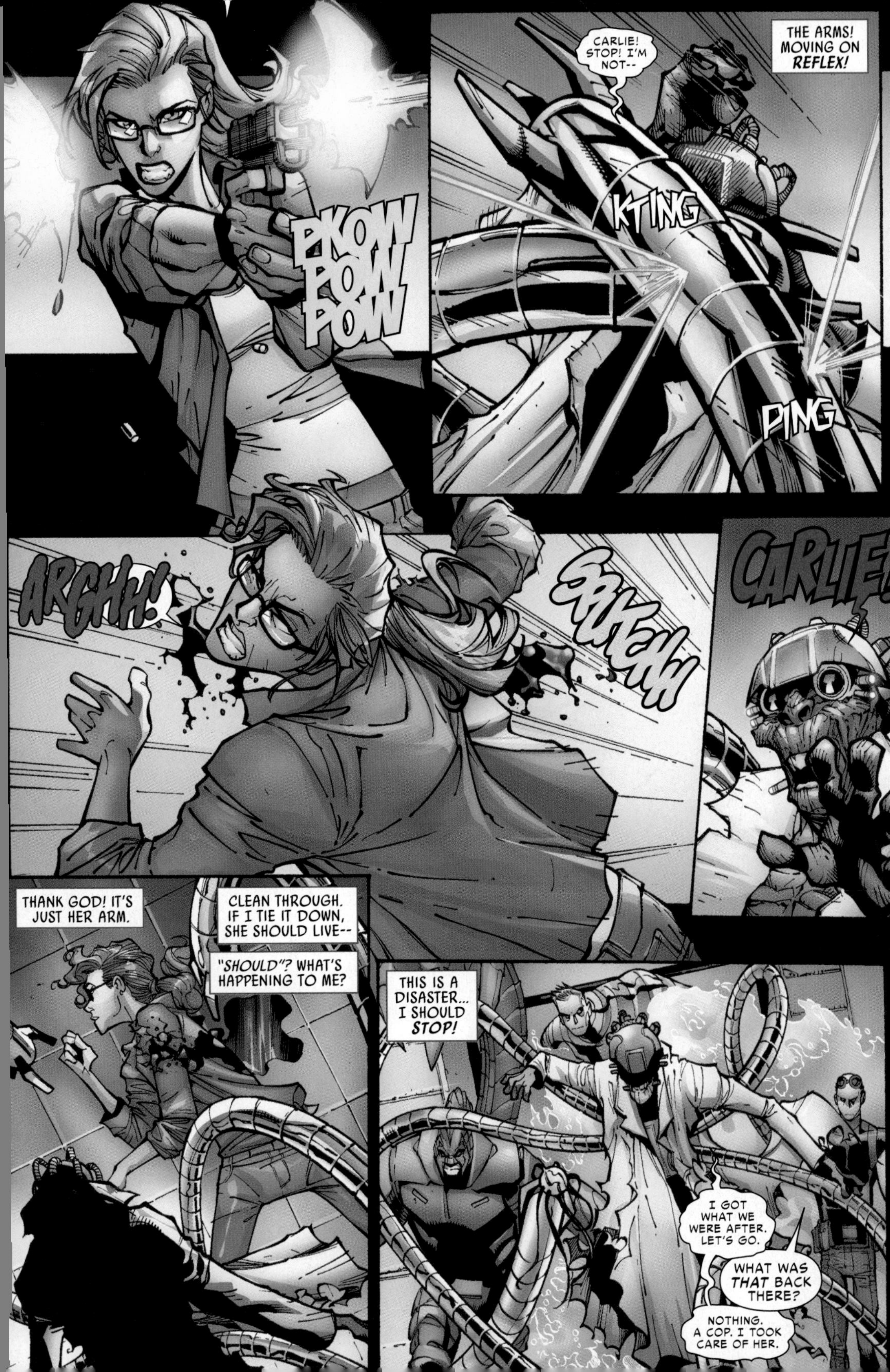
PKOW POW POW
CARLIE! STOP! I'M NOT--
THE ARMS! MOVING ON REFLEX!
KTING
PING
ARGHH!
SPLUTCHH
CARLIE!
THANK GOD! IT'S JUST HER ARM.
CLEAN THROUGH. IF I TIE IT DOWN, SHE SHOULD LIVE--
"SHOULD"? WHAT'S HAPPENING TO ME?
THIS IS A DISASTER... I SHOULD STOP!
I GOT WHAT WE WERE AFTER. LET'S GO.
WHAT WAS THAT BACK THERE?
NOTHING. A COP. I TOOK CARE OF HER.

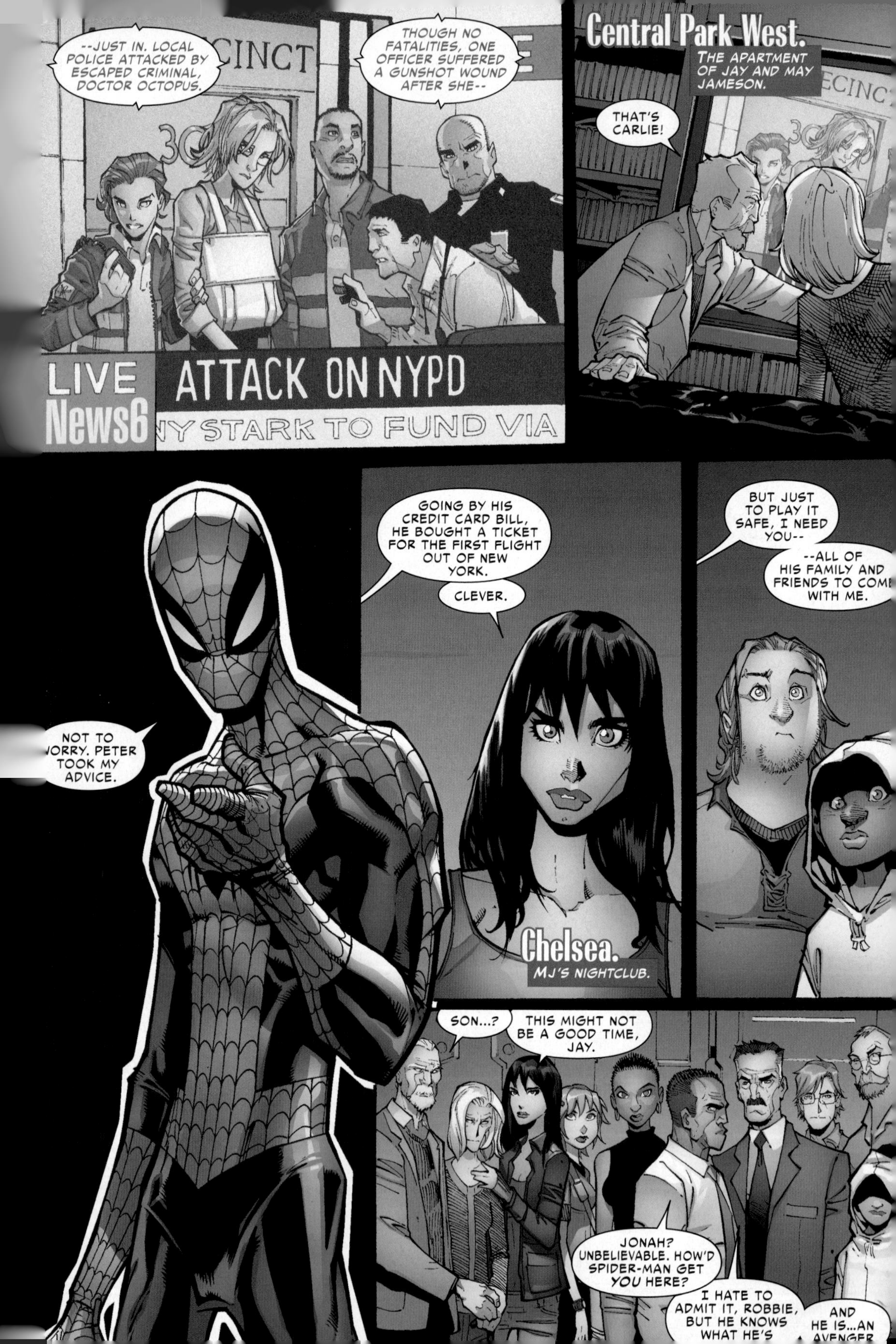
--JUST IN. LOCAL POLICE ATTACKED BY ESCAPED CRIMINAL, DOCTOR OCTOPUS.
THOUGH NO FATALITIES, ONE OFFICER SUFFERED A GUNSHOT WOUND AFTER SHE--
LIVE
News6
ATTACK ON NYPD
NY STARK TO FUND VIA
Central Park West.
THE APARTMENT OF JAY AND MAY JAMESON.
THAT'S CARLIE!
NOT TO WORRY. PETER TOOK MY ADVICE.
GOING BY HIS CREDIT CARD BILL, HE BOUGHT A TICKET FOR THE FIRST FLIGHT OUT OF NEW YORK.
CLEVER.
Chelsea.
MJ'S NIGHTCLUB.
BUT JUST TO PLAY IT SAFE, I NEED YOU--
--ALL OF HIS FAMILY AND FRIENDS TO COME WITH ME.
SON...?
THIS MIGHT NOT BE A GOOD TIME, JAY.
JONAH? UNBELIEVABLE. HOW'D SPIDER-MAN GET YOU HERE?
I HATE TO ADMIT IT, ROBBIE, BUT HE KNOWS WHAT HE'S
AND HE IS...AN AVENGER

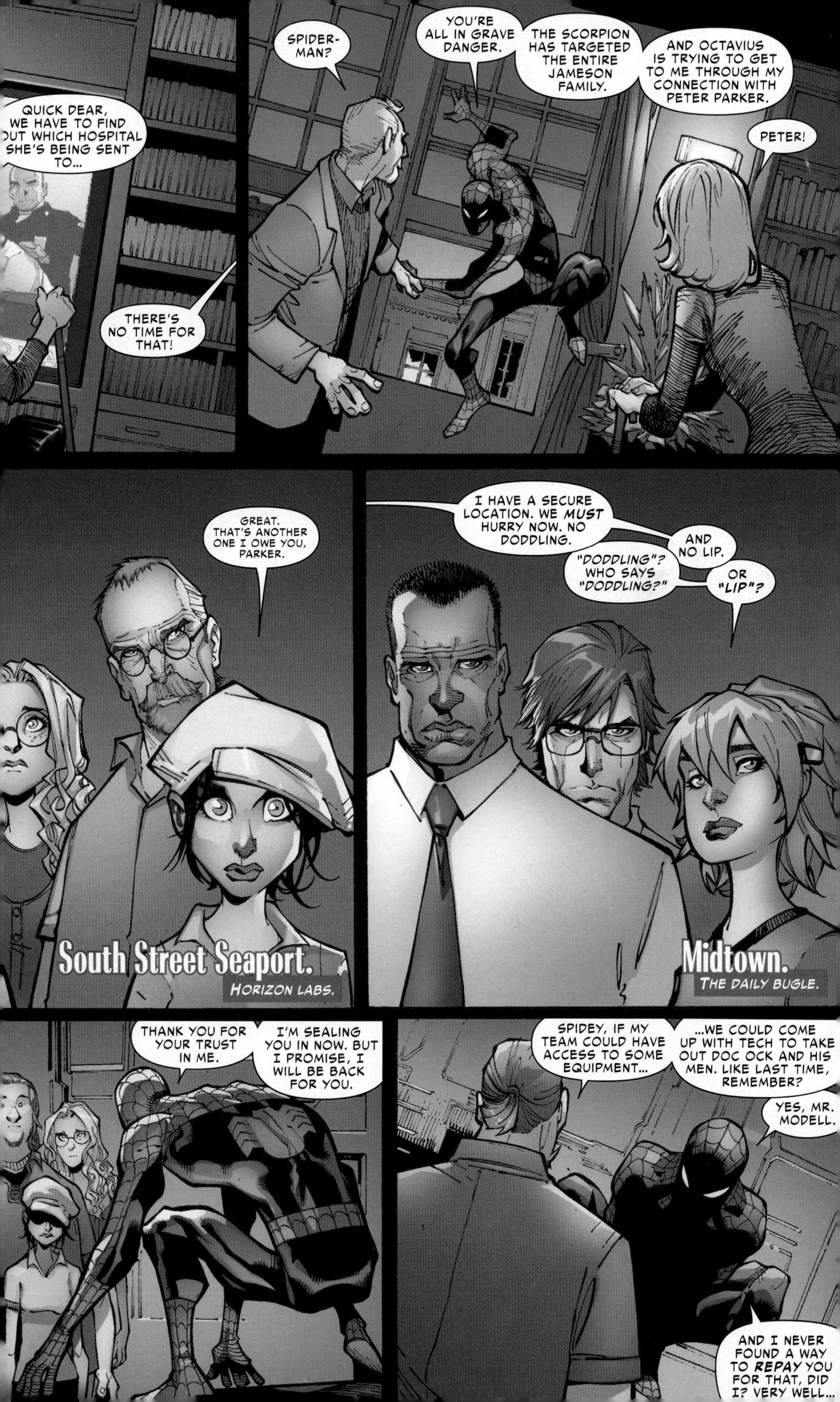
QUICK DEAR, WE HAVE TO FIND OUT WHICH HOSPITAL SHE'S BEING SENT TO...
THERE'S NO TIME FOR THAT!
SPIDER-MAN?
YOU'RE ALL IN GRAVE DANGER.
THE SCORPION HAS TARGETED THE ENTIRE JAMESON FAMILY.
AND OCTAVIUS IS TRYING TO GET TO ME THROUGH MY CONNECTION WITH PETER PARKER.
PETER!
South Street Seaport.
HORIZON LABS.
GREAT. THAT'S ANOTHER ONE I OWE YOU, PARKER.
Midtown.
THE DAILY BUGLE.
I HAVE A SECURE LOCATION. WE MUST HURRY NOW. NO DODDLING.
AND NO LIP.
"DODDLING"? WHO SAYS "DODDLING?"
OR "LIP"?
THANK YOU FOR YOUR TRUST IN ME.
I'M SEALING YOU IN NOW. BUT I PROMISE, I WILL BE BACK FOR YOU.
SPIDEY, IF MY TEAM COULD HAVE ACCESS TO SOME EQUIPMENT...
...WE COULD COME UP WITH TECH TO TAKE OUT DOC OCK AND HIS MEN. LIKE LAST TIME, REMEMBER?
YES, MR. MODELL.
AND I NEVER FOUND A WAY TO REPAY YOU FOR THAT, DID I? VERY WELL...

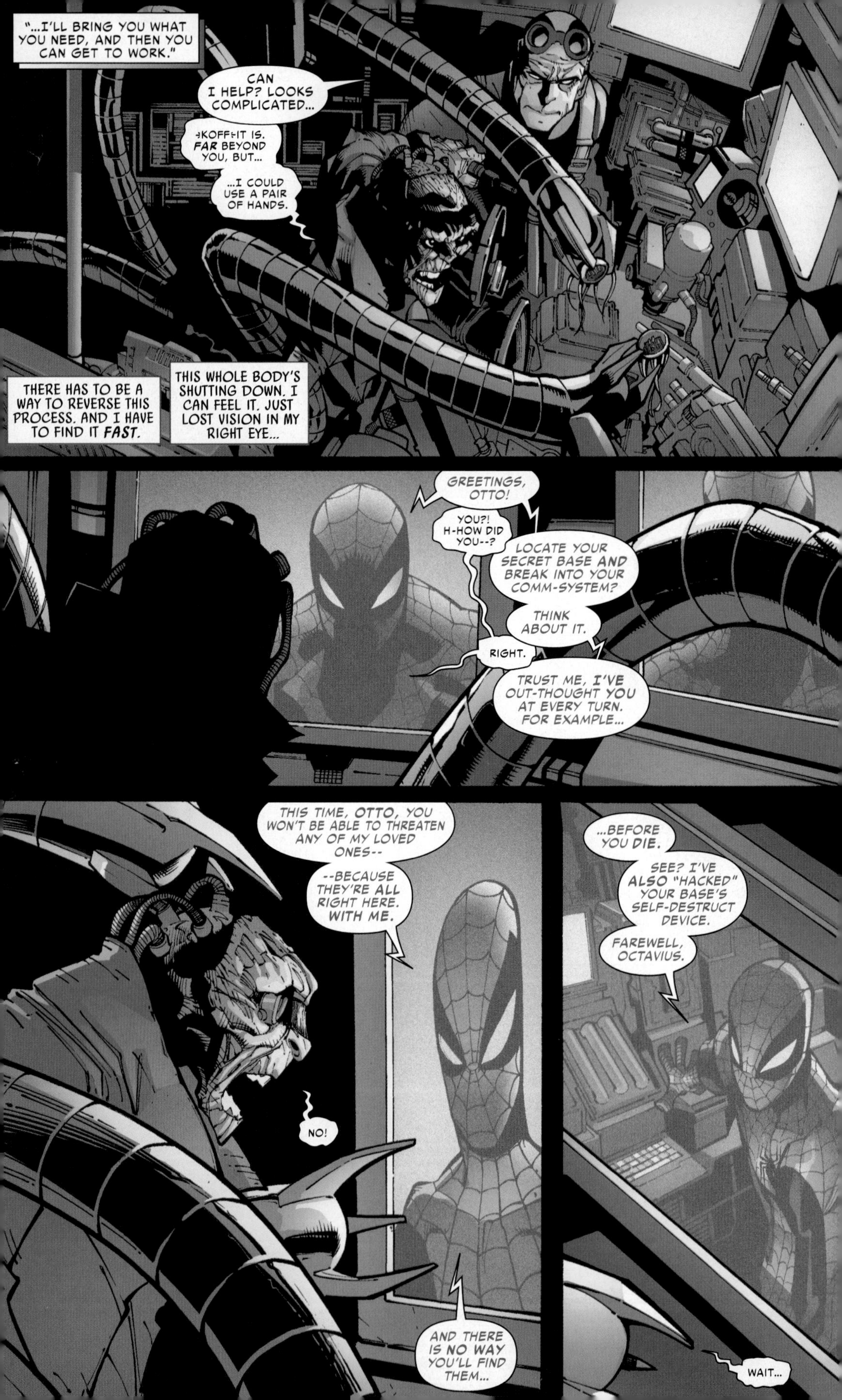
"...I'LL BRING YOU WHAT YOU NEED, AND THEN YOU CAN GET TO WORK."
CAN I HELP? LOOKS COMPLICATED...
÷KOFF÷IT IS. FAR BEYOND YOU, BUT...
...I COULD USE A PAIR OF HANDS.
THERE HAS TO BE A WAY TO REVERSE THIS PROCESS. AND I HAVE TO FIND IT FAST.
THIS WHOLE BODY'S SHUTTING DOWN. I CAN FEEL IT. JUST LOST VISION IN MY RIGHT EYE...
GREETINGS, OTTO!
YOU?! H-HOW DID YOU--?
LOCATE YOUR SECRET BASE AND BREAK INTO YOUR COMM-SYSTEM?
THINK ABOUT IT.
RIGHT.
TRUST ME, I'VE OUT-THOUGHT YOU AT EVERY TURN. FOR EXAMPLE...
THIS TIME, OTTO, YOU WON'T BE ABLE TO THREATEN ANY OF MY LOVED ONES--
--BECAUSE THEY'RE ALL RIGHT HERE. WITH ME.
NO!
AND THERE IS NO WAY YOU'LL FIND THEM...
...BEFORE YOU DIE.
SEE? I'VE ALSO "HACKED" YOUR BASE'S SELF-DESTRUCT DEVICE.
FAREWELL, OCTAVIUS.
WAIT...

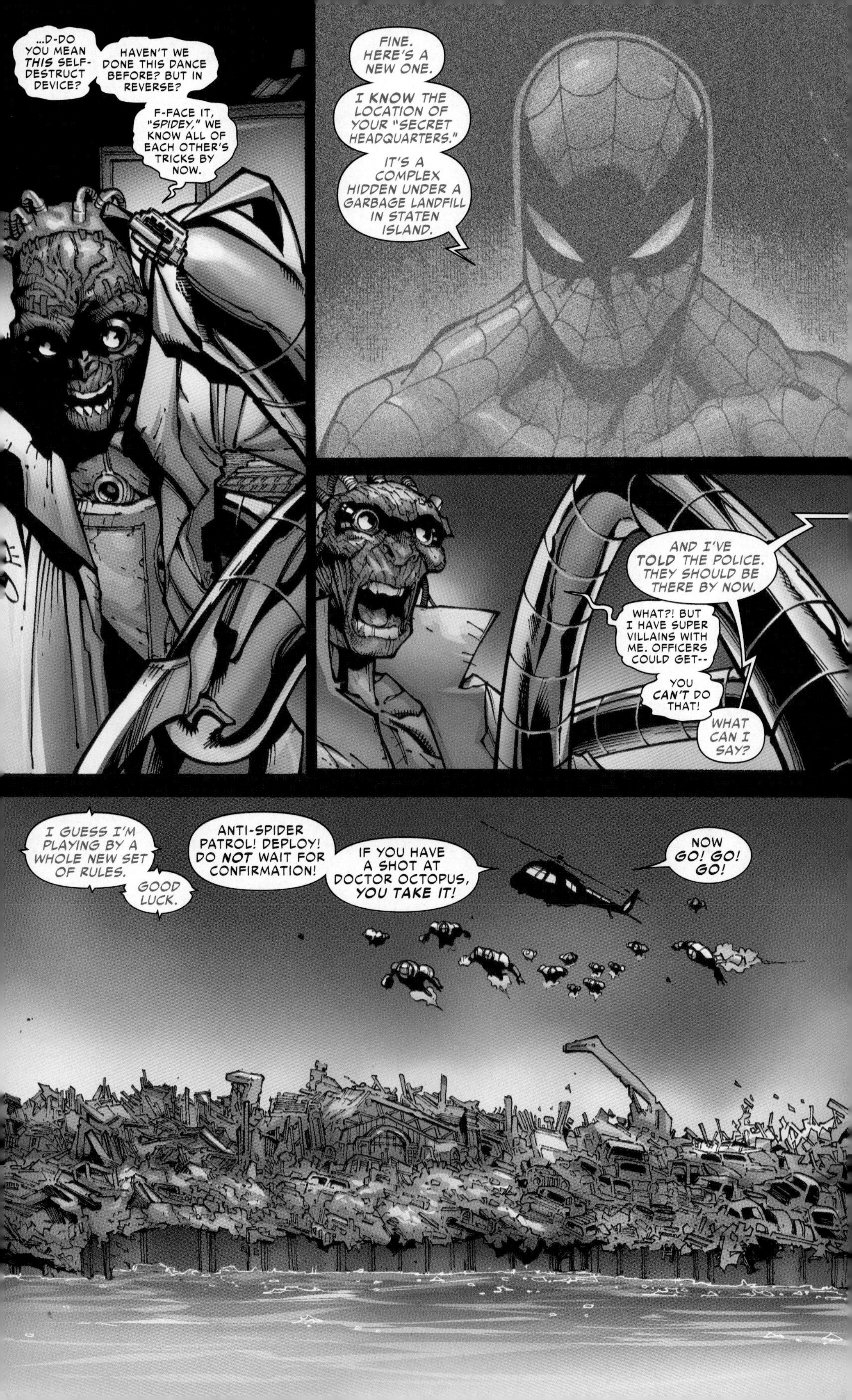
...D-DO YOU MEAN THIS SELF-DESTRUCT DEVICE?
HAVEN'T WE DONE THIS DANCE BEFORE? BUT IN REVERSE?
F-FACE IT, "SPIDEY," WE KNOW ALL OF EACH OTHER'S TRICKS BY NOW.
FINE. HERE'S A NEW ONE.
I KNOW THE LOCATION OF YOUR "SECRET HEADQUARTERS."
IT'S A COMPLEX HIDDEN UNDER A GARBAGE LANDFILL IN STATEN ISLAND.
AND I'VE TOLD THE POLICE. THEY SHOULD BE THERE BY NOW.
WHAT?! BUT I HAVE SUPER VILLAINS WITH ME. OFFICERS COULD GET--
YOU CAN'T DO THAT!
WHAT CAN I SAY?
I GUESS I'M PLAYING BY A WHOLE NEW SET OF RULES.
GOOD LUCK.
ANTI-SPIDER PATROL! DEPLOY! DO NOT WAIT FOR CONFIRMATION!
IF YOU HAVE A SHOT AT DOCTOR OCTOPUS, YOU TAKE IT!
NOW GO! GO! GO!

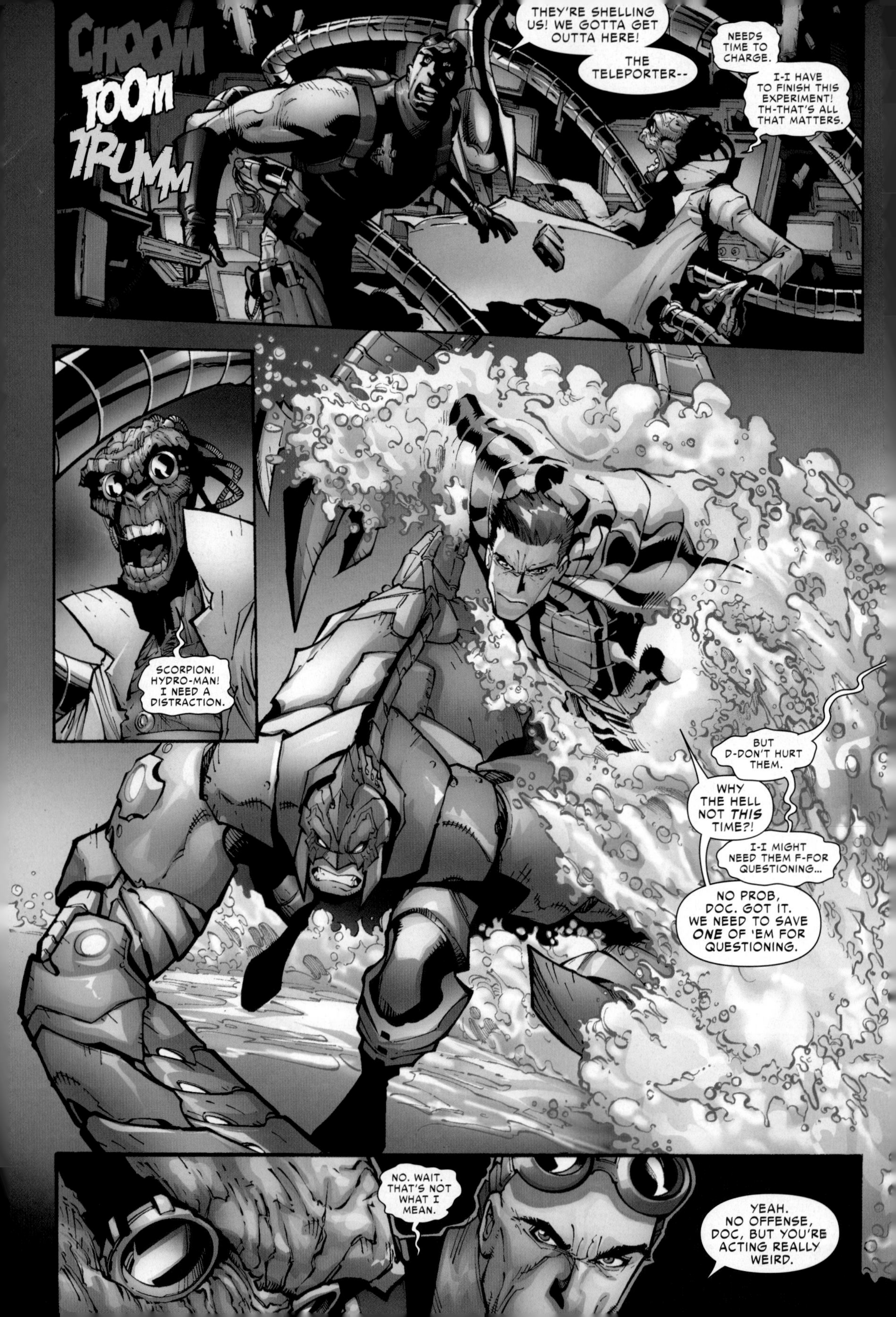
CHOOM
TOOM
TRUMM
THEY'RE SHELLING US! WE GOTTA GET OUTTA HERE!
THE TELEPORTER--
NEEDS TIME TO CHARGE.
I-I HAVE TO FINISH THIS EXPERIMENT! TH-THAT'S ALL THAT MATTERS.
SCORPION! HYDRO-MAN! I NEED A DISTRACTION.
BUT D-DON'T HURT THEM.
WHY THE HELL NOT *THIS* TIME?!
I-I MIGHT NEED THEM F-FOR QUESTIONING...
NO PROB, DOC. GOT IT. WE NEED TO SAVE *ONE* OF 'EM FOR QUESTIONING.
NO. WAIT. THAT'S NOT WHAT I MEAN.
YEAH. NO OFFENSE, DOC, BUT YOU'RE ACTING REALLY WEIRD.

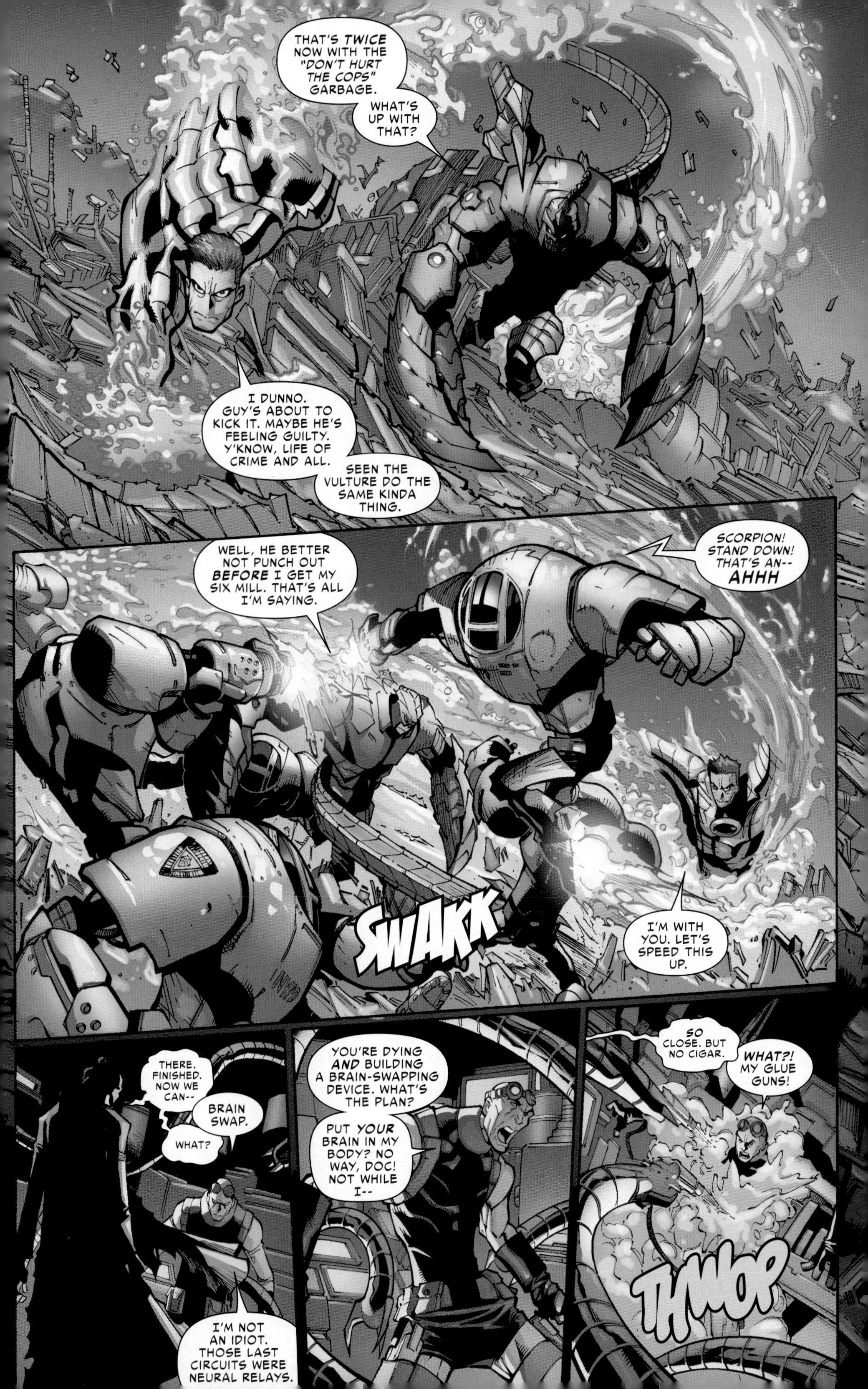
THAT'S *TWICE* NOW WITH THE "DON'T HURT THE COPS" GARBAGE.
WHAT'S UP WITH THAT?
I DUNNO. GUY'S ABOUT TO KICK IT. MAYBE HE'S FEELING GUILTY. Y'KNOW, LIFE OF CRIME AND ALL.
SEEN THE VULTURE DO THE SAME KINDA THING.
WELL, HE BETTER NOT PUNCH OUT *BEFORE* I GET MY SIX MILL. THAT'S ALL I'M SAYING.
SCORPION! STAND DOWN! THAT'S AN-- **AHHH**
SWAKK
I'M WITH YOU. LET'S SPEED THIS UP.
THERE. FINISHED. NOW WE CAN--
BRAIN SWAP.
WHAT?
I'M NOT AN IDIOT. THOSE LAST CIRCUITS WERE NEURAL RELAYS.
YOU'RE DYING *AND* BUILDING A BRAIN-SWAPPING DEVICE. WHAT'S THE PLAN?
PUT *YOUR* BRAIN IN MY BODY? NO WAY, DOC! NOT WHILE I--
SO CLOSE. BUT NO CIGAR.
WHAT?! MY GLUE GUNS!
THWOP

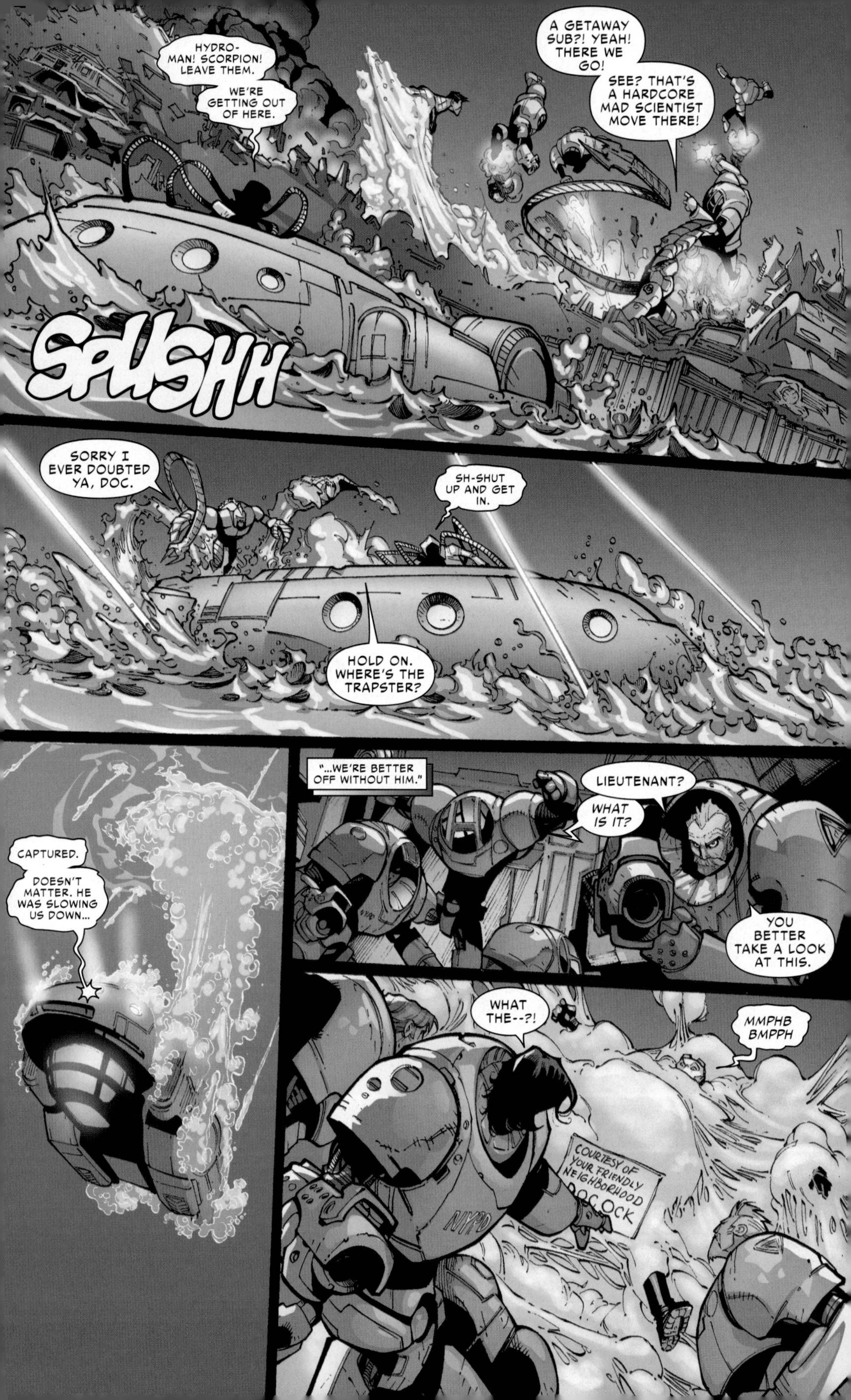
HYDRO-MAN! SCORPION! LEAVE THEM.
WE'RE GETTING OUT OF HERE.
A GETAWAY SUB?! YEAH! THERE WE GO!
SEE? THAT'S A HARDCORE MAD SCIENTIST MOVE THERE!
SPLUSHH
SORRY I EVER DOUBTED YA, DOC.
SH-SHUT UP AND GET IN.
HOLD ON. WHERE'S THE TRAPSTER?
CAPTURED.
DOESN'T MATTER. HE WAS SLOWING US DOWN...
"...WE'RE BETTER OFF WITHOUT HIM."
LIEUTENANT?
WHAT IS IT?
YOU BETTER TAKE A LOOK AT THIS.
WHAT THE--?!
MMPHB BMPPH
COURTESY OF YOUR FRIENDLY NEIGHBORHOOD DOC OCK
NYPD

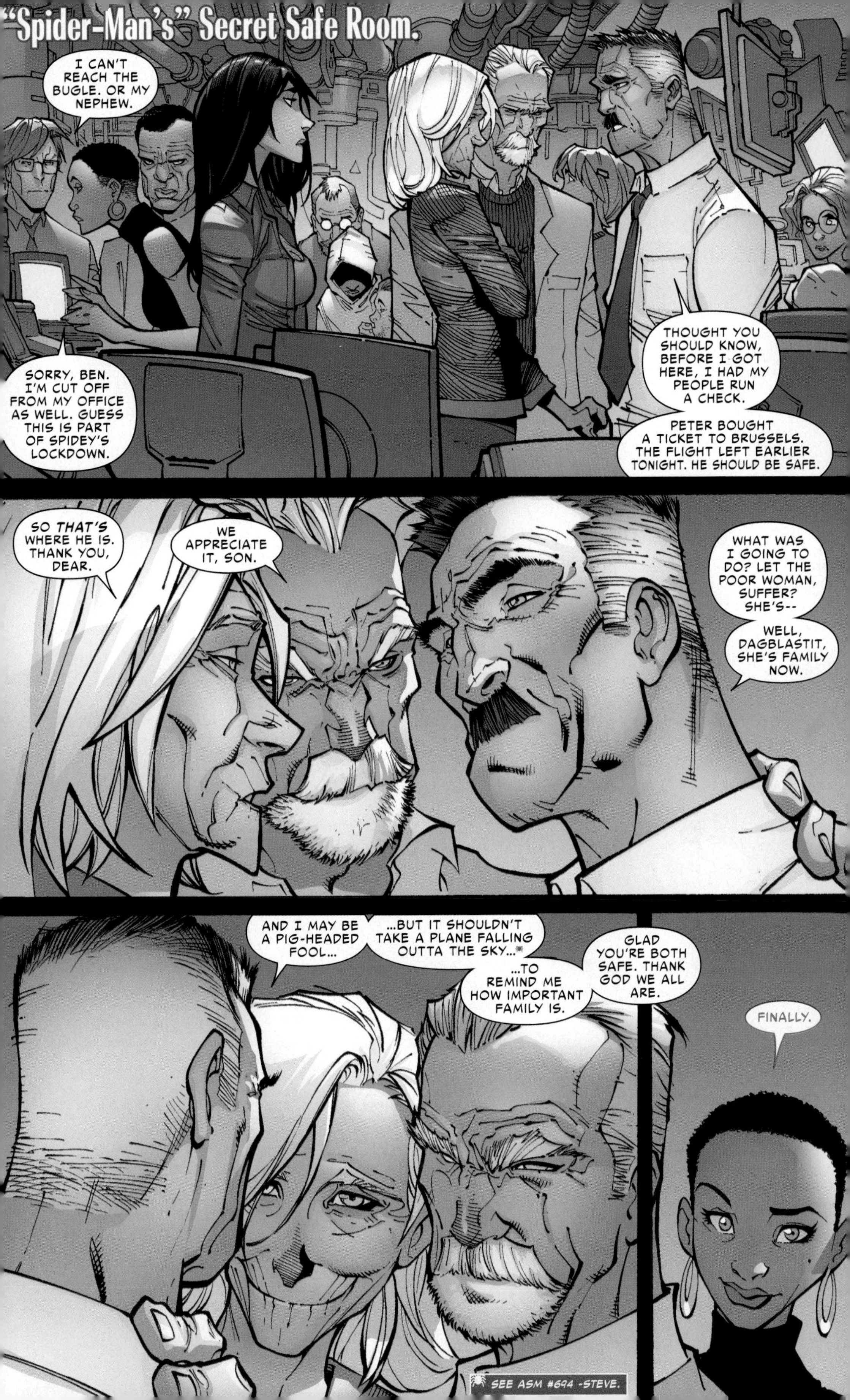
"Spider-Man's" Secret Safe Room.
I CAN'T REACH THE BUGLE. OR MY NEPHEW.
SORRY, BEN. I'M CUT OFF FROM MY OFFICE AS WELL. GUESS THIS IS PART OF SPIDEY'S LOCKDOWN.
THOUGHT YOU SHOULD KNOW, BEFORE I GOT HERE, I HAD MY PEOPLE RUN A CHECK.
PETER BOUGHT A TICKET TO BRUSSELS. THE FLIGHT LEFT EARLIER TONIGHT. HE SHOULD BE SAFE.
SO *THAT'S* WHERE HE IS. THANK YOU, DEAR.
WE APPRECIATE IT, SON.
WHAT WAS I GOING TO DO? LET THE POOR WOMAN, SUFFER? SHE'S--
WELL, DAGBLASTIT, SHE'S FAMILY NOW.
AND I MAY BE A PIG-HEADED FOOL...
...BUT IT SHOULDN'T TAKE A PLANE FALLING OUTTA THE SKY...*
...TO REMIND ME HOW IMPORTANT FAMILY IS.
GLAD YOU'RE BOTH SAFE. THANK GOD WE ALL ARE.
FINALLY.
* SEE ASM #694 -STEVE.

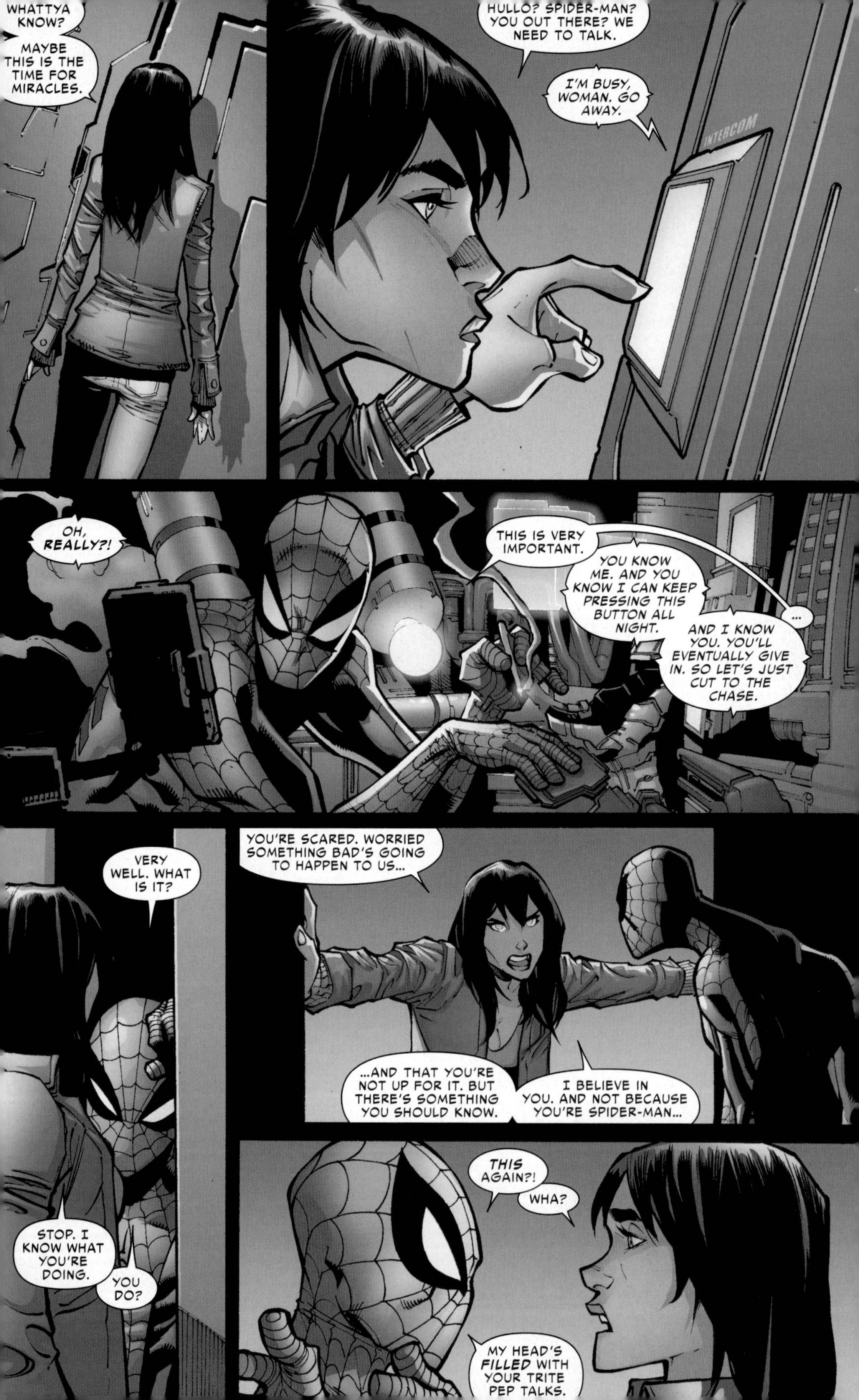
WHATTYA KNOW?
MAYBE THIS IS THE TIME FOR MIRACLES.
HULLO? SPIDER-MAN? YOU OUT THERE? WE NEED TO TALK.
I'M BUSY, WOMAN. GO AWAY.
INTERCOM
OH, REALLY?!
THIS IS VERY IMPORTANT.
YOU KNOW ME. AND YOU KNOW I CAN KEEP PRESSING THIS BUTTON ALL NIGHT.
...
AND I KNOW YOU. YOU'LL EVENTUALLY GIVE IN. SO LET'S JUST CUT TO THE CHASE.
VERY WELL. WHAT IS IT?
YOU'RE SCARED. WORRIED SOMETHING BAD'S GOING TO HAPPEN TO US...
...AND THAT YOU'RE NOT UP FOR IT. BUT THERE'S SOMETHING YOU SHOULD KNOW.
I BELIEVE IN YOU. AND NOT BECAUSE YOU'RE SPIDER-MAN...
STOP. I KNOW WHAT YOU'RE DOING.
YOU DO?
THIS AGAIN?!
WHA?
MY HEAD'S FILLED WITH YOUR TRITE PEP TALKS.

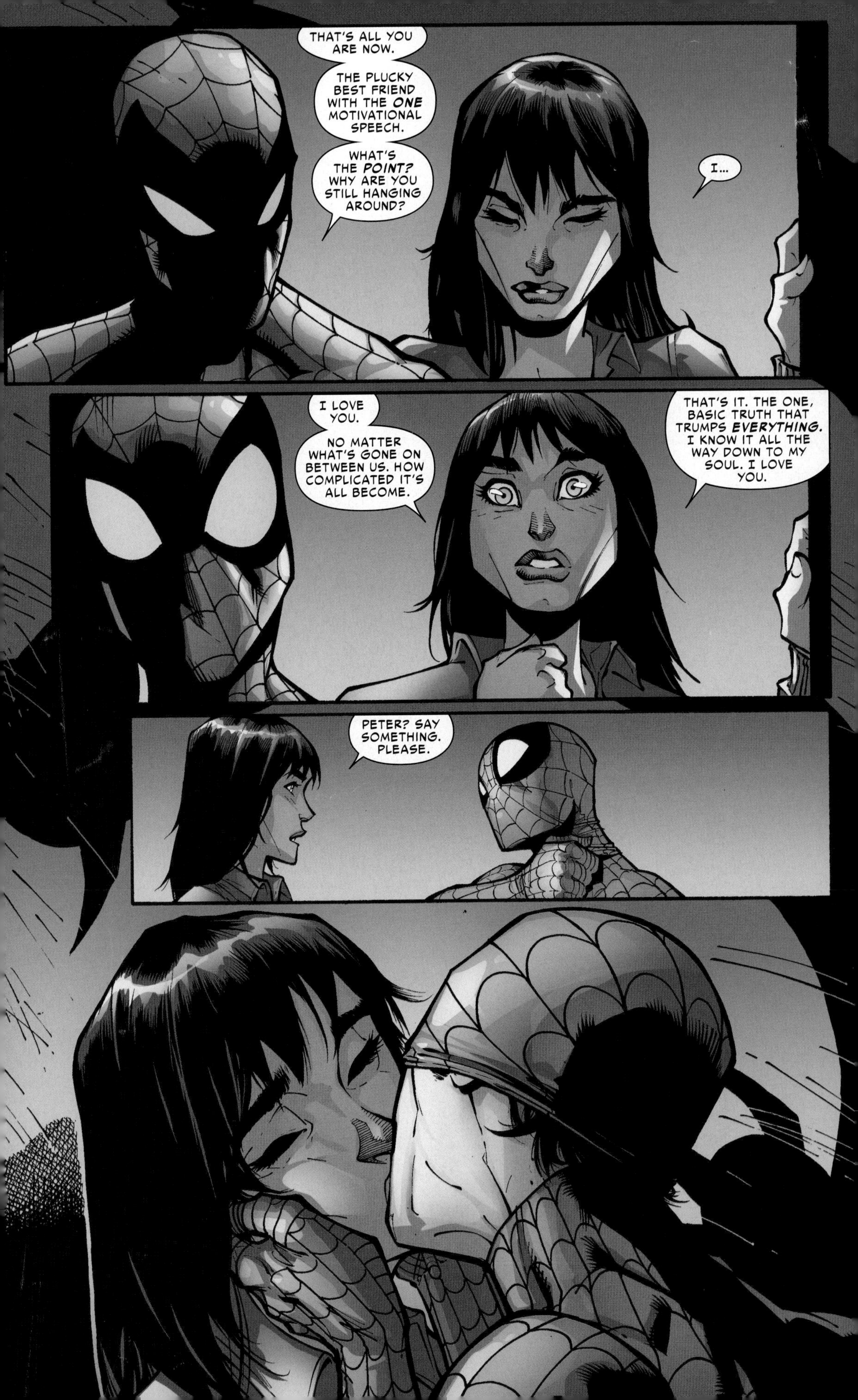
THAT'S ALL YOU ARE NOW.
THE PLUCKY BEST FRIEND WITH THE *ONE* MOTIVATIONAL SPEECH.
WHAT'S THE *POINT?* WHY ARE YOU STILL HANGING AROUND?
I...
I LOVE YOU.
NO MATTER WHAT'S GONE ON BETWEEN US. HOW COMPLICATED IT'S ALL BECOME.
THAT'S IT. THE ONE, BASIC TRUTH THAT TRUMPS *EVERYTHING.* I KNOW IT ALL THE WAY DOWN TO MY SOUL. I LOVE YOU.
PETER? SAY SOMETHING. PLEASE.

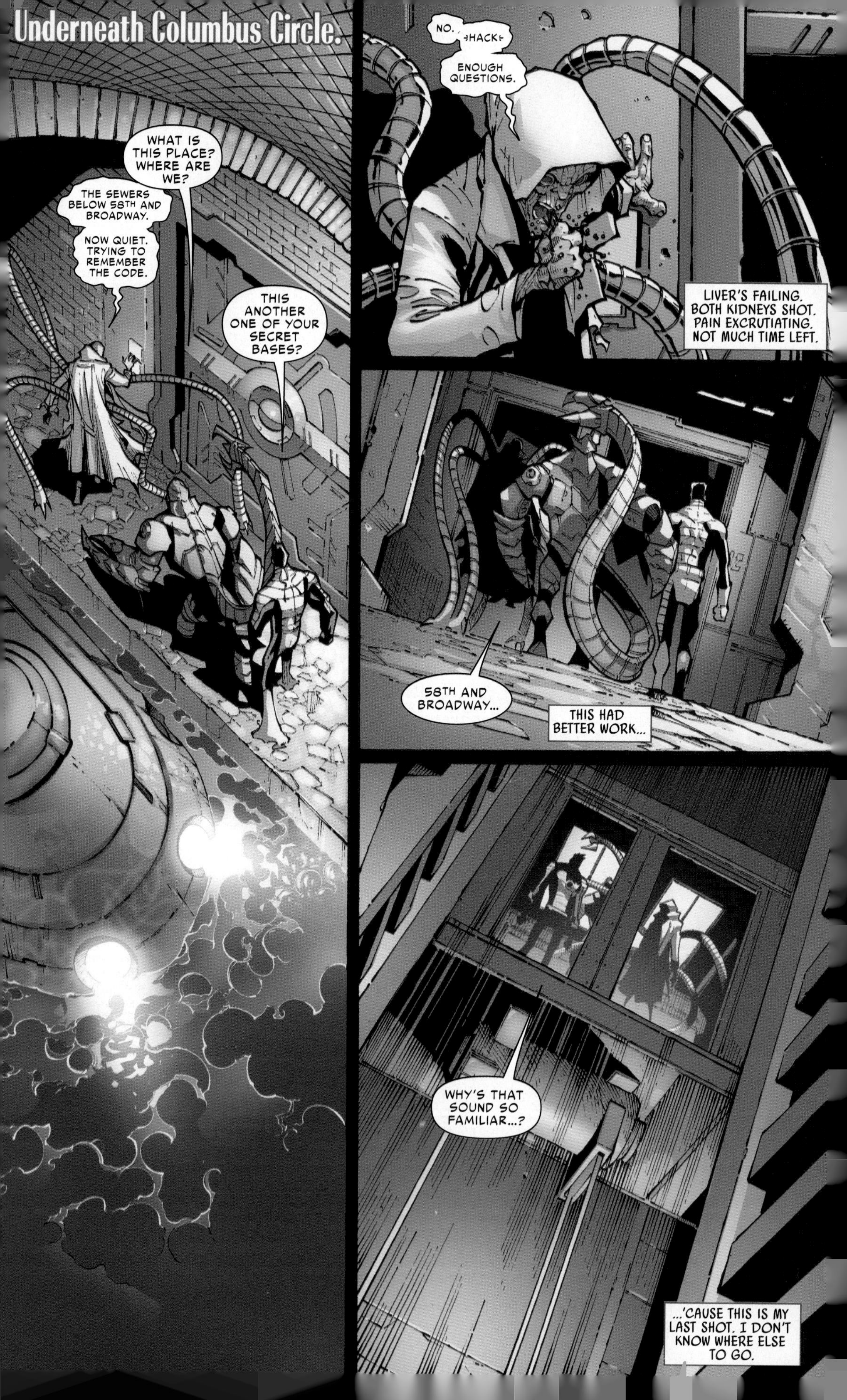
Underneath Columbus Circle.
WHAT IS THIS PLACE? WHERE ARE WE?
THE SEWERS BELOW 58TH AND BROADWAY.
NOW QUIET. TRYING TO REMEMBER THE CODE.
THIS ANOTHER ONE OF YOUR SECRET BASES?
NO. HACK
ENOUGH QUESTIONS.
LIVER'S FAILING. BOTH KIDNEYS SHOT. PAIN EXCRUTIATING. NOT MUCH TIME LEFT.
58TH AND BROADWAY...
THIS HAD BETTER WORK...
WHY'S THAT SOUND SO FAMILIAR...?
...'CAUSE THIS IS MY LAST SHOT. I DON'T KNOW WHERE ELSE TO GO.

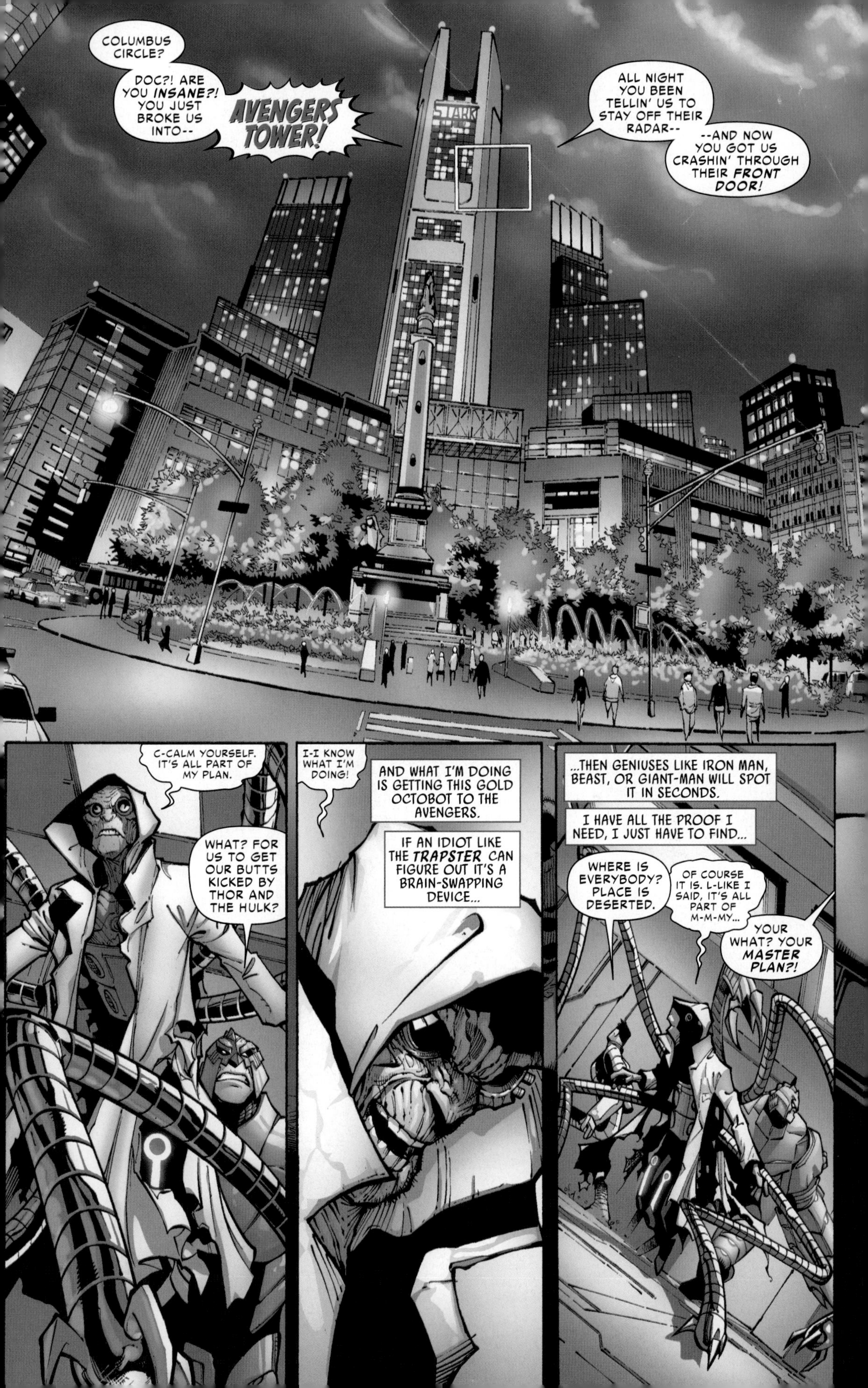
COLUMBUS CIRCLE?
DOC?! ARE YOU INSANE?! YOU JUST BROKE US INTO--
AVENGERS TOWER!
STARK
ALL NIGHT YOU BEEN TELLIN' US TO STAY OFF THEIR RADAR--
--AND NOW YOU GOT US CRASHIN' THROUGH THEIR FRONT DOOR!
C-CALM YOURSELF. IT'S ALL PART OF MY PLAN.
WHAT? FOR US TO GET OUR BUTTS KICKED BY THOR AND THE HULK?
I-I KNOW WHAT I'M DOING!
AND WHAT I'M DOING IS GETTING THIS GOLD OCTOBOT TO THE AVENGERS.
IF AN IDIOT LIKE THE TRAPSTER CAN FIGURE OUT IT'S A BRAIN-SWAPPING DEVICE...
...THEN GENIUSES LIKE IRON MAN, BEAST, OR GIANT-MAN WILL SPOT IT IN SECONDS.
I HAVE ALL THE PROOF I NEED, I JUST HAVE TO FIND...
WHERE IS EVERYBODY? PLACE IS DESERTED.
OF COURSE IT IS. L-LIKE I SAID, IT'S ALL PART OF M-M-MY...
YOUR WHAT? YOUR MASTER PLAN?!

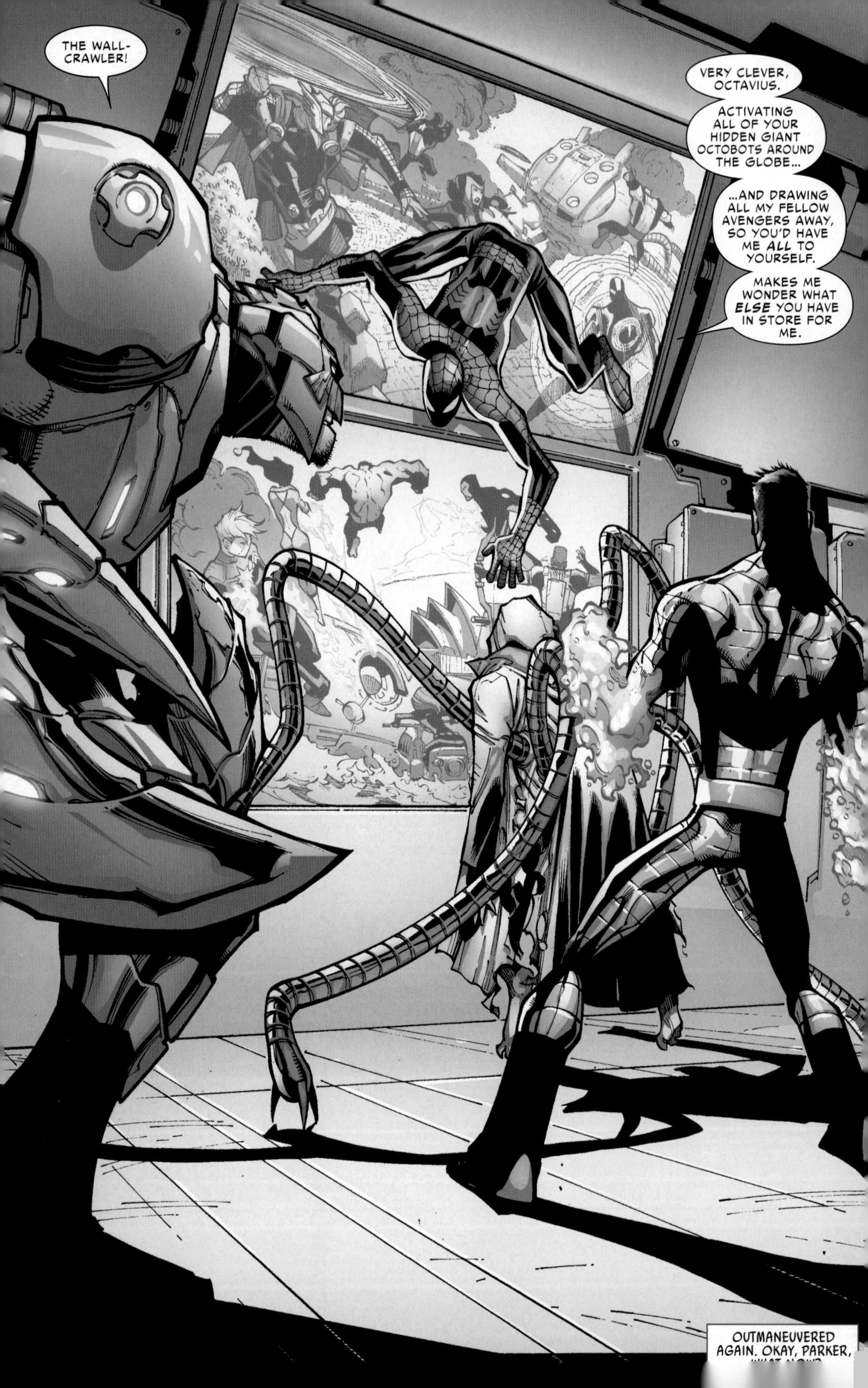
THE WALL-CRAWLER!
VERY CLEVER, OCTAVIUS.
ACTIVATING ALL OF YOUR HIDDEN GIANT OCTOBOTS AROUND THE GLOBE...
...AND DRAWING ALL MY FELLOW AVENGERS AWAY, SO YOU'D HAVE ME ALL TO YOURSELF.
MAKES ME WONDER WHAT ELSE YOU HAVE IN STORE FOR ME.
OUTMANEUVERED AGAIN. OKAY, PARKER,

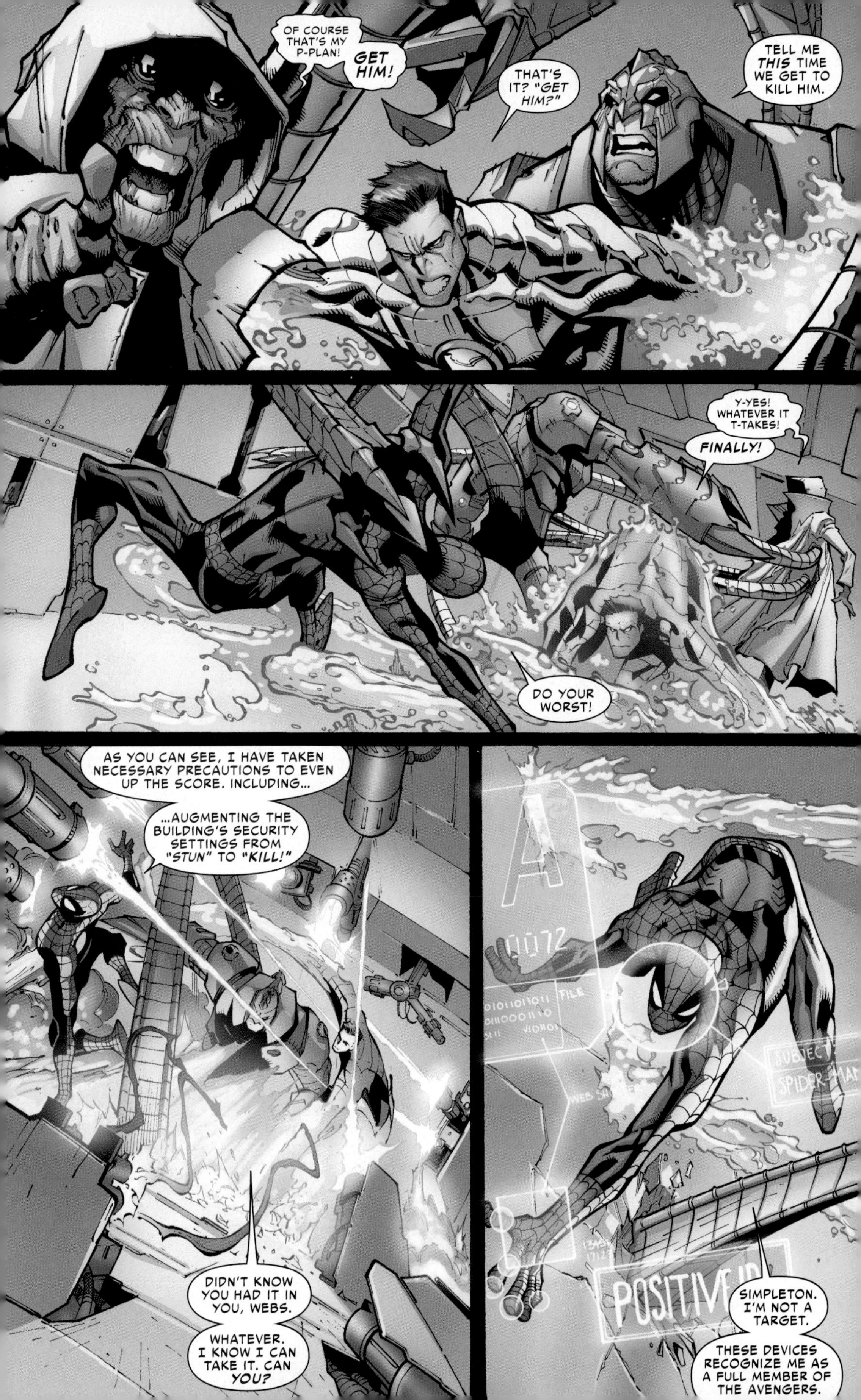
OF COURSE THAT'S MY P-PLAN! GET HIM!
THAT'S IT? "GET HIM?"
TELL ME THIS TIME WE GET TO KILL HIM.
Y-YES! WHATEVER IT T-TAKES!
FINALLY!
DO YOUR WORST!
AS YOU CAN SEE, I HAVE TAKEN NECESSARY PRECAUTIONS TO EVEN UP THE SCORE. INCLUDING...
...AUGMENTING THE BUILDING'S SECURITY SETTINGS FROM "STUN" TO "KILL!"
DIDN'T KNOW YOU HAD IT IN YOU, WEBS.
WHATEVER. I KNOW I CAN TAKE IT. CAN YOU?
FILE
SUBJECT
POSITIVE ID
SIMPLETON. I'M NOT A TARGET.
THESE DEVICES RECOGNIZE ME AS A FULL MEMBER OF THE AVENGERS.

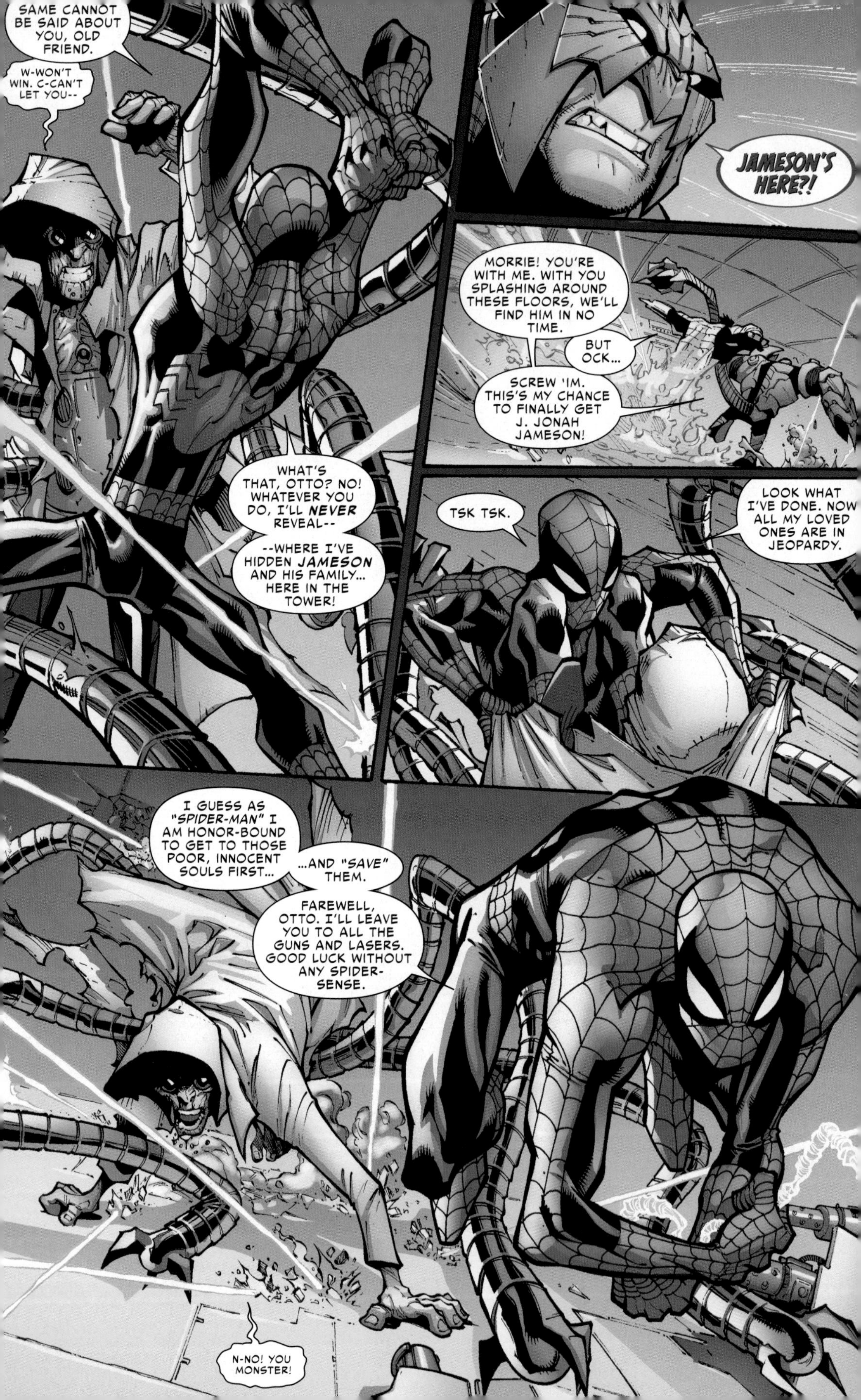
SAME CANNOT BE SAID ABOUT YOU, OLD FRIEND.
W-WON'T WIN. C-CAN'T LET YOU--
JAMESON'S HERE?!
MORRIE! YOU'RE WITH ME. WITH YOU SPLASHING AROUND THESE FLOORS, WE'LL FIND HIM IN NO TIME.
BUT OCK...
SCREW 'IM. THIS'S MY CHANCE TO FINALLY GET J. JONAH JAMESON!
WHAT'S THAT, OTTO? NO! WHATEVER YOU DO, I'LL NEVER REVEAL--
--WHERE I'VE HIDDEN JAMESON AND HIS FAMILY... HERE IN THE TOWER!
TSK TSK.
LOOK WHAT I'VE DONE. NOW ALL MY LOVED ONES ARE IN JEOPARDY.
I GUESS AS "SPIDER-MAN" I AM HONOR-BOUND TO GET TO THOSE POOR, INNOCENT SOULS FIRST...
...AND "SAVE" THEM.
FAREWELL, OTTO. I'LL LEAVE YOU TO ALL THE GUNS AND LASERS. GOOD LUCK WITHOUT ANY SPIDER-SENSE.
N-NO! YOU MONSTER!

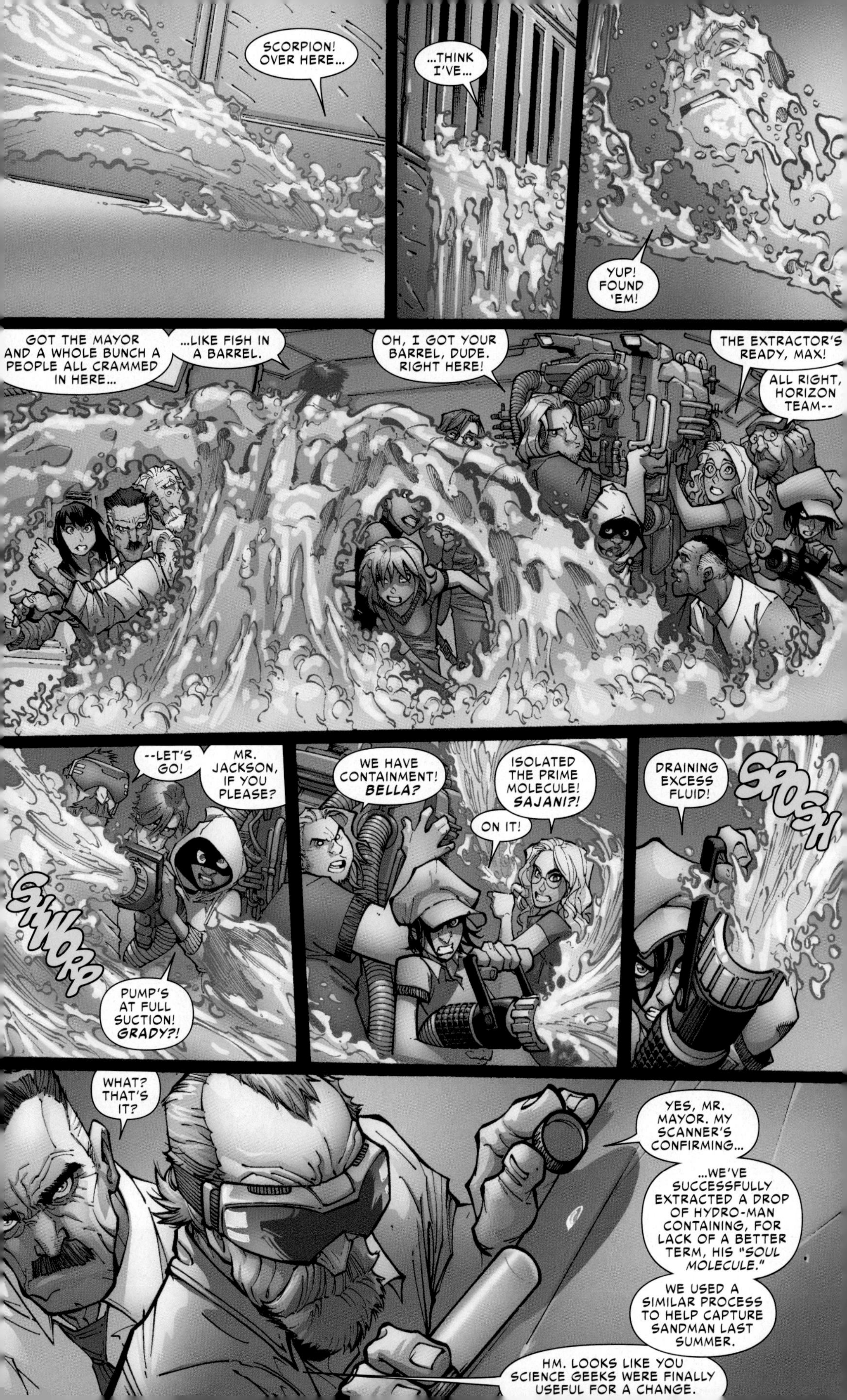
SCORPION! OVER HERE...
...THINK I'VE...
YUP! FOUND 'EM!
GOT THE MAYOR AND A WHOLE BUNCH A PEOPLE ALL CRAMMED IN HERE...
...LIKE FISH IN A BARREL.
OH, I GOT YOUR BARREL, DUDE. RIGHT HERE!
THE EXTRACTOR'S READY, MAX!
ALL RIGHT, HORIZON TEAM--
--LET'S GO!
MR. JACKSON, IF YOU PLEASE?
SHHORP
PUMP'S AT FULL SUCTION! GRADY?!
WE HAVE CONTAINMENT! BELLA?
ISOLATED THE PRIME MOLECULE! SAJANI?!
ON IT!
DRAINING EXCESS FLUID!
SPOSH
WHAT? THAT'S IT?
YES, MR. MAYOR. MY SCANNER'S CONFIRMING...
...WE'VE SUCCESSFULLY EXTRACTED A DROP OF HYDRO-MAN CONTAINING, FOR LACK OF A BETTER TERM, HIS "SOUL MOLECULE."
WE USED A SIMILAR PROCESS TO HELP CAPTURE SANDMAN LAST SUMMER.
HM. LOOKS LIKE YOU SCIENCE GEEKS WERE FINALLY USEFUL FOR A CHANGE.

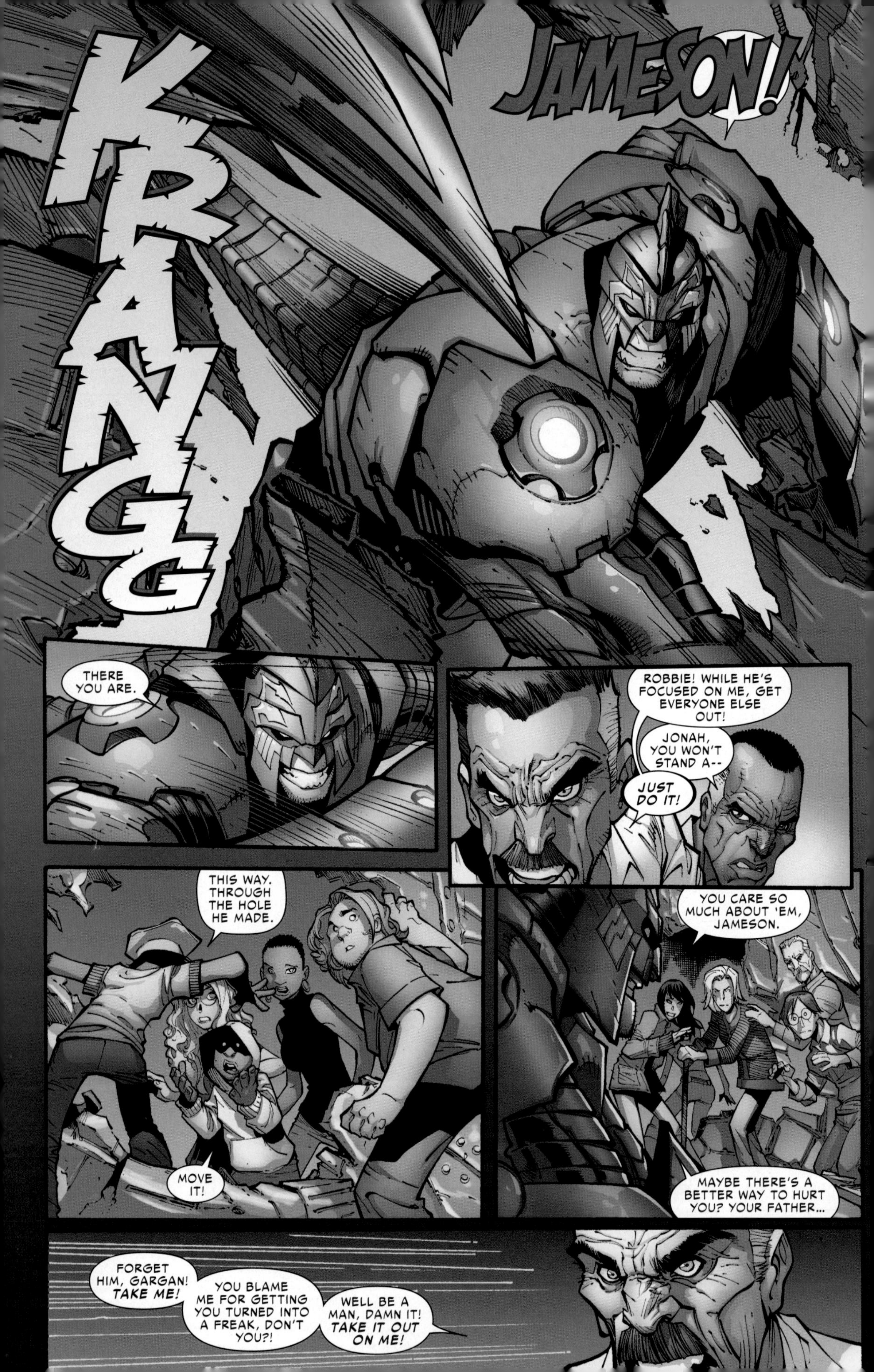
KRANGG
JAMESON!
THERE YOU ARE.
ROBBIE! WHILE HE'S FOCUSED ON ME, GET EVERYONE ELSE OUT!
JONAH, YOU WON'T STAND A--
JUST DO IT!
THIS WAY. THROUGH THE HOLE HE MADE.
MOVE IT!
YOU CARE SO MUCH ABOUT 'EM, JAMESON.
MAYBE THERE'S A BETTER WAY TO HURT YOU? YOUR FATHER...
FORGET HIM, GARGAN! TAKE ME!
YOU BLAME ME FOR GETTING YOU TURNED INTO A FREAK, DON'T YOU?!
WELL BE A MAN, DAMN IT! TAKE IT OUT ON ME!

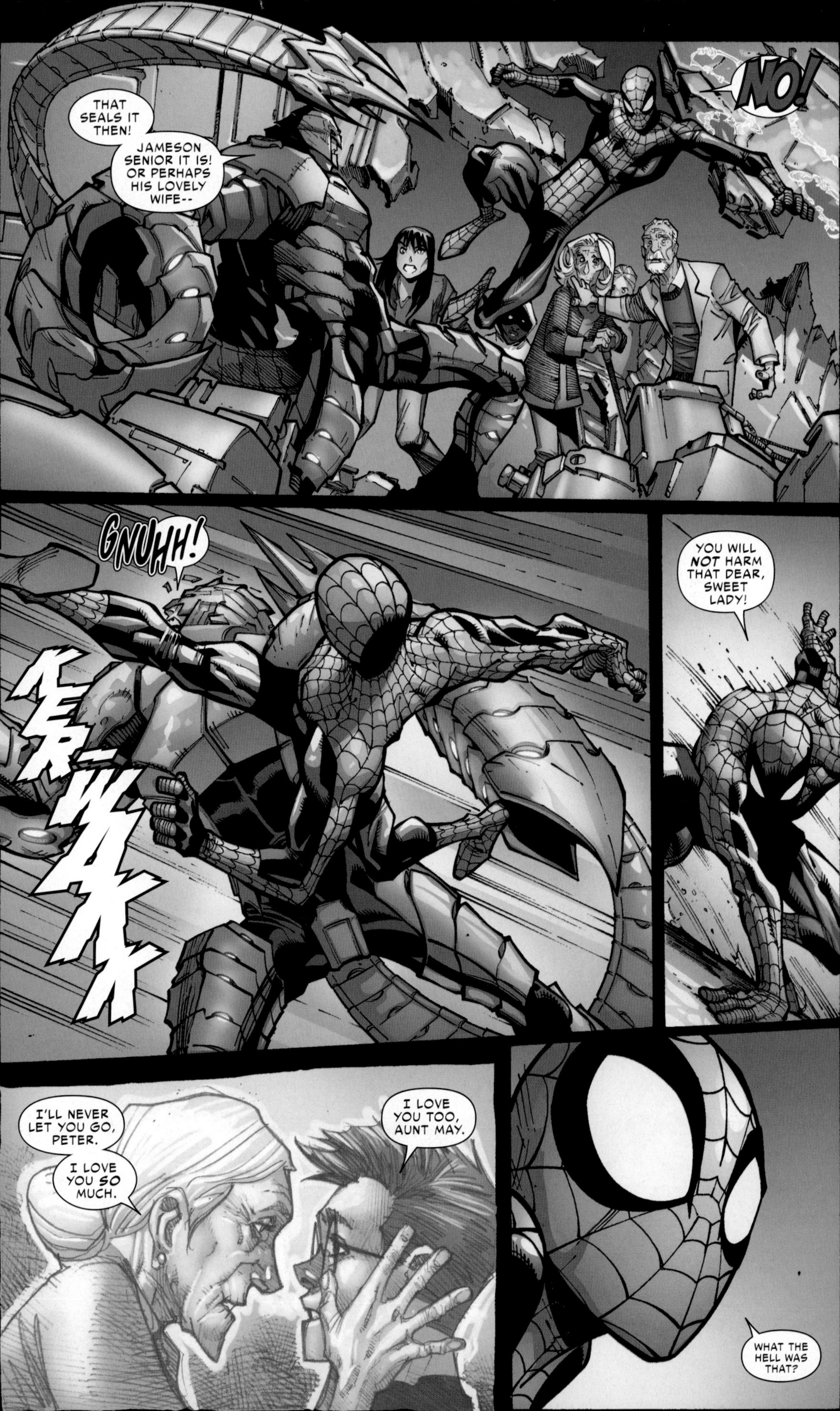
THAT SEALS IT THEN!
JAMESON SENIOR IT IS! OR PERHAPS HIS LOVELY WIFE--
NO!
GNUHH!
KER-WAKK
YOU WILL NOT HARM THAT DEAR, SWEET LADY!
I'LL NEVER LET YOU GO, PETER.
I LOVE YOU SO MUCH.
I LOVE YOU TOO, AUNT MAY.
WHAT THE HELL WAS THAT?

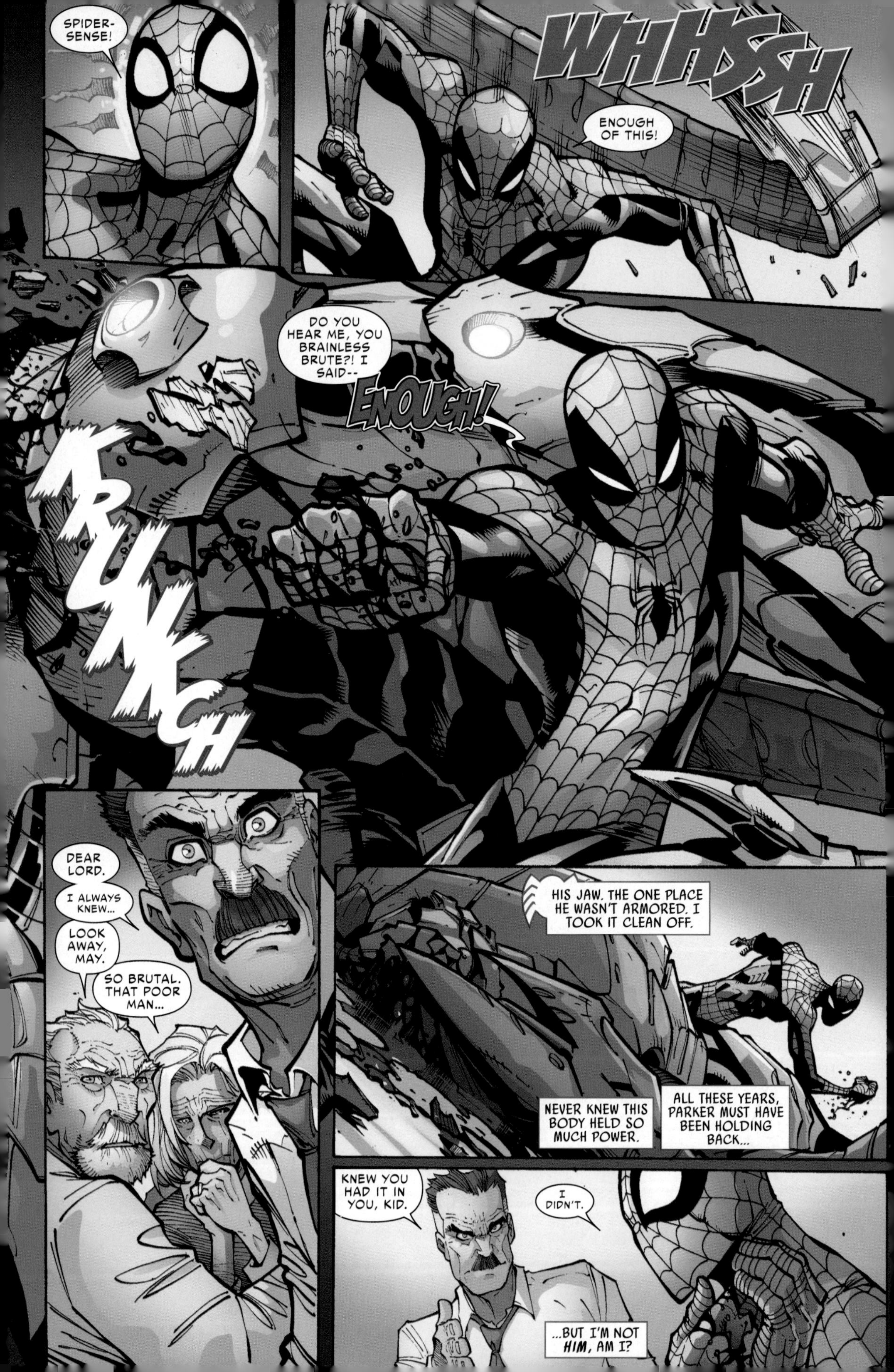
SPIDER-SENSE!
WHHSSH
ENOUGH OF THIS!
DO YOU HEAR ME, YOU BRAINLESS BRUTE?! I SAID--
ENOUGH!
KRUNCH
DEAR LORD.
I ALWAYS KNEW...
LOOK AWAY, MAY.
SO BRUTAL. THAT POOR MAN...
HIS JAW. THE ONE PLACE HE WASN'T ARMORED. I TOOK IT CLEAN OFF.
NEVER KNEW THIS BODY HELD SO MUCH POWER.
ALL THESE YEARS, PARKER MUST HAVE BEEN HOLDING BACK...
KNEW YOU HAD IT IN YOU, KID.
I DIDN'T.
...BUT I'M NOT *HIM*, AM I?

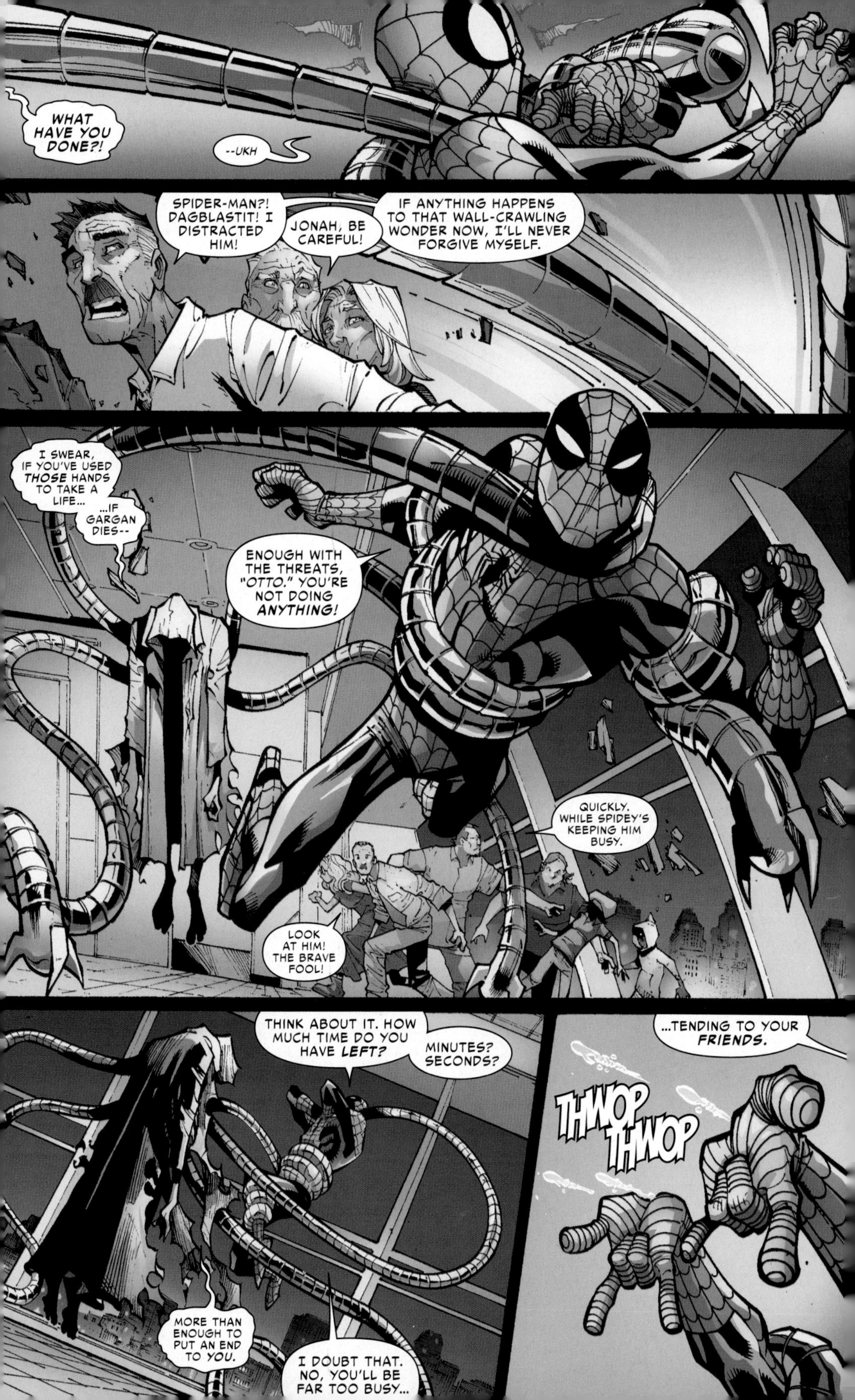
WHAT HAVE YOU DONE?!
--UKH
SPIDER-MAN?! DAGBLASTIT! I DISTRACTED HIM!
JONAH, BE CAREFUL!
IF ANYTHING HAPPENS TO THAT WALL-CRAWLING WONDER NOW, I'LL NEVER FORGIVE MYSELF.
I SWEAR, IF YOU'VE USED THOSE HANDS TO TAKE A LIFE...
...IF GARGAN DIES--
ENOUGH WITH THE THREATS, "OTTO." YOU'RE NOT DOING ANYTHING!
QUICKLY. WHILE SPIDEY'S KEEPING HIM BUSY.
LOOK AT HIM! THE BRAVE FOOL!
THINK ABOUT IT. HOW MUCH TIME DO YOU HAVE LEFT?
MINUTES? SECONDS?
MORE THAN ENOUGH TO PUT AN END TO YOU.
I DOUBT THAT. NO, YOU'LL BE FAR TOO BUSY...
...TENDING TO YOUR FRIENDS.
THWOP THWOP

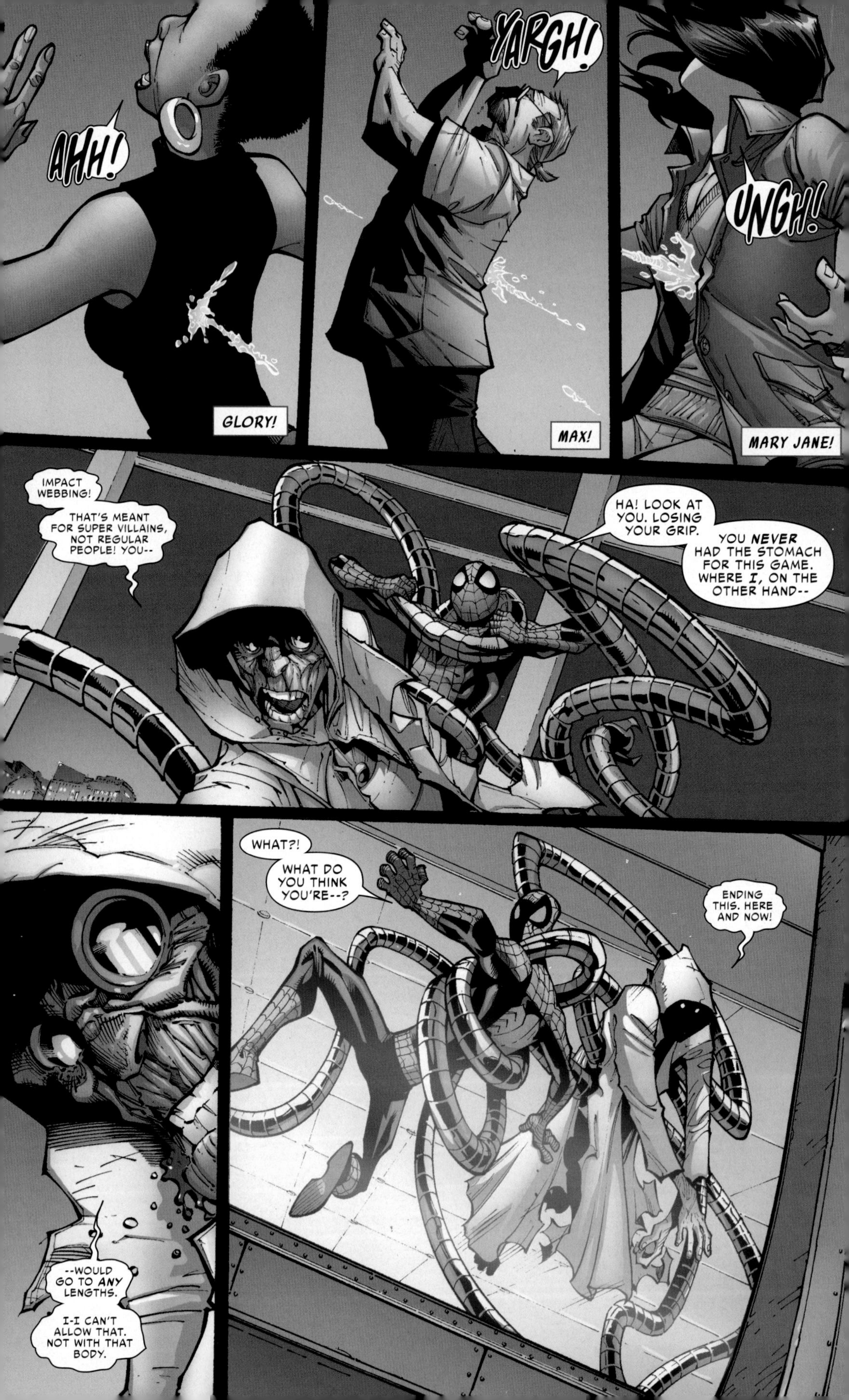
AHH!
GLORY!
YARGH!
MAX!
UNGH!
MARY JANE!
IMPACT WEBBING!
THAT'S MEANT FOR SUPER VILLAINS, NOT REGULAR PEOPLE! YOU--
HA! LOOK AT YOU. LOSING YOUR GRIP.
YOU NEVER HAD THE STOMACH FOR THIS GAME. WHERE I, ON THE OTHER HAND--
--WOULD GO TO ANY LENGTHS.
I-I CAN'T ALLOW THAT. NOT WITH THAT BODY.
WHAT?!
WHAT DO YOU THINK YOU'RE--?
ENDING THIS. HERE AND NOW!

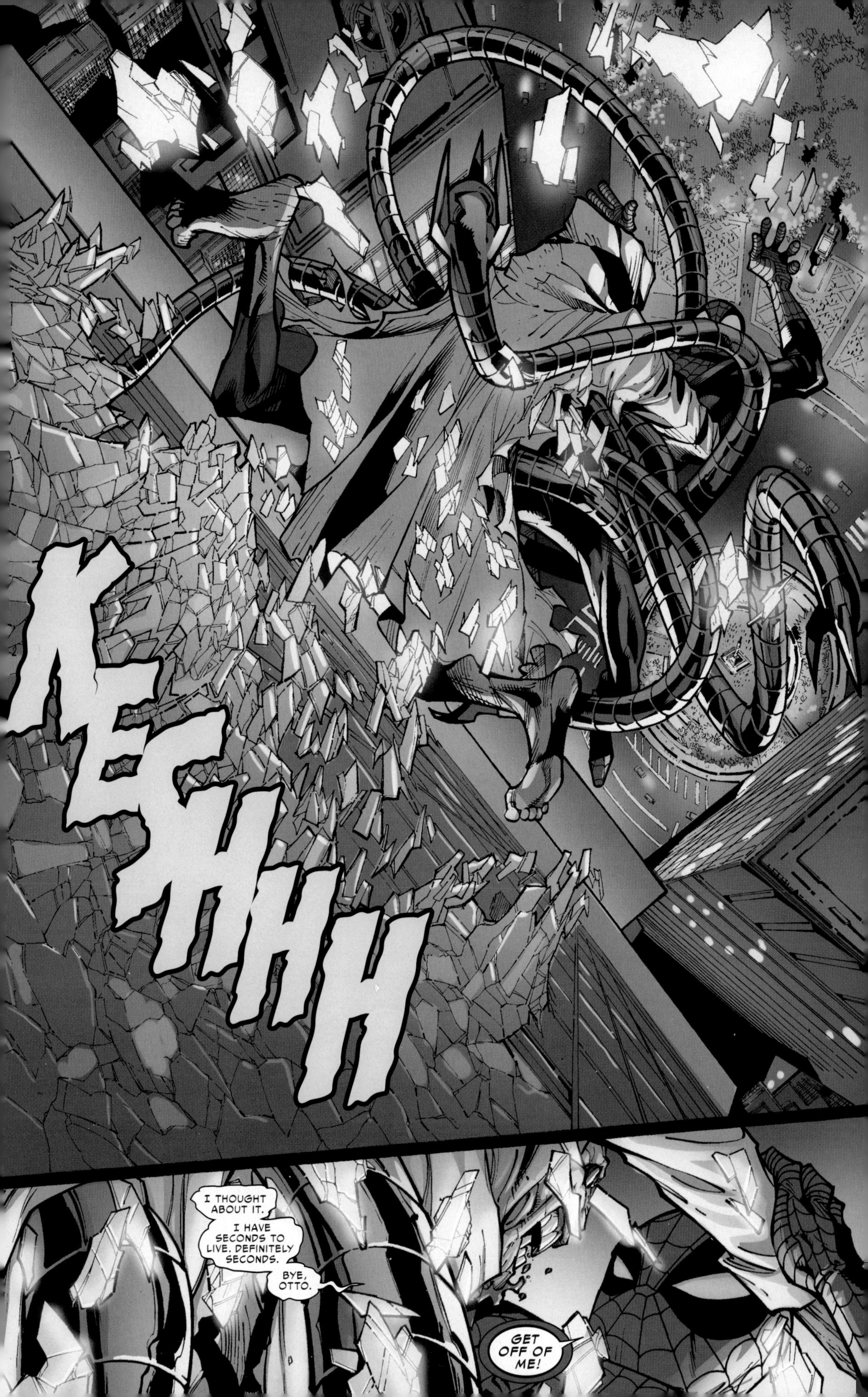
I THOUGHT ABOUT IT.
I HAVE SECONDS TO LIVE. DEFINITELY SECONDS.
BYE, OTTO.
GET OFF OF ME!

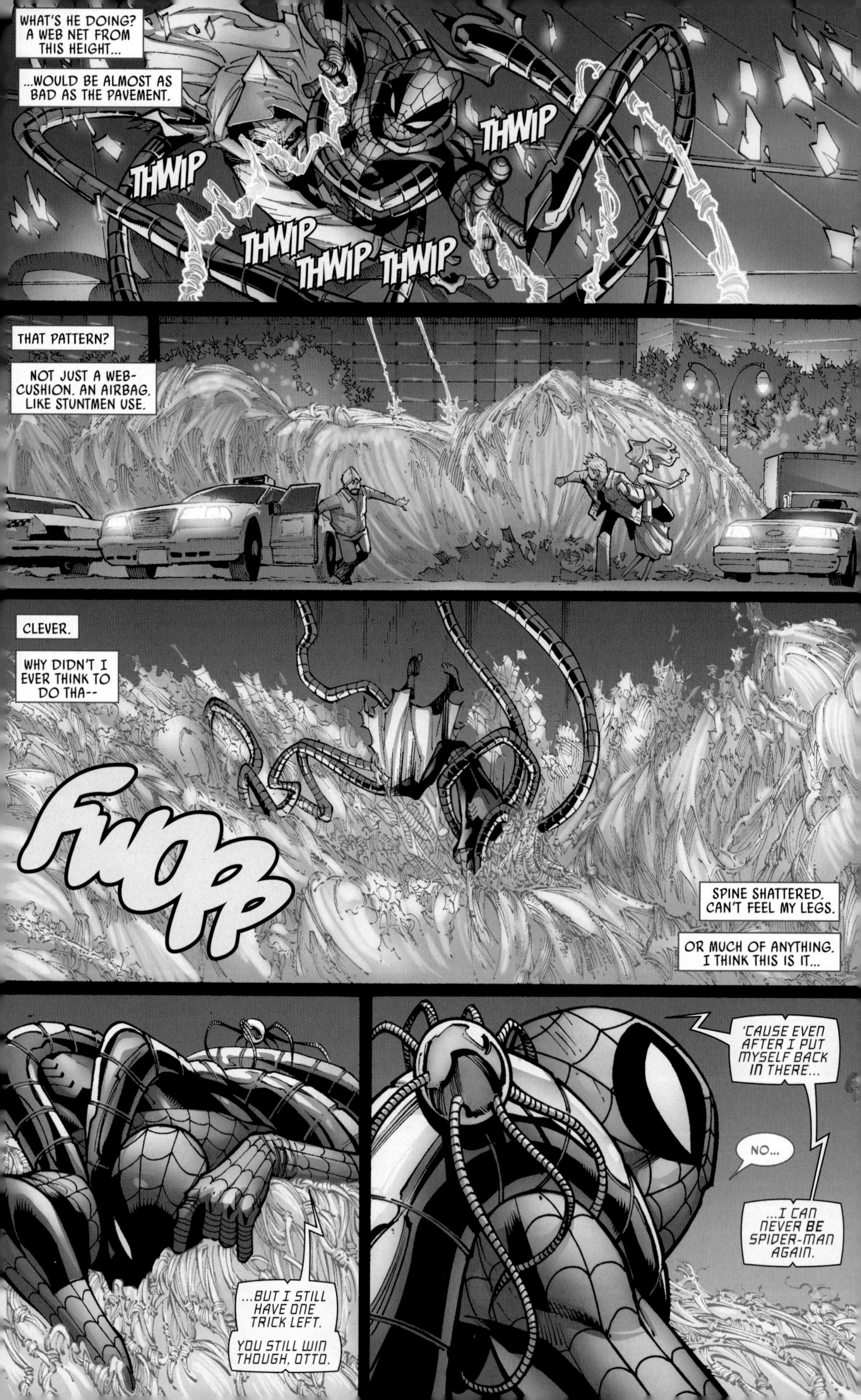
WHAT'S HE DOING? A WEB NET FROM THIS HEIGHT...
...WOULD BE ALMOST AS BAD AS THE PAVEMENT.
THWIP
THWIP
THWIP
THWIP
THWIP
THAT PATTERN?
NOT JUST A WEB-CUSHION. AN AIRBAG. LIKE STUNTMEN USE.
CLEVER.
WHY DIDN'T I EVER THINK TO DO THA--
FWOOP
SPINE SHATTERED. CAN'T FEEL MY LEGS.
OR MUCH OF ANYTHING. I THINK THIS IS IT...
...BUT I STILL HAVE ONE TRICK LEFT.
YOU STILL WIN THOUGH, OTTO.
'CAUSE EVEN AFTER I PUT MYSELF BACK IN THERE...
NO...
...I CAN NEVER BE SPIDER-MAN AGAIN.

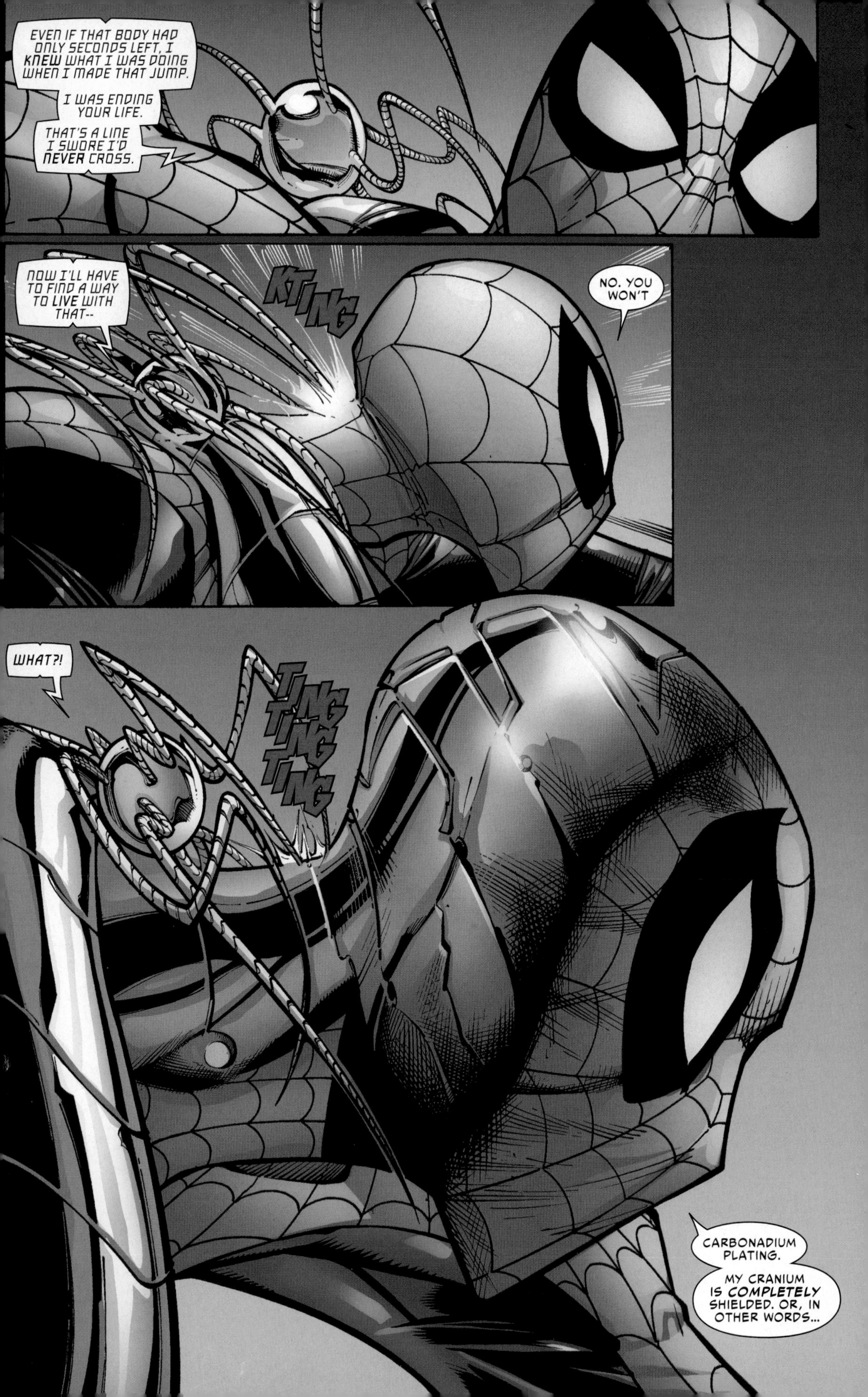
EVEN IF THAT BODY HAD ONLY SECONDS LEFT, I KNEW WHAT I WAS DOING WHEN I MADE THAT JUMP.
I WAS ENDING YOUR LIFE.
THAT'S A LINE I SWORE I'D NEVER CROSS.
NOW I'LL HAVE TO FIND A WAY TO LIVE WITH THAT--
KTING
NO. YOU WON'T
WHAT?!
TING TING TING
CARBONADIUM PLATING.
MY CRANIUM IS COMPLETELY SHIELDED. OR, IN OTHER WORDS...

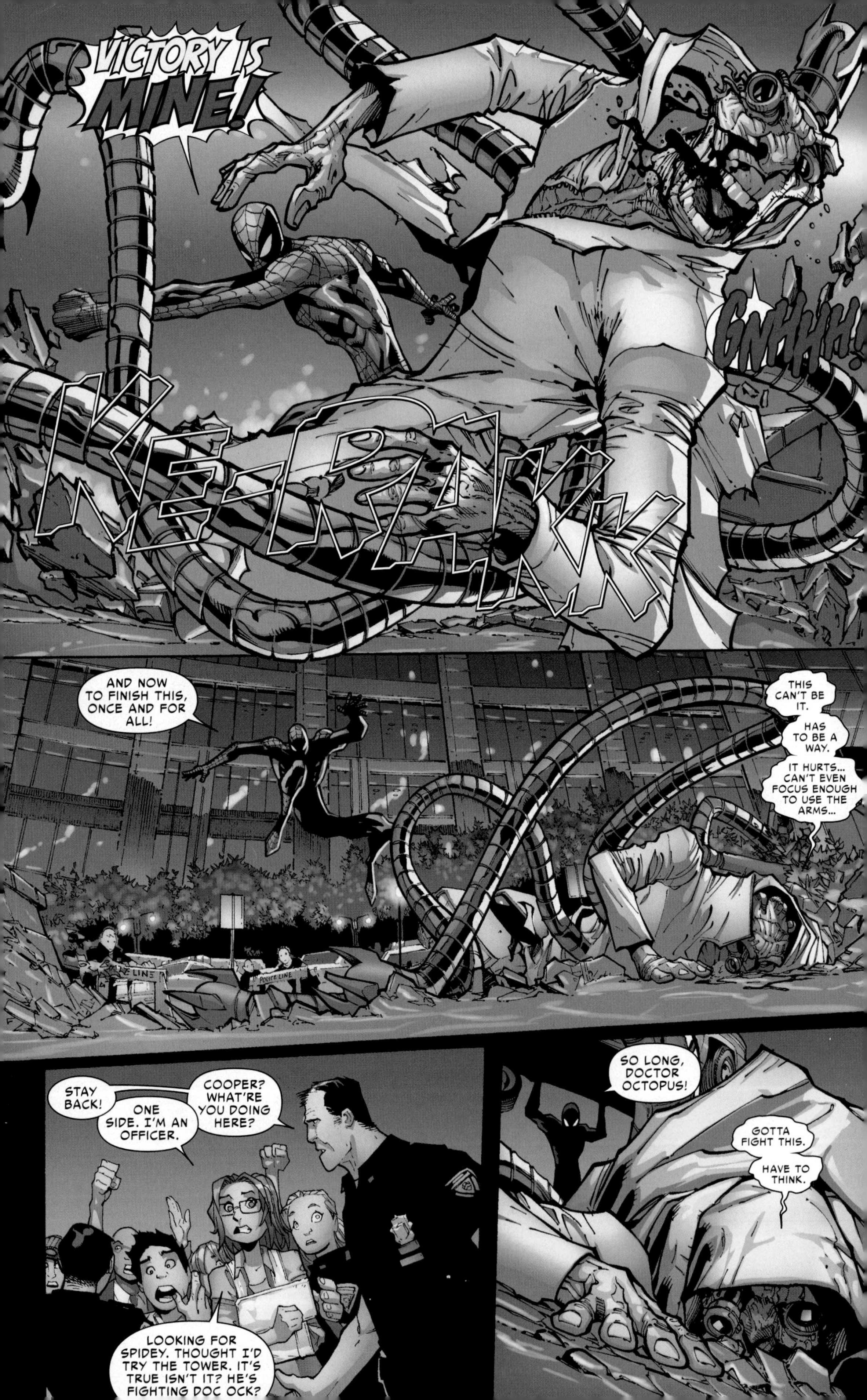
VICTORY IS MINE!
GNHHH!
KE-RANK
AND NOW TO FINISH THIS, ONCE AND FOR ALL!
THIS CAN'T BE IT.
HAS TO BE A WAY.
IT HURTS... CAN'T EVEN FOCUS ENOUGH TO USE THE ARMS...
STAY BACK!
ONE SIDE. I'M AN OFFICER.
COOPER? WHAT'RE YOU DOING HERE?
LOOKING FOR SPIDEY. THOUGHT I'D TRY THE TOWER. IT'S TRUE ISN'T IT? HE'S FIGHTING DOC OCK?
SO LONG, DOCTOR OCTOPUS!
GOTTA FIGHT THIS.
HAVE TO THINK.

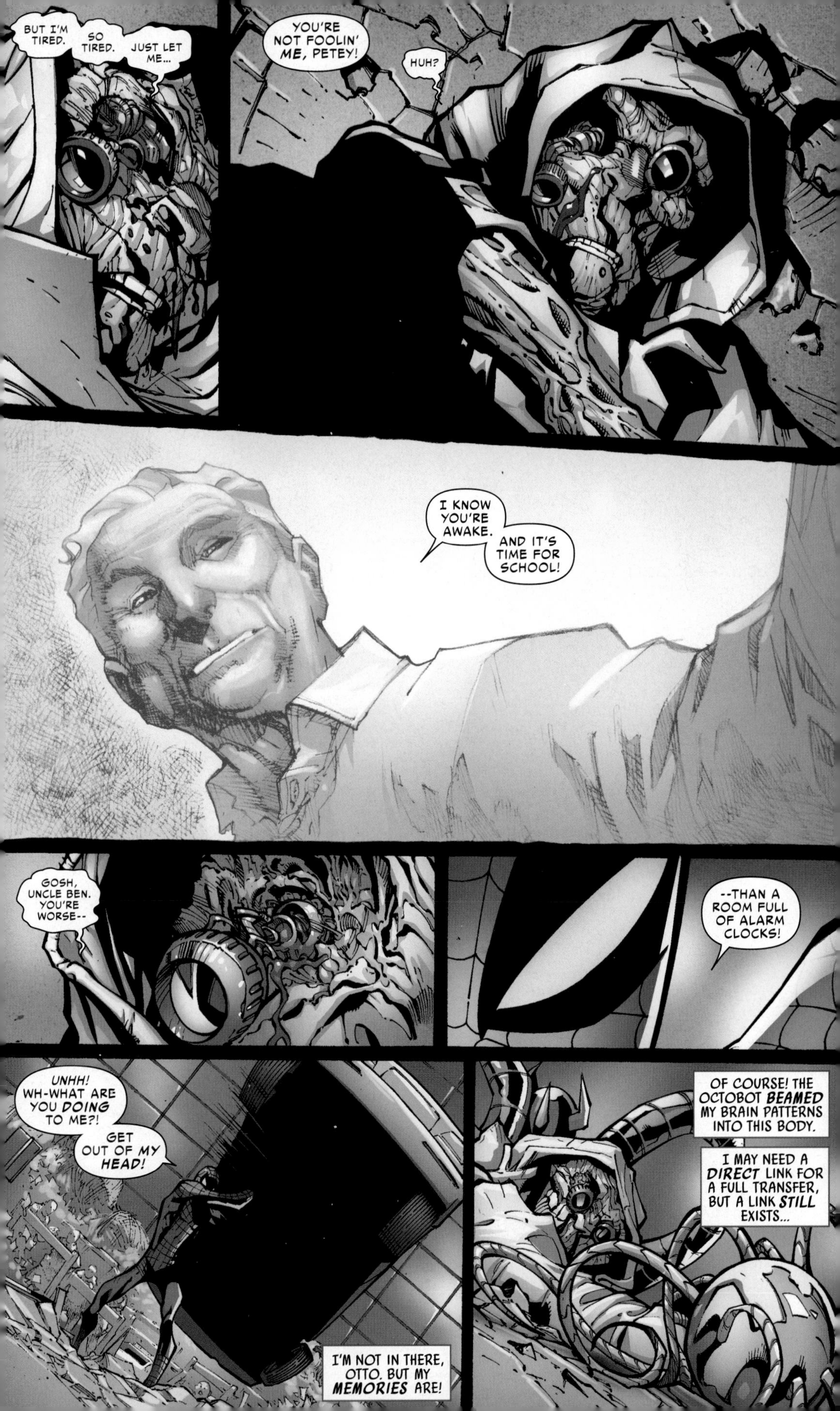
BUT I'M TIRED.
SO TIRED.
JUST LET ME...
YOU'RE NOT FOOLIN' ME, PETEY!
HUH?
I KNOW YOU'RE AWAKE.
AND IT'S TIME FOR SCHOOL!
GOSH, UNCLE BEN. YOU'RE WORSE--
--THAN A ROOM FULL OF ALARM CLOCKS!
UNHH! WH-WHAT ARE YOU DOING TO ME?!
GET OUT OF MY HEAD!
I'M NOT IN THERE, OTTO. BUT MY MEMORIES ARE!
OF COURSE! THE OCTOBOT BEAMED MY BRAIN PATTERNS INTO THIS BODY.
I MAY NEED A DIRECT LINK FOR A FULL TRANSFER, BUT A LINK STILL EXISTS...

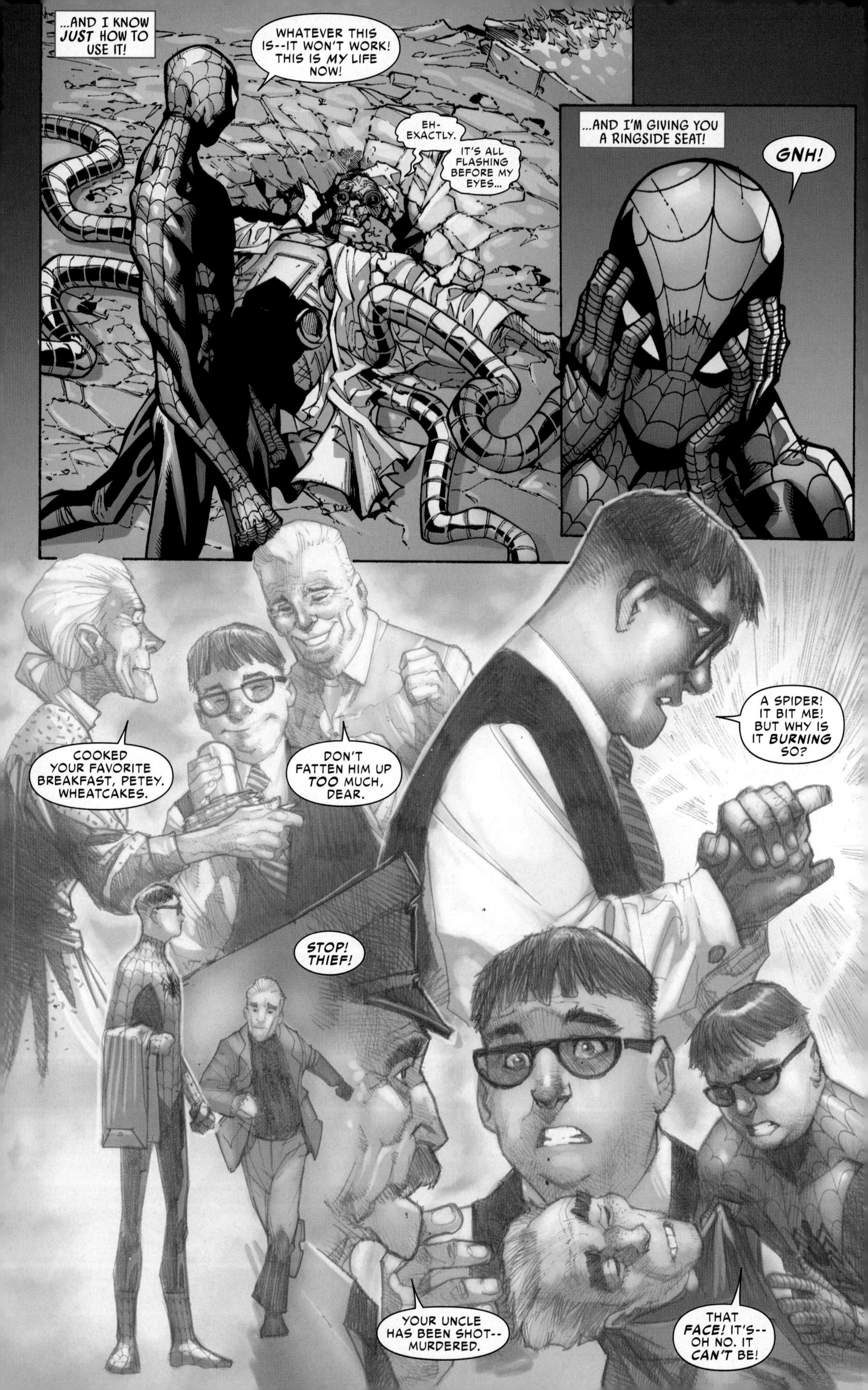

...AND I KNOW JUST HOW TO USE IT!
WHATEVER THIS IS--IT WON'T WORK! THIS IS MY LIFE NOW!
EH- EXACTLY.
IT'S ALL FLASHING BEFORE MY EYES...
...AND I'M GIVING YOU A RINGSIDE SEAT!
GNH!
COOKED YOUR FAVORITE BREAKFAST, PETEY. WHEATCAKES.
DON'T FATTEN HIM UP TOO MUCH, DEAR.
A SPIDER! IT BIT ME! BUT WHY IS IT BURNING SO?
STOP! THIEF!
YOUR UNCLE HAS BEEN SHOT-- MURDERED.
THAT FACE! IT'S-- OH NO. IT CAN'T BE!

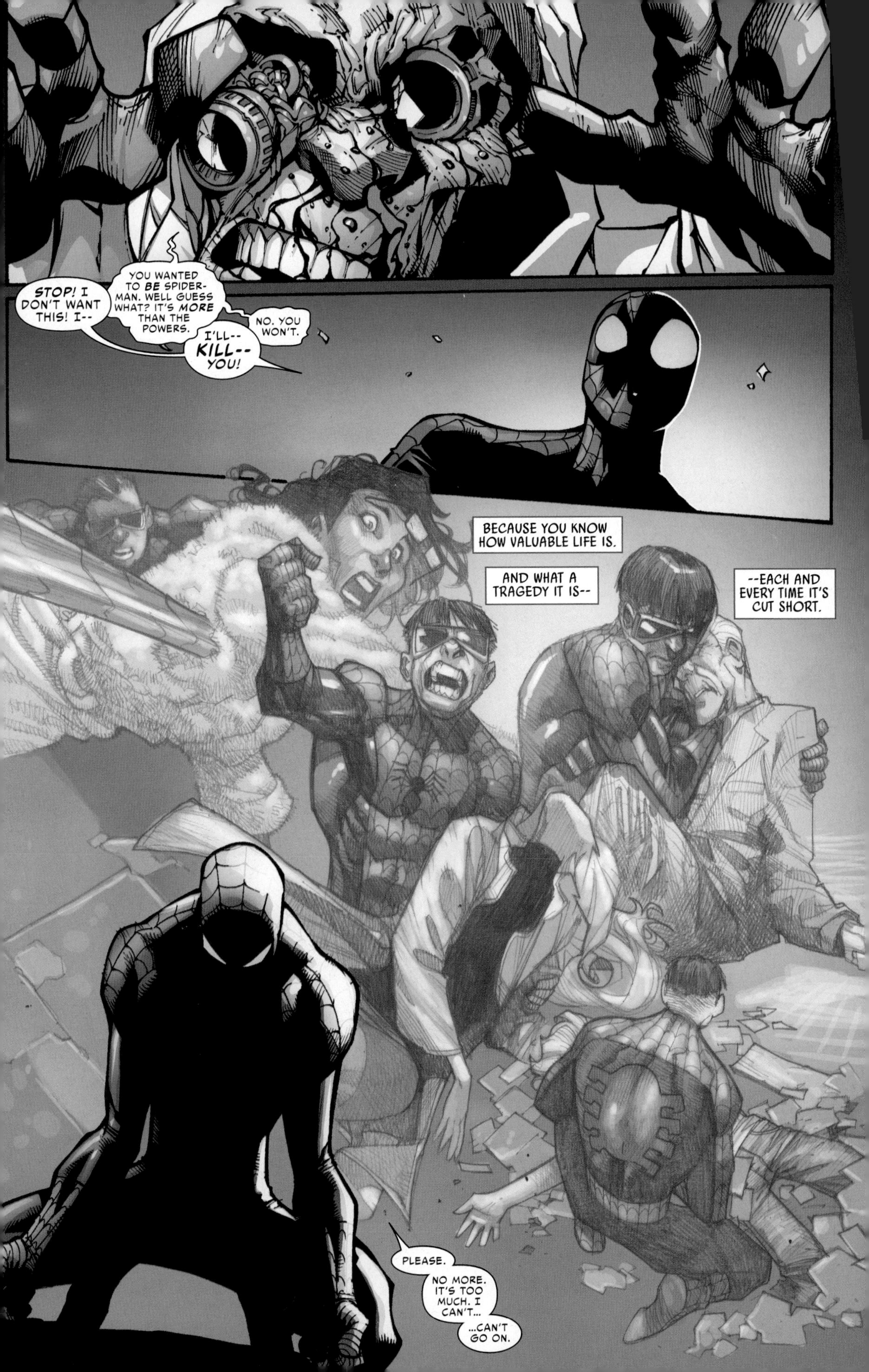
STOP! I DON'T WANT THIS! I--
YOU WANTED TO BE SPIDER-MAN. WELL GUESS WHAT? IT'S MORE THAN THE POWERS.
I'LL-- KILL-- YOU!
NO. YOU WON'T.
BECAUSE YOU KNOW HOW VALUABLE LIFE IS.
AND WHAT A TRAGEDY IT IS--
--EACH AND EVERY TIME IT'S CUT SHORT.
PLEASE.
NO MORE. IT'S TOO MUCH. I CAN'T...
...CAN'T GO ON.

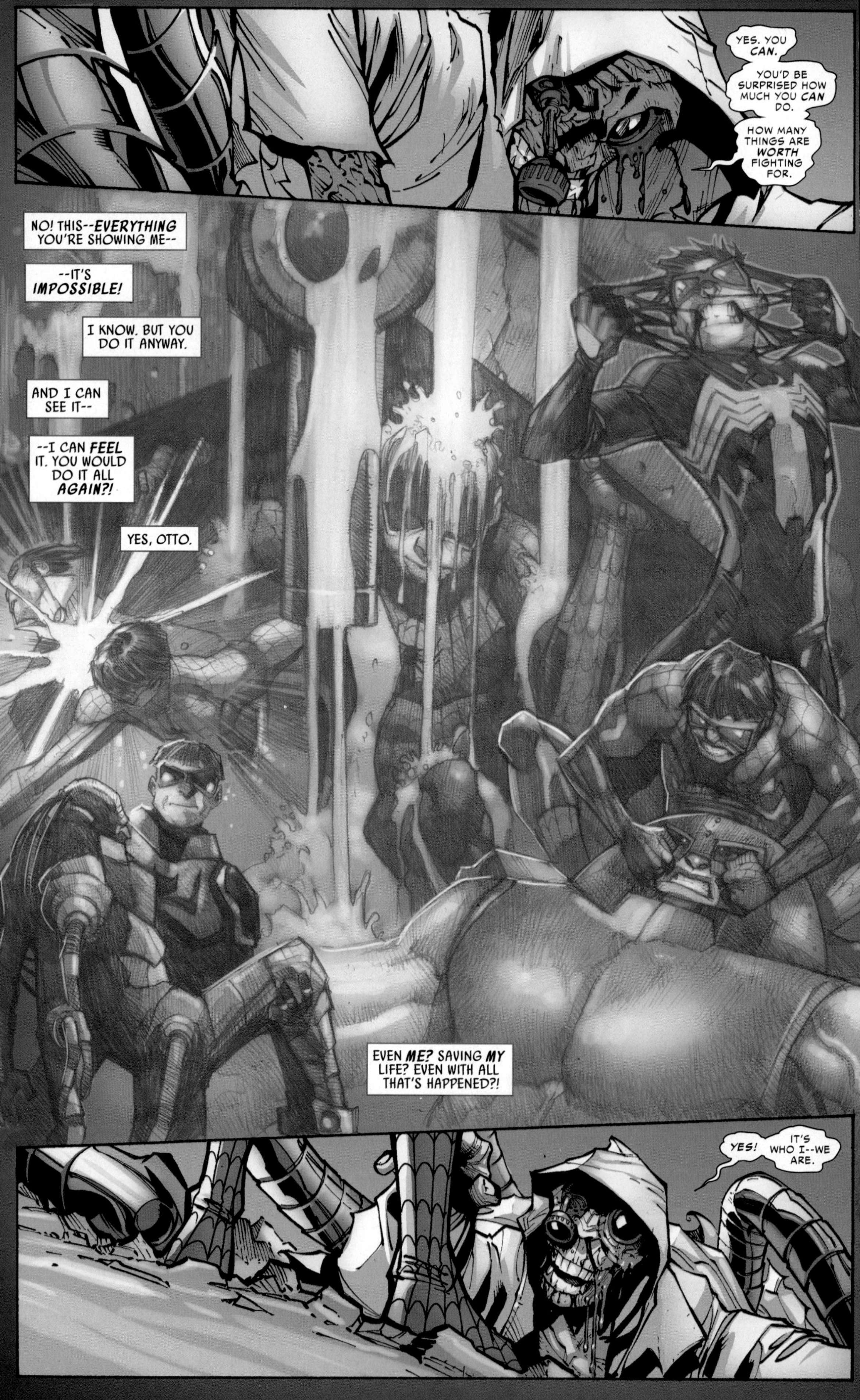
YES. YOU CAN.
YOU'D BE SURPRISED HOW MUCH YOU CAN DO.
HOW MANY THINGS ARE WORTH FIGHTING FOR.
NO! THIS--EVERYTHING YOU'RE SHOWING ME--
--IT'S IMPOSSIBLE!
I KNOW. BUT YOU DO IT ANYWAY.
AND I CAN SEE IT--
--I CAN FEEL IT. YOU WOULD DO IT ALL AGAIN?!
YES, OTTO.
EVEN ME? SAVING MY LIFE? EVEN WITH ALL THAT'S HAPPENED?!
YES!
IT'S WHO I--WE ARE.

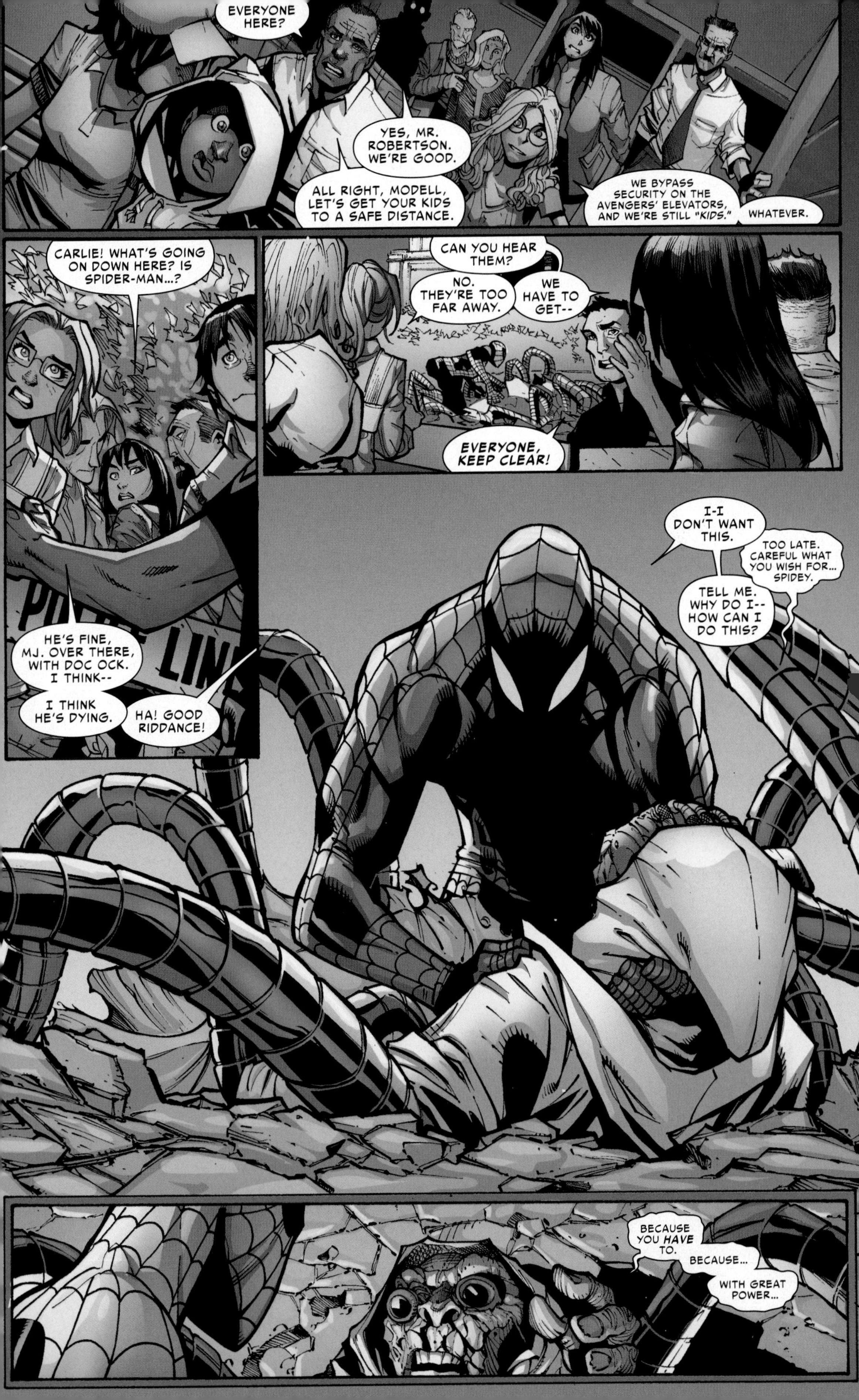
EVERYONE HERE?
YES, MR. ROBERTSON. WE'RE GOOD.
ALL RIGHT, MODELL, LET'S GET YOUR KIDS TO A SAFE DISTANCE.
WE BYPASS SECURITY ON THE AVENGERS' ELEVATORS, AND WE'RE STILL "KIDS."
WHATEVER.
CARLIE! WHAT'S GOING ON DOWN HERE? IS SPIDER-MAN...?
HE'S FINE, MJ. OVER THERE, WITH DOC OCK. I THINK--
I THINK HE'S DYING.
HA! GOOD RIDDANCE!
CAN YOU HEAR THEM?
NO. THEY'RE TOO FAR AWAY.
WE HAVE TO GET--
EVERYONE, KEEP CLEAR!
I-I DON'T WANT THIS.
TOO LATE. CAREFUL WHAT YOU WISH FOR... SPIDEY.
TELL ME. WHY DO I-- HOW CAN I DO THIS?
BECAUSE YOU HAVE TO.
BECAUSE...
WITH GREAT POWER...

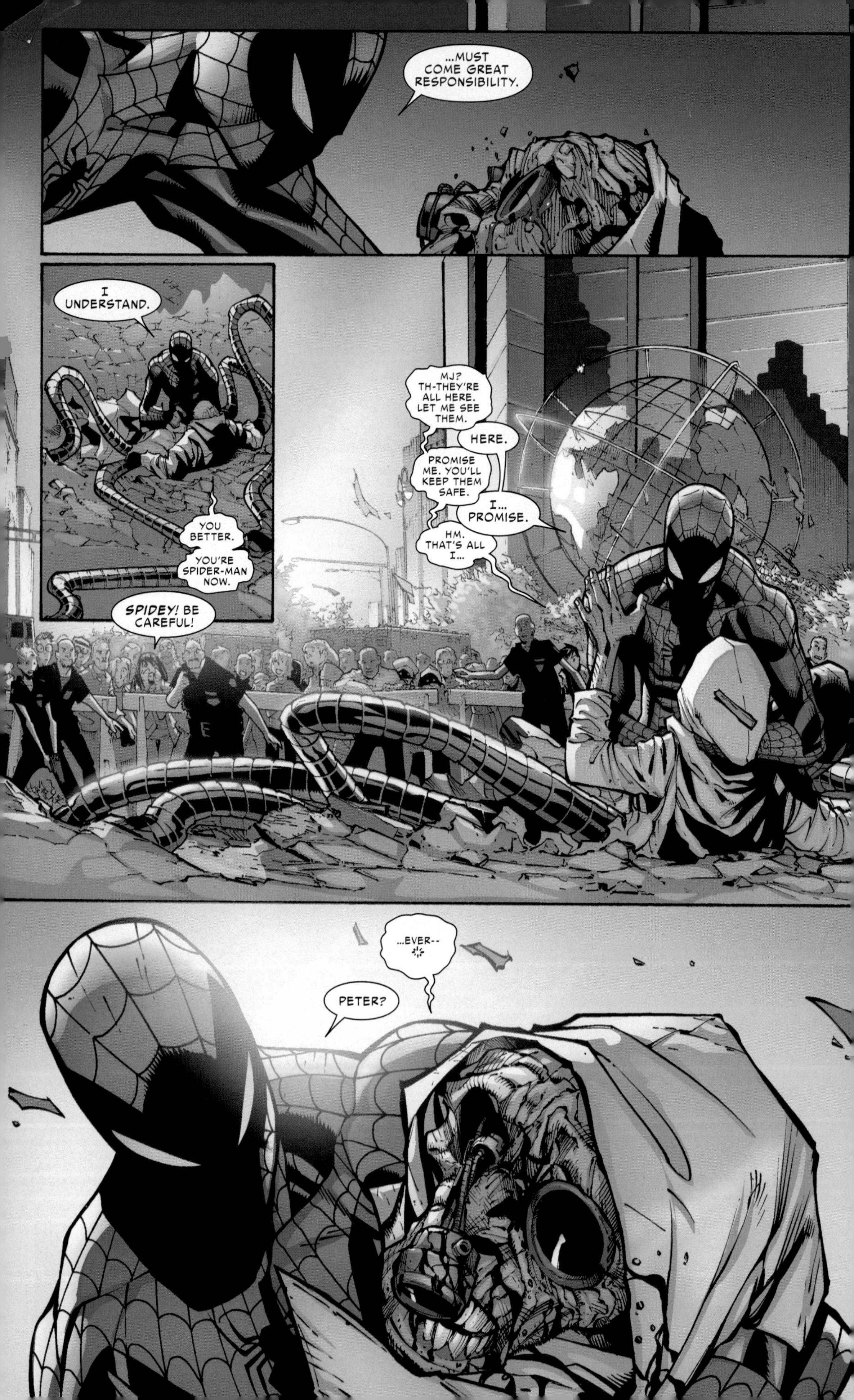
...MUST COME GREAT RESPONSIBILITY.
I UNDERSTAND.
YOU BETTER.
YOU'RE SPIDER-MAN NOW.
SPIDEY! BE CAREFUL!
MJ? TH-THEY'RE ALL HERE. LET ME SEE THEM.
HERE.
PROMISE ME. YOU'LL KEEP THEM SAFE.
I... PROMISE.
HM. THAT'S ALL I...
...EVER--
PETER?

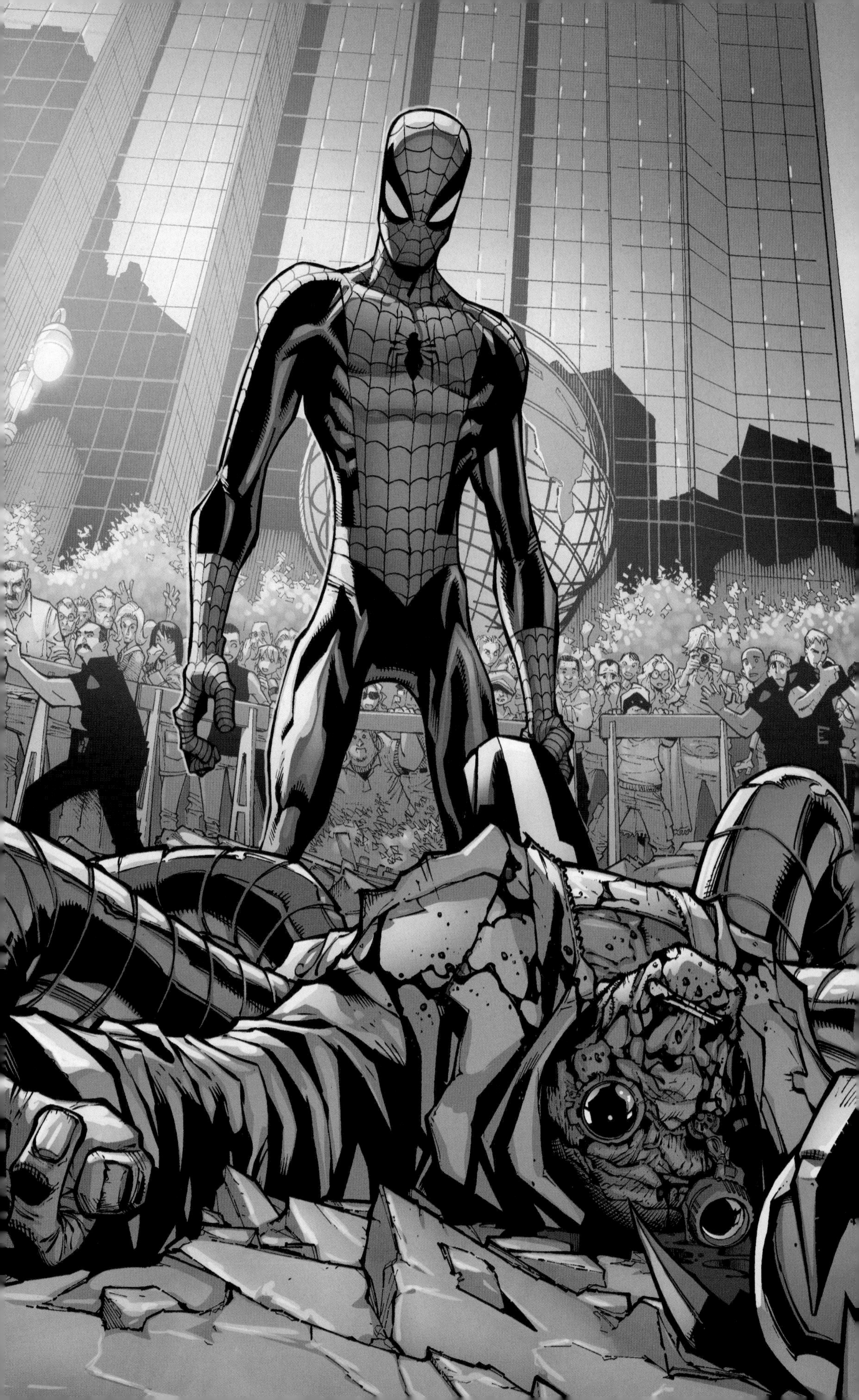

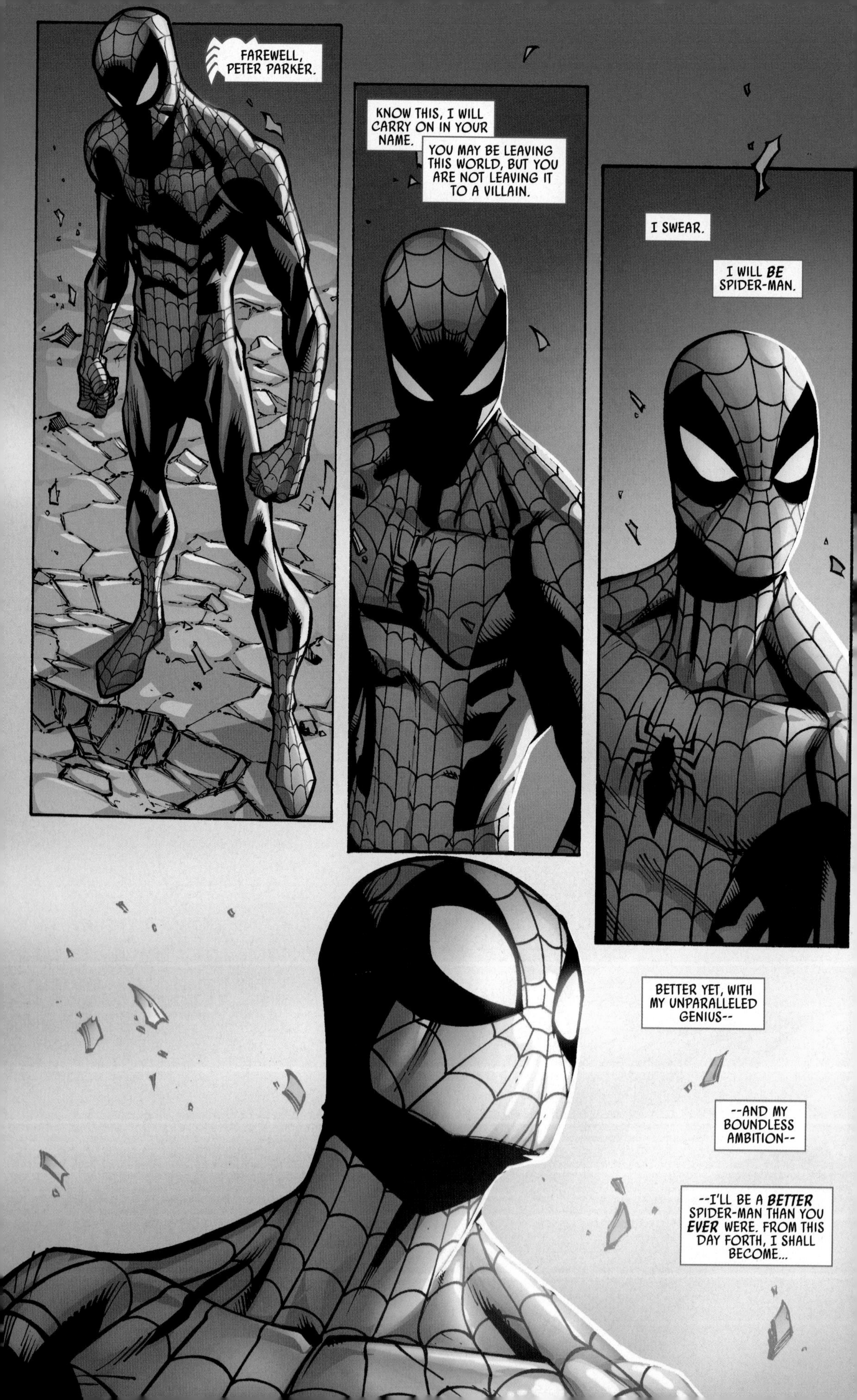
FAREWELL, PETER PARKER.
KNOW THIS, I WILL CARRY ON IN YOUR NAME.
YOU MAY BE LEAVING THIS WORLD, BUT YOU ARE NOT LEAVING IT TO A VILLAIN.
I SWEAR.
I WILL BE SPIDER-MAN.
BETTER YET, WITH MY UNPARALLELED GENIUS--
--AND MY BOUNDLESS AMBITION--
--I'LL BE A BETTER SPIDER-MAN THAN YOU EVER WERE. FROM THIS DAY FORTH, I SHALL BECOME...

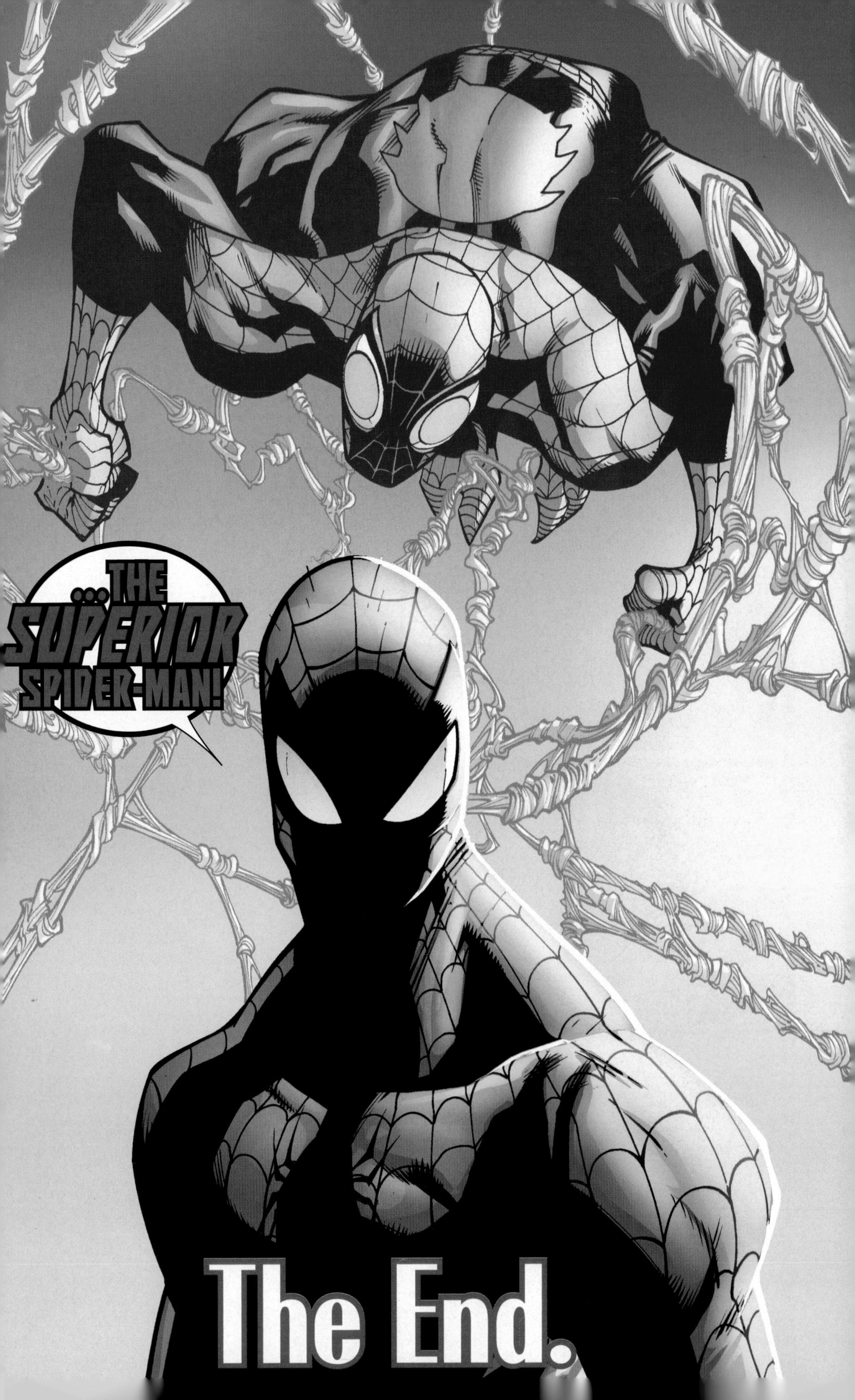
...THE SUPERIOR SPIDER-MAN!
The End.

AMAZING SPIDER-MAN #700

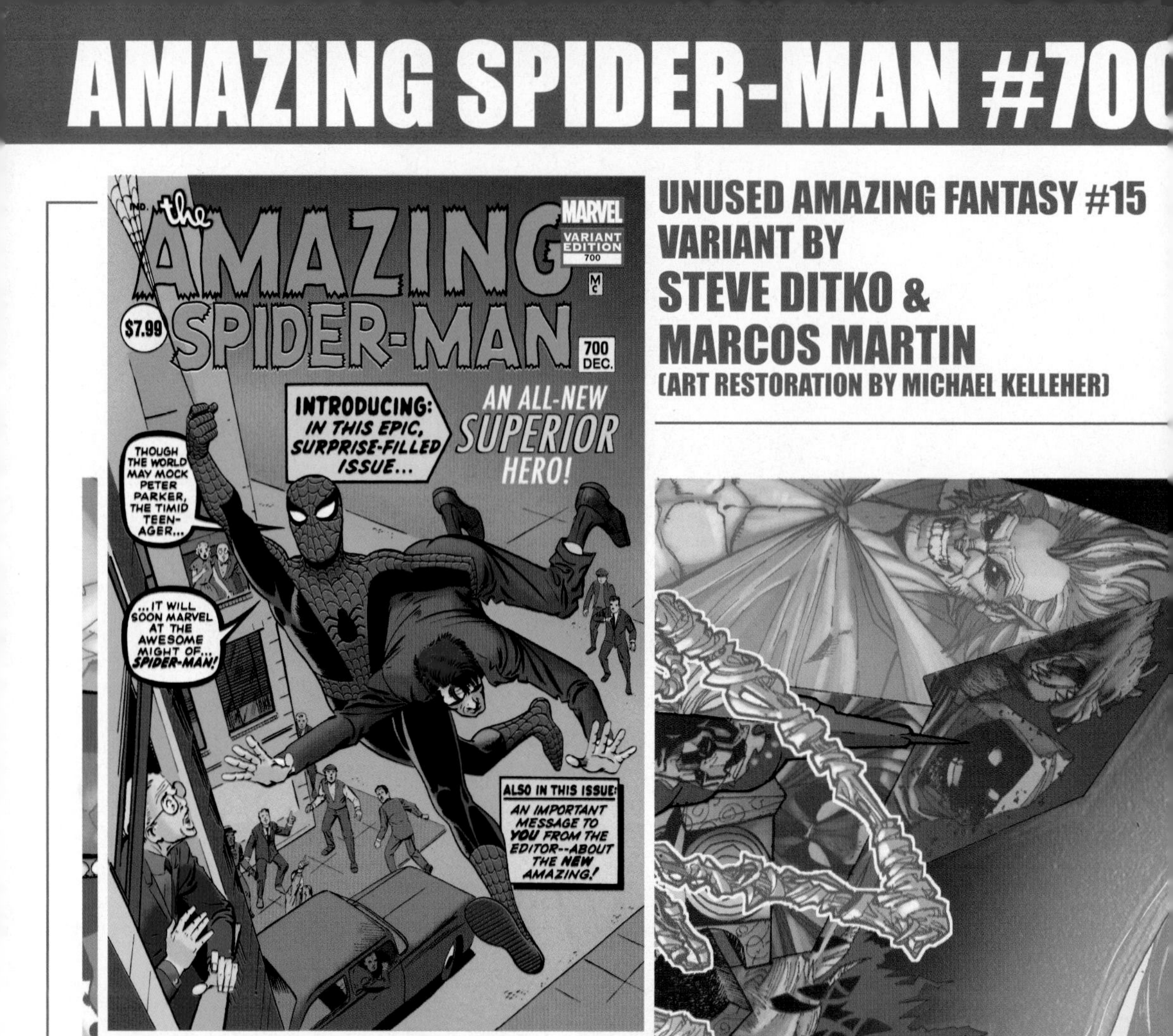

IND.
the AMAZING SPIDER-MAN
MARVEL
VARIANT EDITION 700
MC
$7.99
700 DEC.
INTRODUCING: IN THIS EPIC, SURPRISE-FILLED ISSUE...
AN ALL-NEW SUPERIOR HERO!
THOUGH THE WORLD MAY MOCK PETER PARKER, THE TIMID TEEN-AGER...
...IT WILL SOON MARVEL AT THE AWESOME MIGHT OF... SPIDER-MAN!
ALSO IN THIS ISSUE: AN IMPORTANT MESSAGE TO YOU FROM THE EDITOR--ABOUT THE NEW AMAZING!

UNUSED AMAZING FANTASY #15 VARIANT BY
STEVE DITKO &
MARCOS MARTIN
(ART RESTORATION BY MICHAEL KELLEHER)

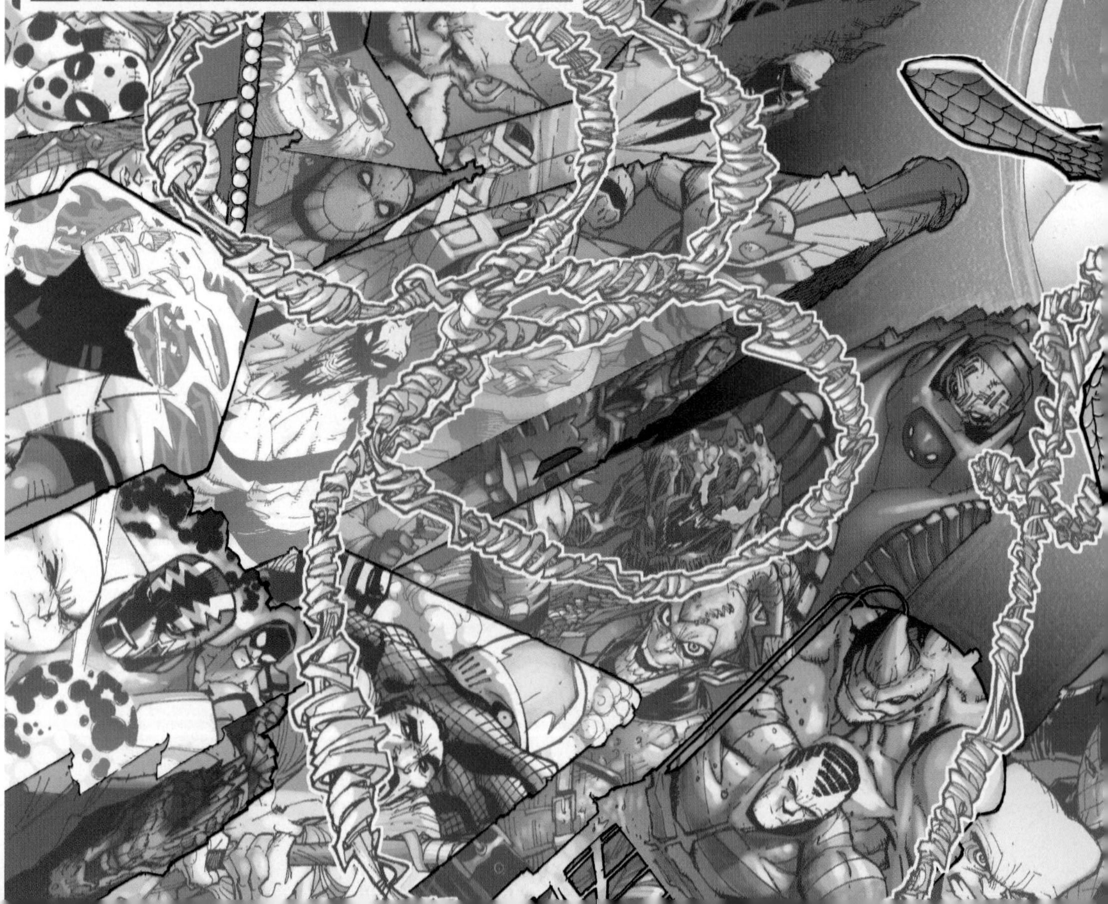

VARIANT COVER GALLERY

MARCOS MARTIN

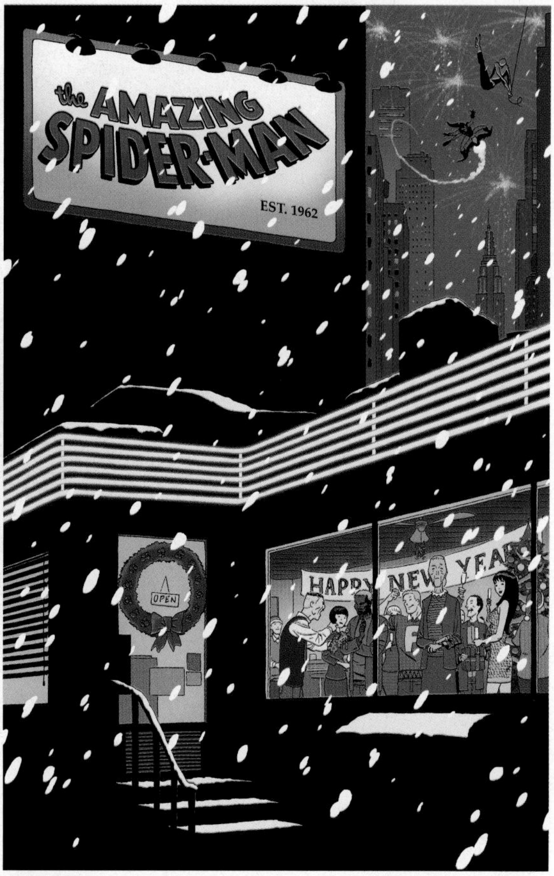
the AMAZING SPIDER-MAN
EST. 1962
OPEN

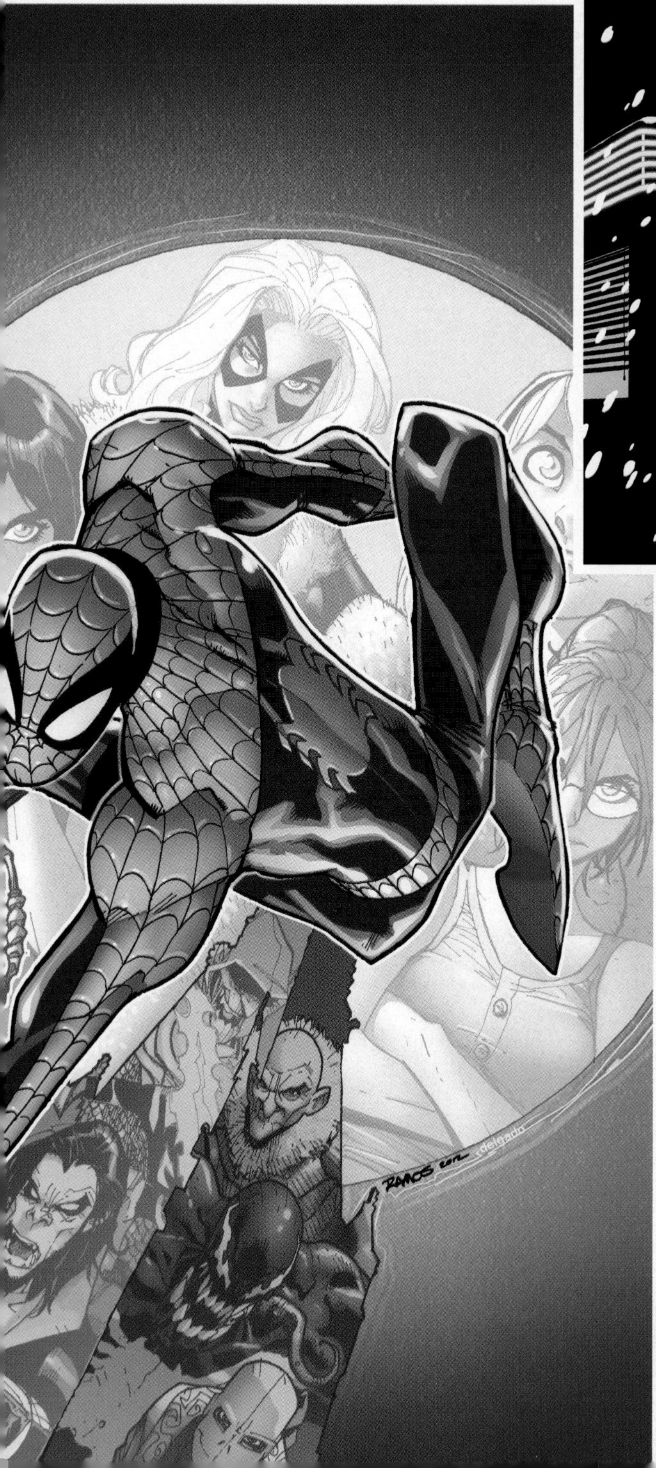
RAMOS
delgado

HUMBERTO RAMOS & EDGAR DELGADO

JOE QUESADA, DANNY MIKI & MORRY HOLLOWELL

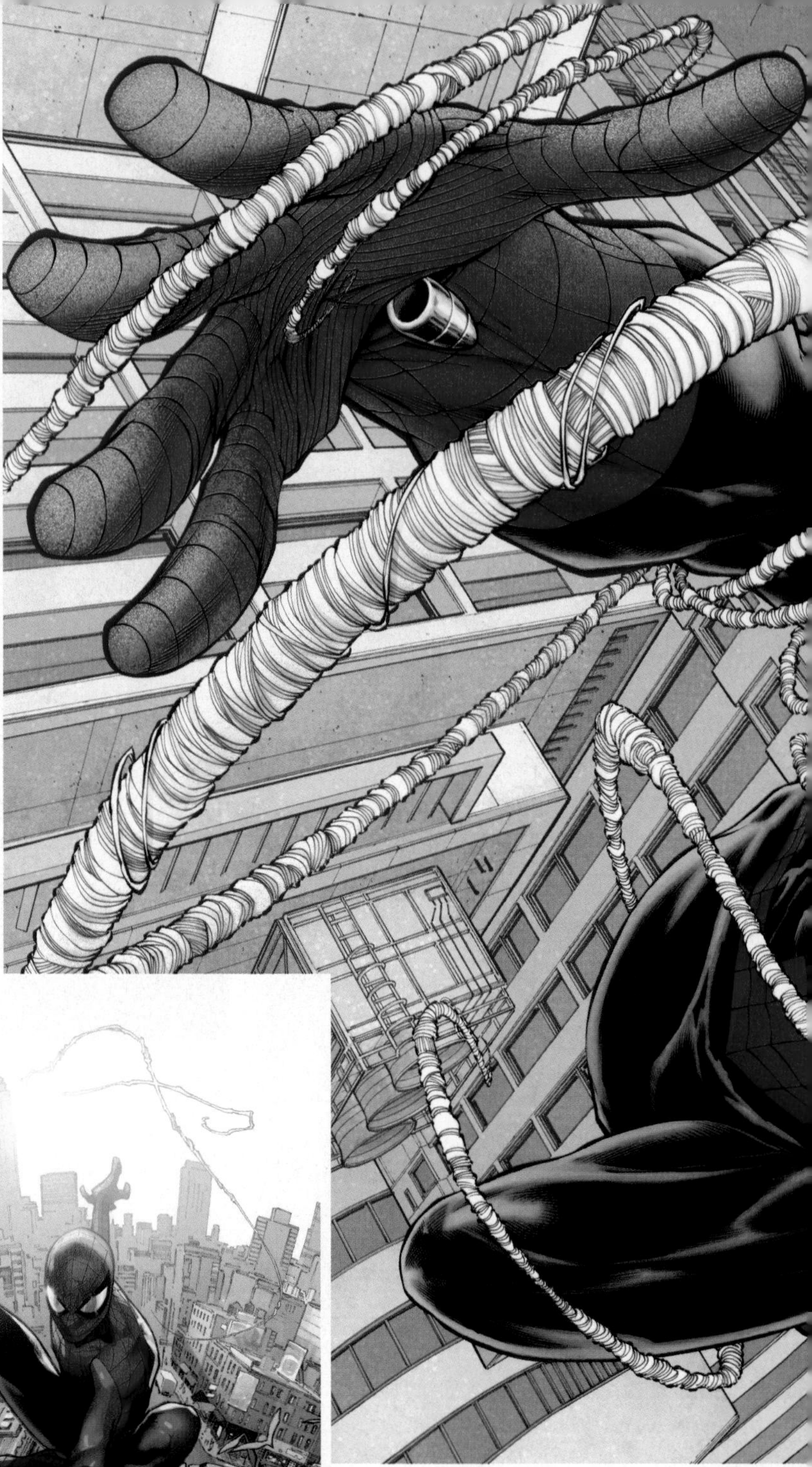

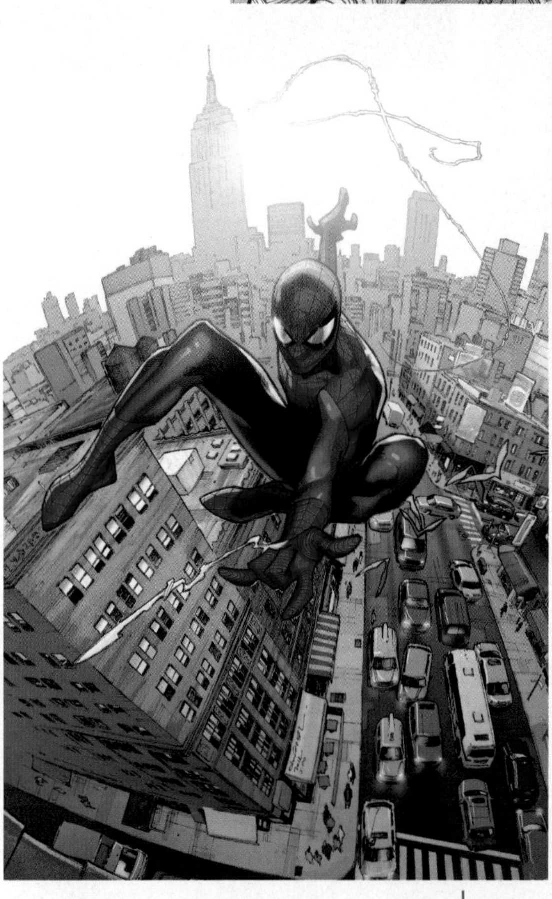

OLIVIER COIPEL & JUSTIN PONSOR

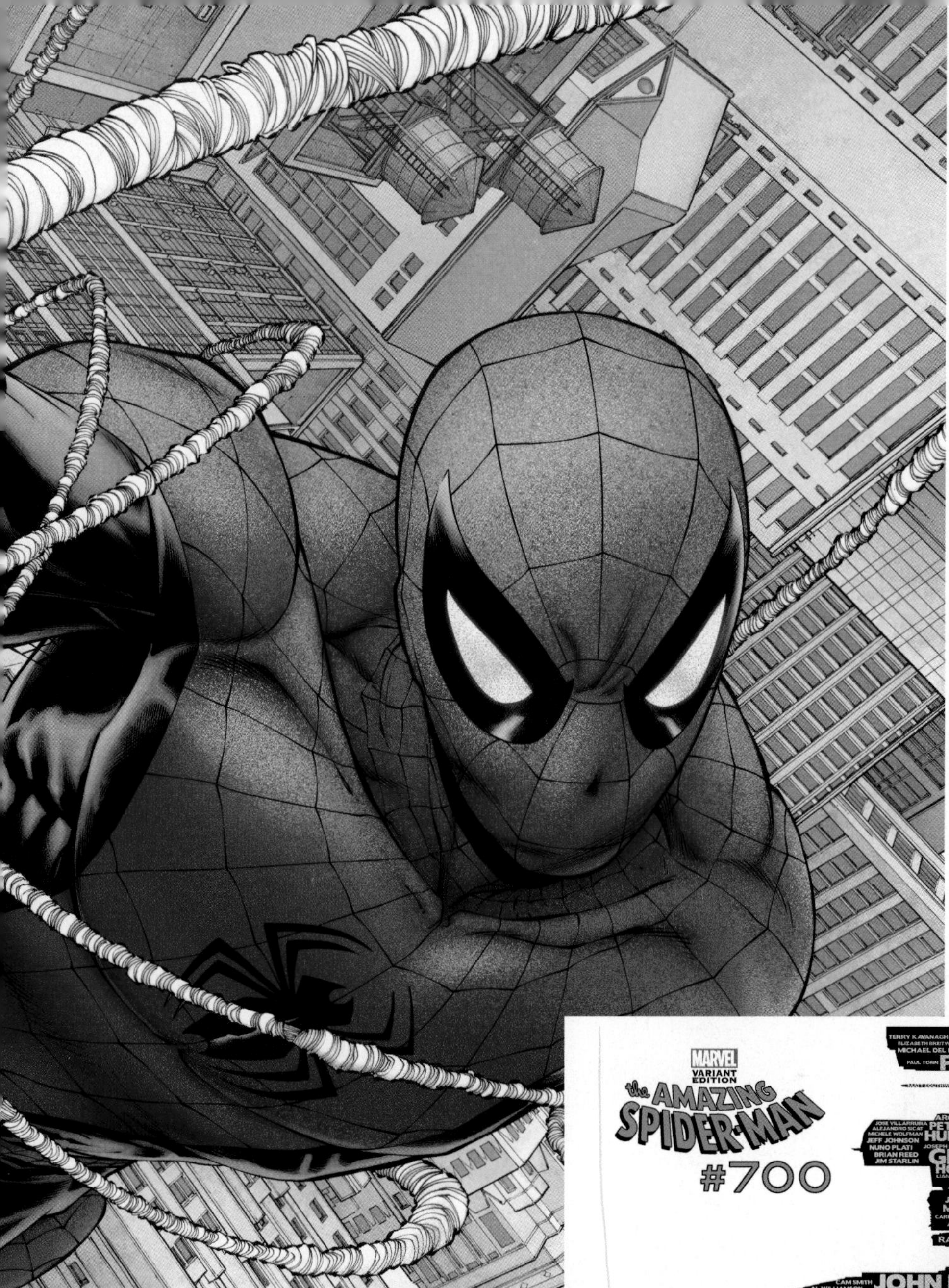

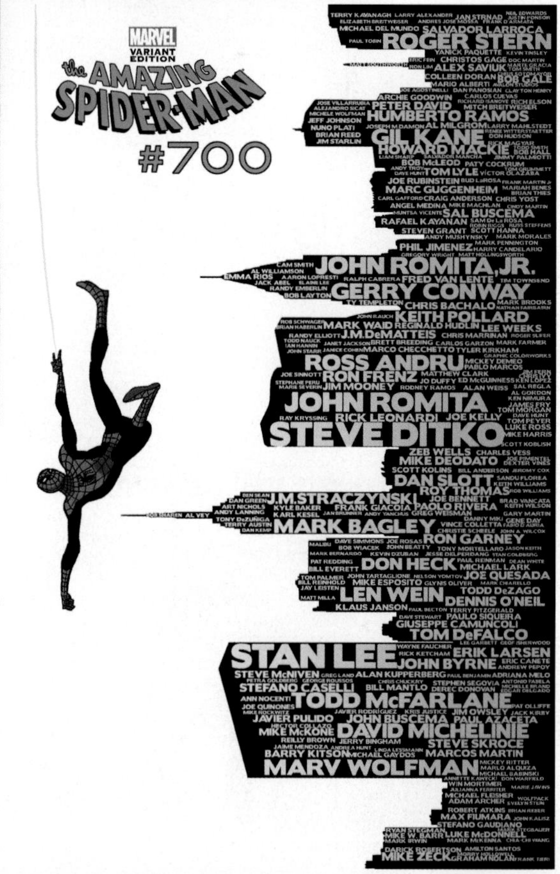

MARVEL
VARIANT EDITION
the AMAZING SPIDER-MAN
#700
ROGER STERN
SALVADOR LARROCA
ALEX SAVIUK
PETER DAVID
HUMBERTO RAMOS
GIL KANE
HOWARD MACKIE
TOM LYLE
MARC GUGGENHEIM
SAL BUSCEMA
PHIL JIMENEZ
JOHN ROMITA, JR.
GERRY CONWAY
KEITH POLLARD
J.M.DeMATTEIS
ROSS ANDRU
RON FRENZ
JIM MOONEY
JOHN ROMITA
STEVE DITKO
MIKE DEODATO
DAN SLOTT
ROY THOMAS
J.M.STRACZYNSKI
MARK BAGLEY
RON GARNEY
DON HECK
JOE QUESADA
LEN WEIN
DENNIS O'NEIL
TOM DeFALCO
STAN LEE
JOHN BYRNE
ERIK LARSEN
TODD McFARLANE
DAVID MICHELINIE
STEVE SKROCE
MARCOS MARTIN
MARV WOLFMAN

MARCOS MARTIN

Hey, I'm Proclamatin' Here!

Back in October during the massive New York Comic Convention, NYC Mayor Michael Bloomberg proclaimed Sunday was officially "Spider-Man Day" complete with official ceremony! Presented here for the first time is that official proclamation for all Spidey fans to behold! Be proud, Spidey fans! YOU made this happen (well, along with Marvel Marketing guru Arune Singh!)!

Office of the Mayor
CITY OF NEW YORK

Proclamation

WHEREAS: NEW YORK CITY BOASTS MANY HOMETOWN HEROES, BUT ONLY ONE IS OFFICIALLY AMAZING. THE AMAZING SPIDER-MAN, THAT IS—A NATIVE OF FOREST HILLS WHOSE BIRTHDAY IS OCTOBER 14TH, PETER PARKER, THROUGH HIS ARACHNID ALTER EGO, EPITOMIZES CIVIC DUTY IN LIVING OUT HIS UNCLE BEN'S MAXIM, "WITH GREAT POWER COMES GREAT RESPONSIBILITY." SPIDEY IS KNOWN FOR ALWAYS PUTTING THE SAFETY OF OUR CITY AND ITS PEOPLE FIRST, AND HIS SPIRIT OF SERVICE—NOT TO MENTION HIS VERY COOL WEB-SHOOTERS—INSPIRE NEW YORKERS YOUNG AND OLD TO BE EVERYDAY HEROES IN THEIR OWN COMMUNITIES. THAT'S WHY WE'RE GLAD TO JOIN IN CELEBRATING SPIDER-MAN'S BIRTHDAY AT NEW YORK COMIC CON.

WHEREAS: THE SPIDER-MAN FILMS ALWAYS SHOWCASE THE BEAUTY OF OUR GREAT CITY, AND THIS YEAR'S *THE AMAZING SPIDER-MAN* WAS NO EXCEPTION. FROM WEB-SWINGING ALONG THE RIVERSIDE DRIVE VIADUCT TO SEIZING CARS FALLING OFF THE WILLIAMSBURG BRIDGE WITH HIS WEB-LINES, THE EXPLOITS OF THIS FAMOUS RED-AND-BLUE-SUITED WALL-CRAWLER WERE SPECTACULARLY SET AGAINST SOME OF THE CITY'S MOST STUNNING BACKDROPS. IN THE LATEST TWIST TO HIS LIFE IN NEW YORK, A NEW MARVEL COMIC BOOK FINDS SPIDER-MAN LIVING IN A BROOKLYN BROWNSTONE, WHERE HE FIGHTS BEDBUGS, POLLUTION, AND EVICTION WITH HIS FRIENDS, THE BROOKLYN AVENGERS. AND THE GREAT WEB-SLINGER EMBODIES NOT ONLY ATHLETIC BUT ALSO INTELLECTUAL PROWESS. PHOTOGRAPHER, TEACHER, AND SCIENTIST, THIS ALL-AROUND RESOURCEFUL AND INVENTIVE TEEN-AGER EXCELS IN CHEMISTRY AND PHYSICS, PROVING THAT HEROISM AND STUDYING HARD DO INDEED GO HAND-IN-HAND.

WHEREAS: *THE AMAZING SPIDER-MAN* IS THE LONGEST-LASTING COMIC PRODUCED BY MARVEL, AND IT IS WONDERFUL THAT NOW, 50 YEARS AFTER THE WEB-HEAD'S DEBUT IN THE AUGUST 1962 ISSUE OF *AMAZING FANTASY #15*, HE IS THE SUBJECT OF A HIT BROADWAY MUSICAL, *TURN OFF THE DARK*. (IN FACT, THE PLAY INSPIRED ME TO DROP ONTO A STAGE FROM THE CEILING, SPIDEY-FASHION AND SPIDEY-COSTUMED, DURING A BENEFIT SHOW FOR CHARITY A FEW YEARS AGO.) THIS YEAR'S COMIC CON PROVIDES A WONDERFUL OPPORTUNITY TO CELEBRATE THE BIRTHDAY OF ONE OF OUR GREATEST FICTIONAL HOMETOWN HEROES IN ALL HIS INCARNATIONS ON THE PAGE, SCREEN, AND STAGE, AND TO COME TOGETHER TO HONOR A FIGURE WHO HAS ALWAYS COME TO NEW YORK CITY'S RESCUE.

NOW THEREFORE, I, MICHAEL R. BLOOMBERG, MAYOR OF THE CITY OF NEW YORK, IN RECOGNITION OF SPIDER-MAN'S BIRTHDAY, DO HEREBY PROCLAIM SUNDAY, OCTOBER 14TH, 2012 IN THE CITY OF NEW YORK AS:

"NYC SPIDER-MAN DAY"

Michael R. Bloomberg

MICHAEL R. BLOOMBERG
MAYOR

IN WITNESS... ...HAVE HEREUNTO
SET MY HAN... ...SED THE SEAL OF
THE CITY OF... ...K TO BE AFFIXED.

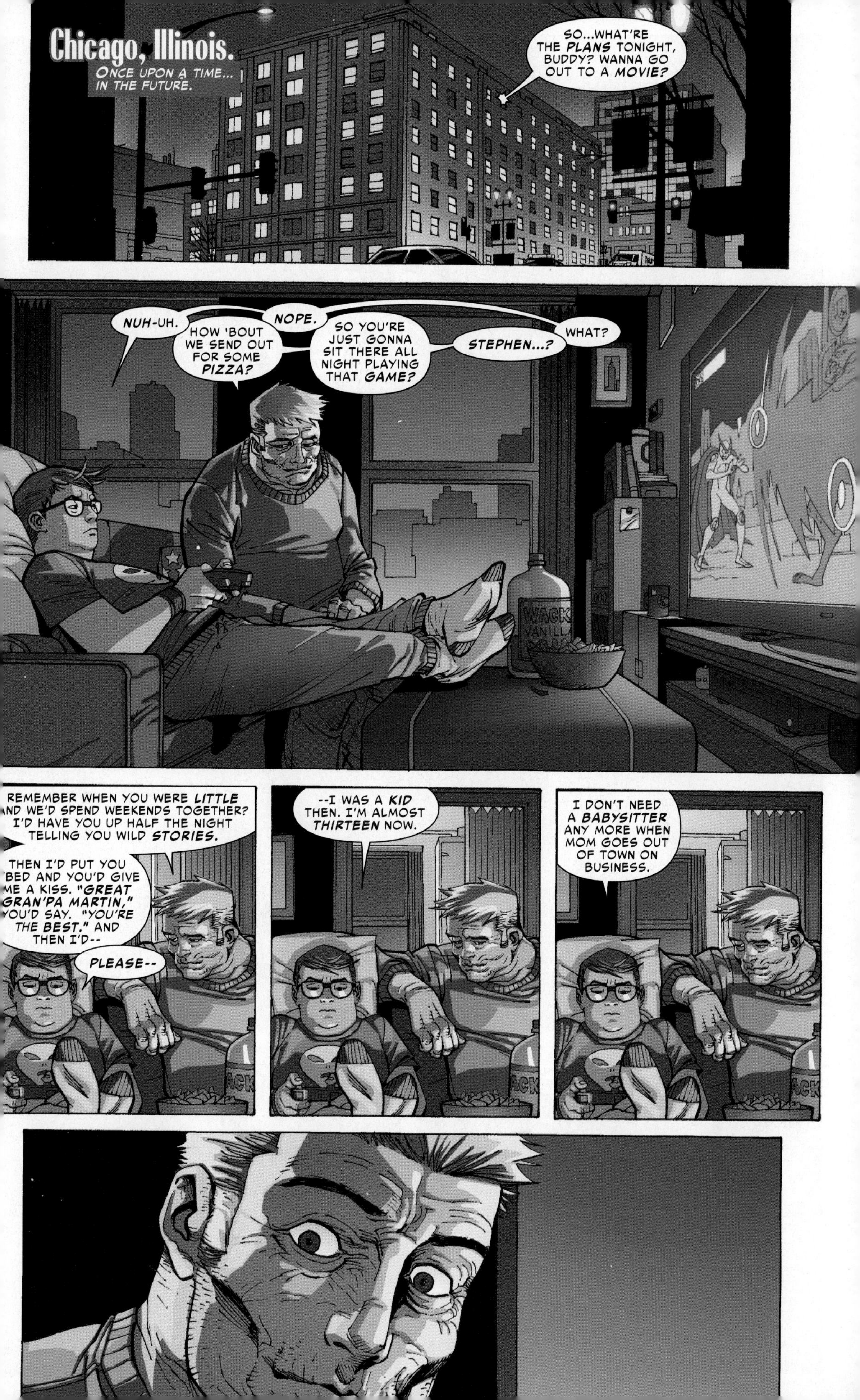

Chicago, Illinois.
ONCE UPON A TIME... IN THE FUTURE.
SO...WHAT'RE THE PLANS TONIGHT, BUDDY? WANNA GO OUT TO A MOVIE?
NUH-UH.
HOW 'BOUT WE SEND OUT FOR SOME PIZZA?
NOPE.
SO YOU'RE JUST GONNA SIT THERE ALL NIGHT PLAYING THAT GAME?
STEPHEN...?
WHAT?
REMEMBER WHEN YOU WERE LITTLE ND WE'D SPEND WEEKENDS TOGETHER? I'D HAVE YOU UP HALF THE NIGHT TELLING YOU WILD STORIES.
THEN I'D PUT YOU BED AND YOU'D GIVE ME A KISS. "GREAT GRAN'PA MARTIN," YOU'D SAY. "YOU'RE THE BEST." AND THEN I'D--
PLEASE--
--I WAS A KID THEN. I'M ALMOST THIRTEEN NOW.
I DON'T NEED A BABYSITTER ANY MORE WHEN MOM GOES OUT OF TOWN ON BUSINESS.

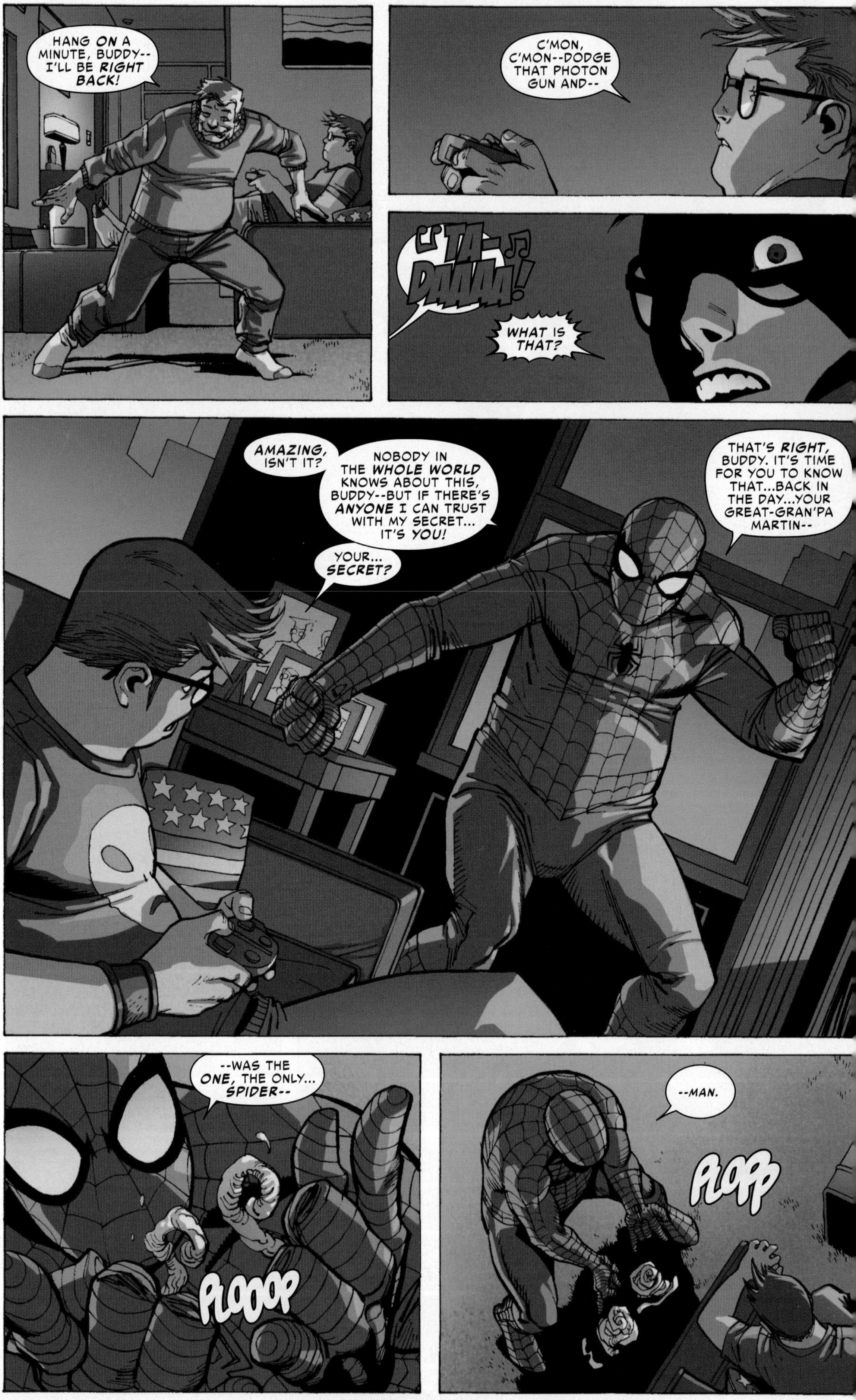
HANG ON A MINUTE, BUDDY-- I'LL BE RIGHT BACK!
C'MON, C'MON--DODGE THAT PHOTON GUN AND--
TA-DAAAA!
WHAT IS THAT?
AMAZING, ISN'T IT?
NOBODY IN THE WHOLE WORLD KNOWS ABOUT THIS, BUDDY--BUT IF THERE'S ANYONE I CAN TRUST WITH MY SECRET... IT'S YOU!
YOUR... SECRET?
THAT'S RIGHT, BUDDY. IT'S TIME FOR YOU TO KNOW THAT...BACK IN THE DAY...YOUR GREAT-GRAN'PA MARTIN--
--WAS THE ONE, THE ONLY... SPIDER--
PLOOOP
--MAN.
PLOPP

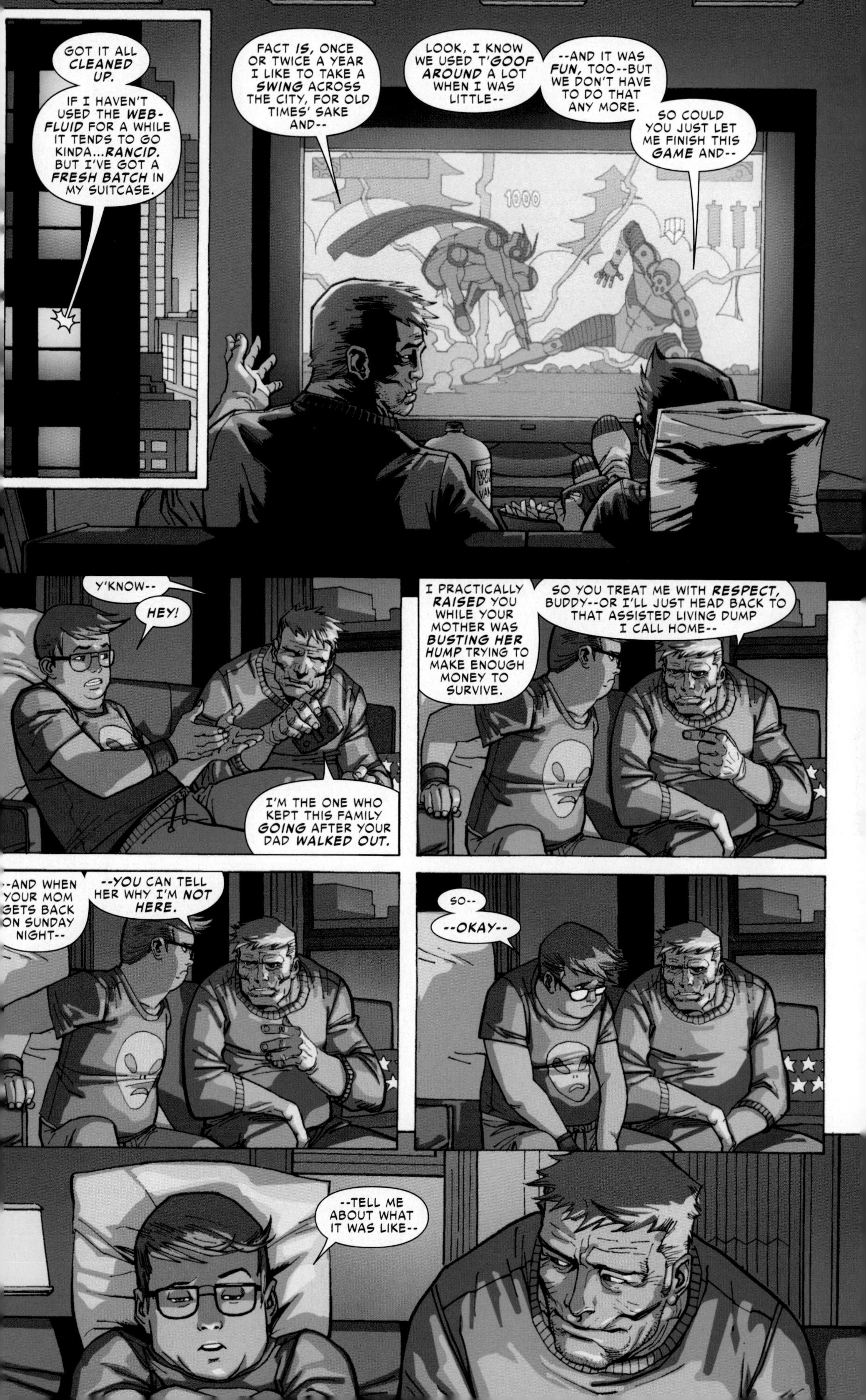
GOT IT ALL CLEANED UP.
IF I HAVEN'T USED THE WEB-FLUID FOR A WHILE IT TENDS TO GO KINDA...RANCID. BUT I'VE GOT A FRESH BATCH IN MY SUITCASE.
FACT IS, ONCE OR TWICE A YEAR I LIKE TO TAKE A SWING ACROSS THE CITY, FOR OLD TIMES' SAKE AND--
LOOK, I KNOW WE USED T'GOOF AROUND A LOT WHEN I WAS LITTLE--
--AND IT WAS FUN, TOO--BUT WE DON'T HAVE TO DO THAT ANY MORE.
SO COULD YOU JUST LET ME FINISH THIS GAME AND--
1000
Y'KNOW--
HEY!
I'M THE ONE WHO KEPT THIS FAMILY GOING AFTER YOUR DAD WALKED OUT.
I PRACTICALLY RAISED YOU WHILE YOUR MOTHER WAS BUSTING HER HUMP TRYING TO MAKE ENOUGH MONEY TO SURVIVE.
SO YOU TREAT ME WITH RESPECT, BUDDY--OR I'LL JUST HEAD BACK TO THAT ASSISTED LIVING DUMP I CALL HOME--
--AND WHEN YOUR MOM GETS BACK ON SUNDAY NIGHT--
--YOU CAN TELL HER WHY I'M NOT HERE.
SO--
--OKAY--
--TELL ME ABOUT WHAT IT WAS LIKE--

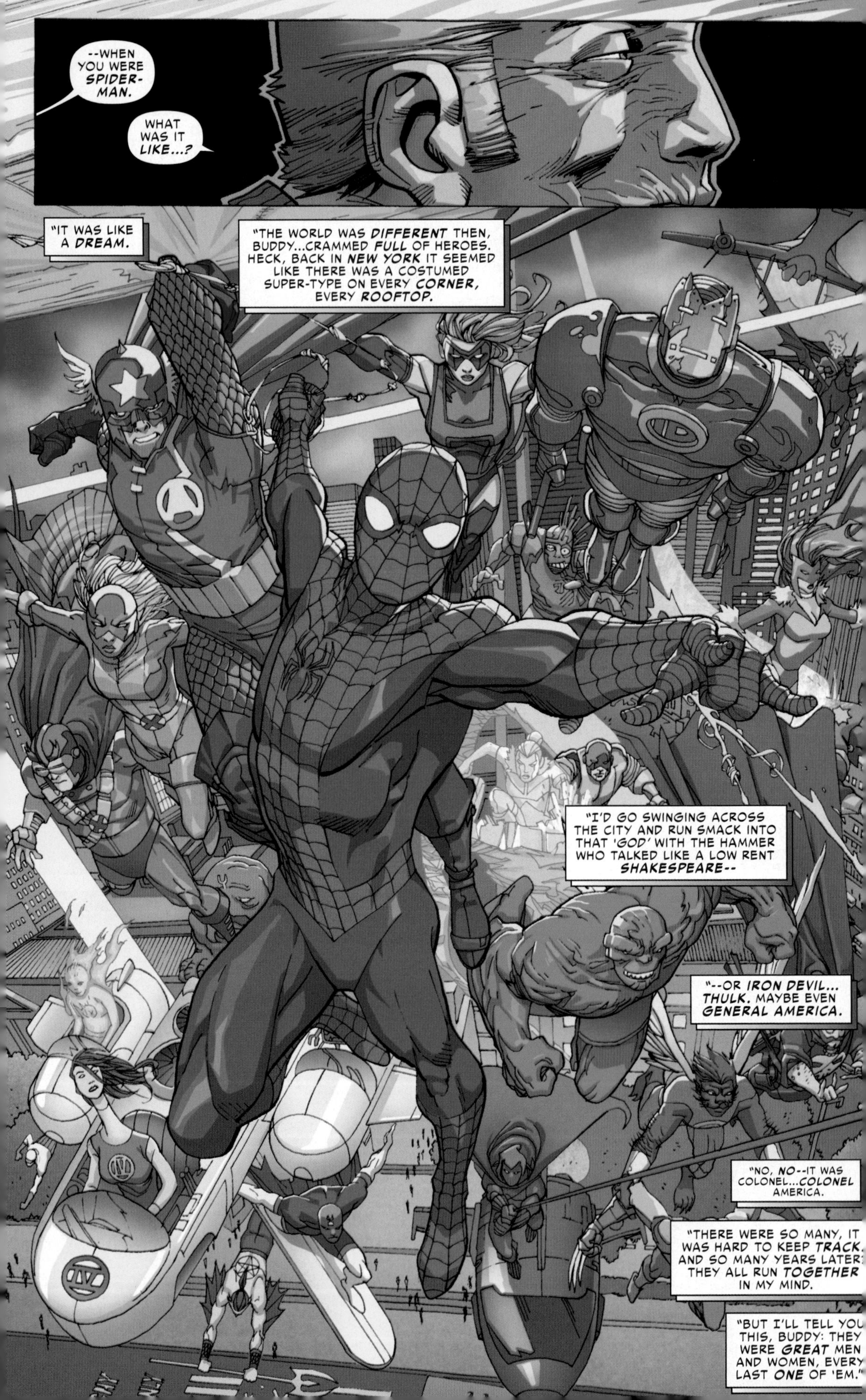

--WHEN YOU WERE SPIDER-MAN.
WHAT WAS IT LIKE...?
"IT WAS LIKE A DREAM.
"THE WORLD WAS DIFFERENT THEN, BUDDY...CRAMMED FULL OF HEROES. HECK, BACK IN NEW YORK IT SEEMED LIKE THERE WAS A COSTUMED SUPER-TYPE ON EVERY CORNER, EVERY ROOFTOP.
"I'D GO SWINGING ACROSS THE CITY AND RUN SMACK INTO THAT 'GOD' WITH THE HAMMER WHO TALKED LIKE A LOW RENT SHAKESPEARE--
"--OR IRON DEVIL... THULK. MAYBE EVEN GENERAL AMERICA.
"NO, NO--IT WAS COLONEL...COLONEL AMERICA.
"THERE WERE SO MANY, IT WAS HARD TO KEEP TRACK. AND SO MANY YEARS LATER, THEY ALL RUN TOGETHER IN MY MIND.
"BUT I'LL TELL YOU THIS, BUDDY: THEY WERE GREAT MEN AND WOMEN, EVERY LAST ONE OF 'EM."

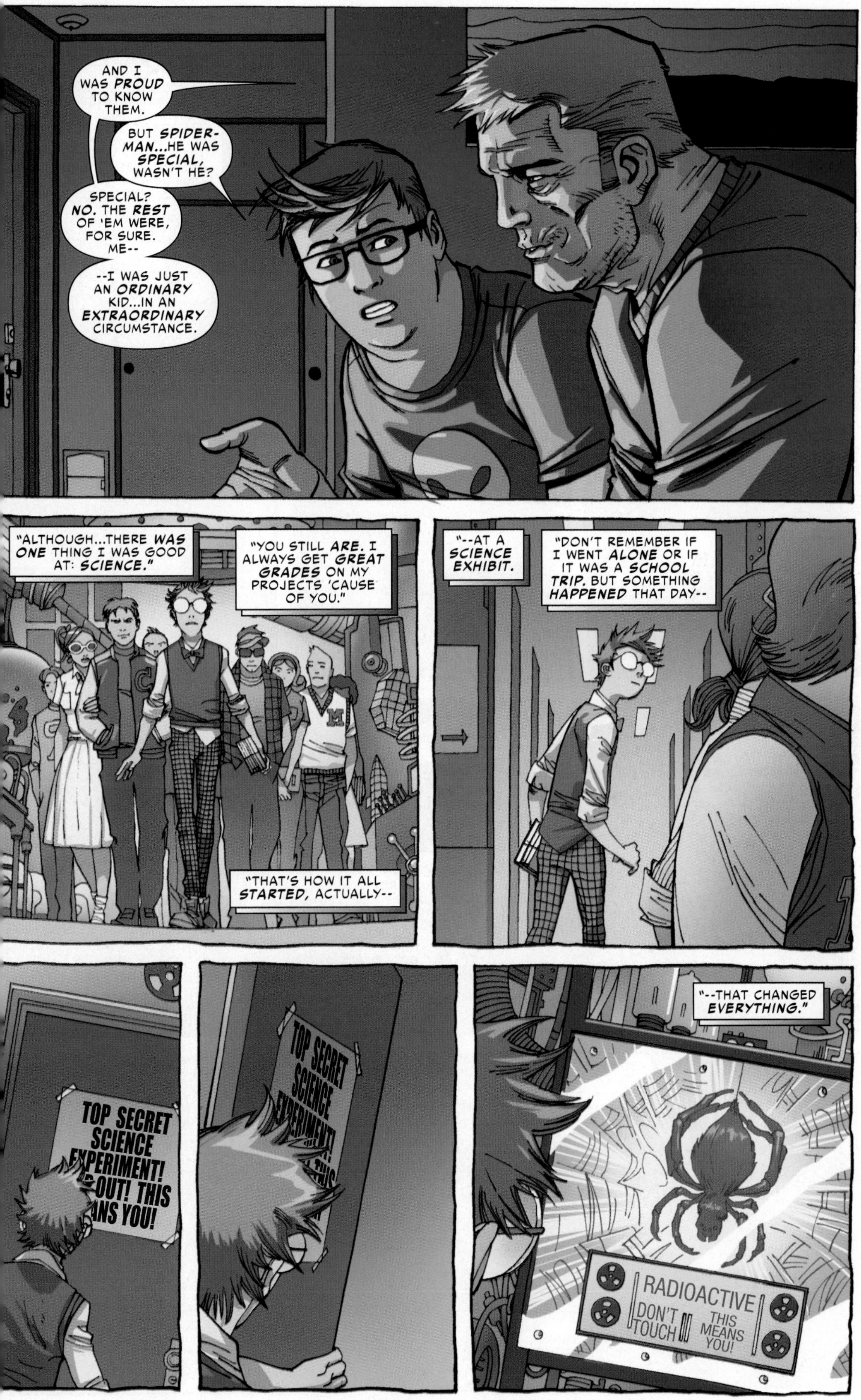
AND I WAS PROUD TO KNOW THEM.
BUT SPIDER-MAN...HE WAS SPECIAL, WASN'T HE?
SPECIAL? NO. THE REST OF 'EM WERE, FOR SURE. ME--
--I WAS JUST AN ORDINARY KID...IN AN EXTRAORDINARY CIRCUMSTANCE.
"ALTHOUGH...THERE WAS ONE THING I WAS GOOD AT: SCIENCE."
"YOU STILL ARE. I ALWAYS GET GREAT GRADES ON MY PROJECTS 'CAUSE OF YOU."
"THAT'S HOW IT ALL STARTED, ACTUALLY--
"--AT A SCIENCE EXHIBIT.
"DON'T REMEMBER IF I WENT ALONE OR IF IT WAS A SCHOOL TRIP. BUT SOMETHING HAPPENED THAT DAY--
TOP SECRET SCIENCE EXPERIMENT!
TOP SECRET SCIENCE EXPERIMENT!
"--THAT CHANGED EVERYTHING."
RADIOACTIVE
DON'T TOUCH
THIS MEANS YOU!

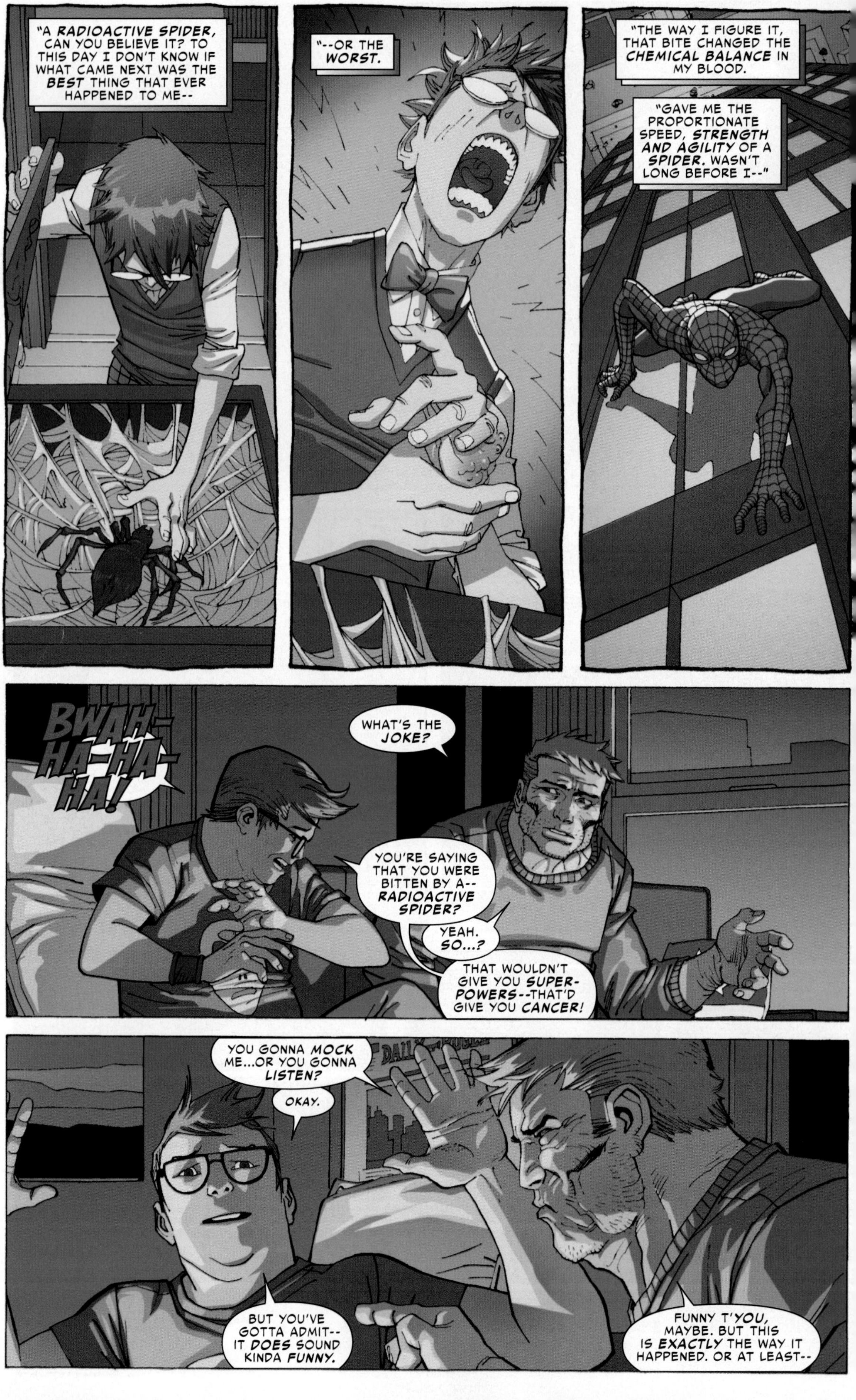
"A RADIOACTIVE SPIDER, CAN YOU BELIEVE IT? TO THIS DAY I DON'T KNOW IF WHAT CAME NEXT WAS THE BEST THING THAT EVER HAPPENED TO ME--
"--OR THE WORST.
"THE WAY I FIGURE IT, THAT BITE CHANGED THE CHEMICAL BALANCE IN MY BLOOD.
"GAVE ME THE PROPORTIONATE SPEED, STRENGTH AND AGILITY OF A SPIDER. WASN'T LONG BEFORE I--"
BWAH-HA-HA-HA!
WHAT'S THE JOKE?
YOU'RE SAYING THAT YOU WERE BITTEN BY A--RADIOACTIVE SPIDER?
YEAH. SO...?
THAT WOULDN'T GIVE YOU SUPER-POWERS--THAT'D GIVE YOU CANCER!
YOU GONNA MOCK ME...OR YOU GONNA LISTEN?
OKAY.
BUT YOU'VE GOTTA ADMIT--IT DOES SOUND KINDA FUNNY.
FUNNY T'YOU, MAYBE. BUT THIS IS EXACTLY THE WAY IT HAPPENED. OR AT LEAST--

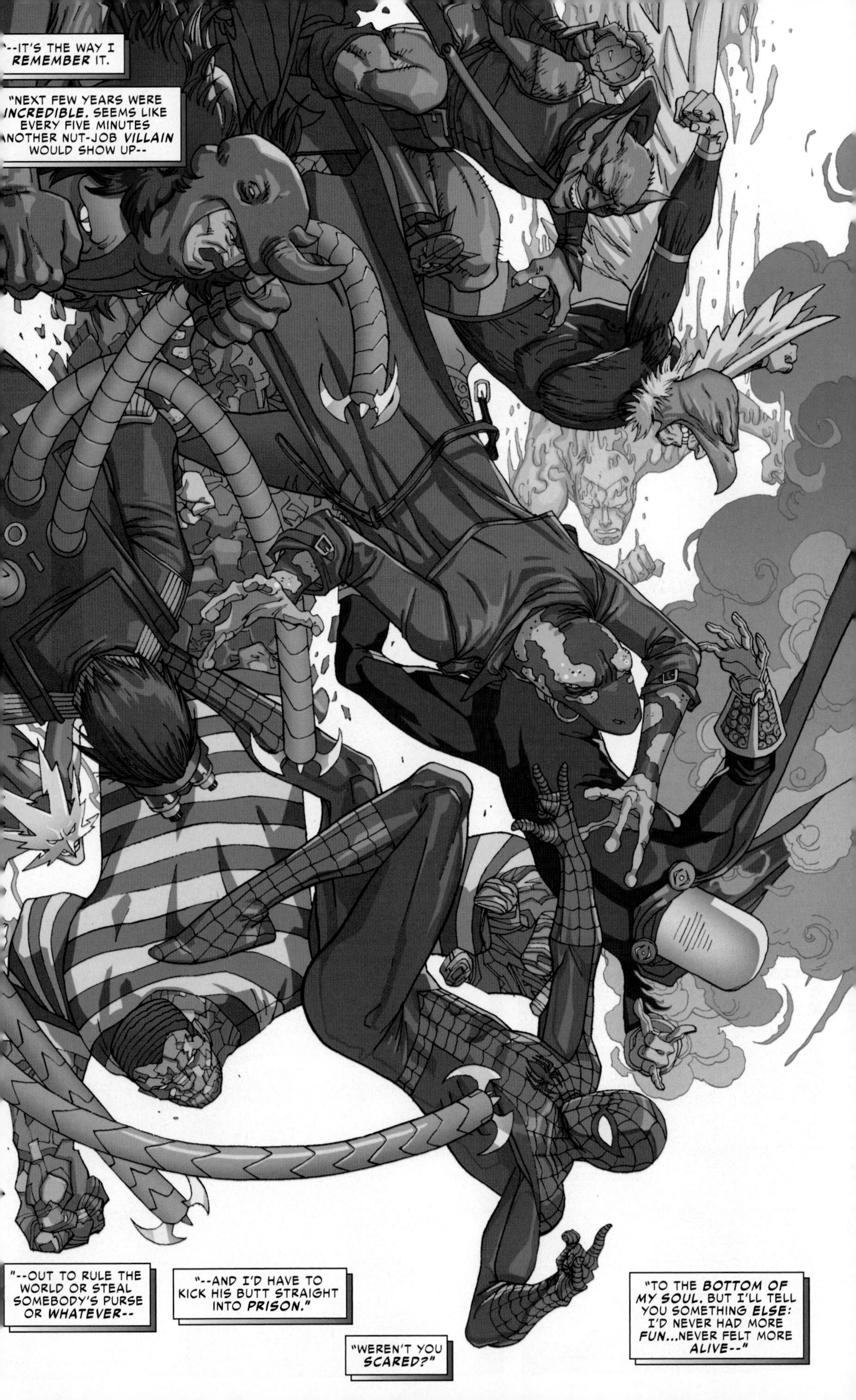
"--IT'S THE WAY I REMEMBER IT.
"NEXT FEW YEARS WERE INCREDIBLE. SEEMS LIKE EVERY FIVE MINUTES ANOTHER NUT-JOB VILLAIN WOULD SHOW UP--
"--OUT TO RULE THE WORLD OR STEAL SOMEBODY'S PURSE OR WHATEVER--
"--AND I'D HAVE TO KICK HIS BUTT STRAIGHT INTO PRISON."
"WEREN'T YOU SCARED?"
"TO THE BOTTOM OF MY SOUL. BUT I'LL TELL YOU SOMETHING ELSE: I'D NEVER HAD MORE FUN...NEVER FELT MORE ALIVE--"

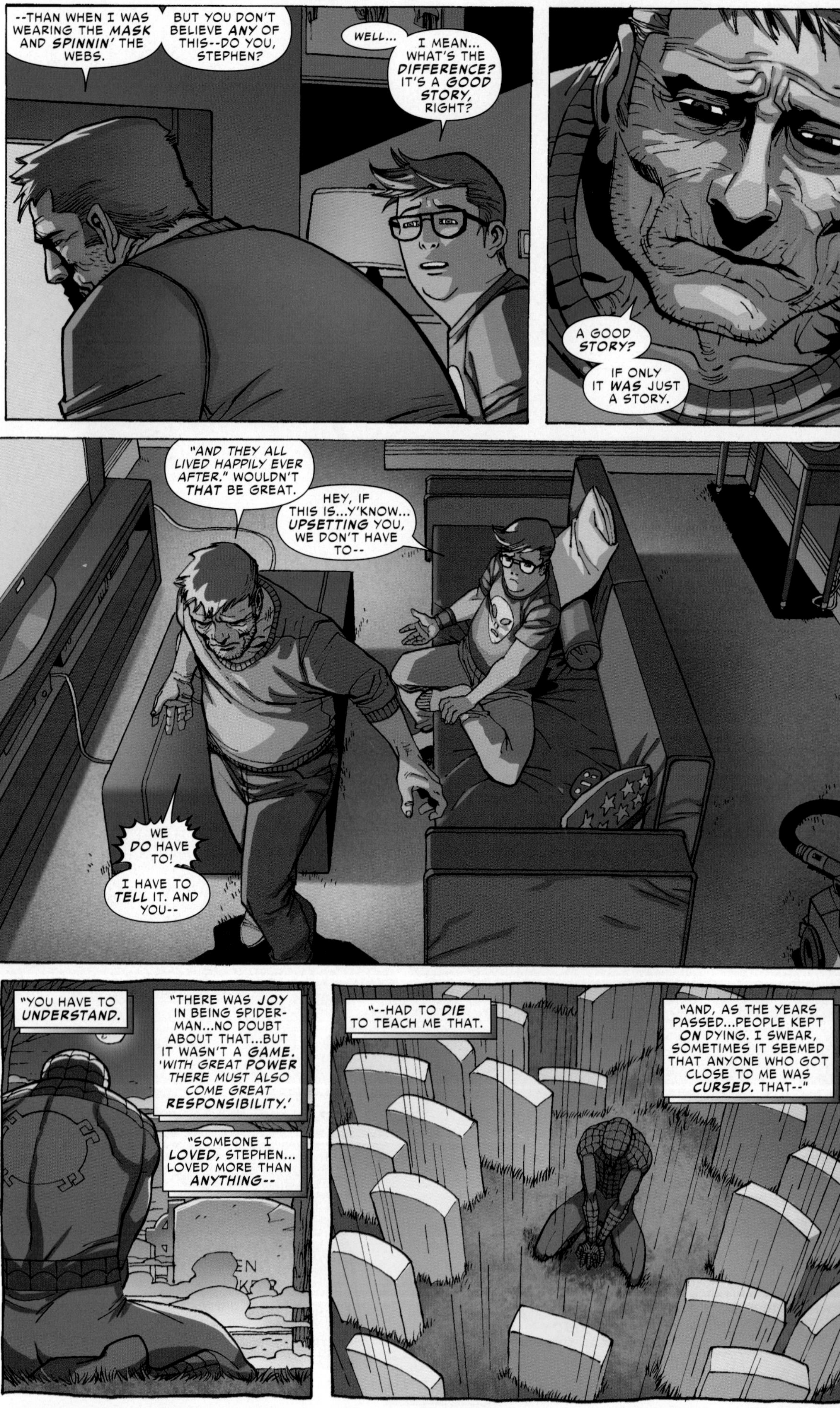

--THAN WHEN I WAS WEARING THE MASK AND SPINNIN' THE WEBS.
BUT YOU DON'T BELIEVE ANY OF THIS--DO YOU, STEPHEN?
WELL...
I MEAN... WHAT'S THE DIFFERENCE? IT'S A GOOD STORY, RIGHT?
A GOOD STORY?
IF ONLY IT WAS JUST A STORY.
"AND THEY ALL LIVED HAPPILY EVER AFTER." WOULDN'T THAT BE GREAT.
HEY, IF THIS IS...Y'KNOW... UPSETTING YOU, WE DON'T HAVE TO--
WE DO HAVE TO!
I HAVE TO TELL IT. AND YOU--
"YOU HAVE TO UNDERSTAND.
"THERE WAS JOY IN BEING SPIDER-MAN...NO DOUBT ABOUT THAT...BUT IT WASN'T A GAME. 'WITH GREAT POWER THERE MUST ALSO COME GREAT RESPONSIBILITY.'
"SOMEONE I LOVED, STEPHEN... LOVED MORE THAN ANYTHING--
"--HAD TO DIE TO TEACH ME THAT.
"AND, AS THE YEARS PASSED...PEOPLE KEPT ON DYING. I SWEAR, SOMETIMES IT SEEMED THAT ANYONE WHO GOT CLOSE TO ME WAS CURSED. THAT--"

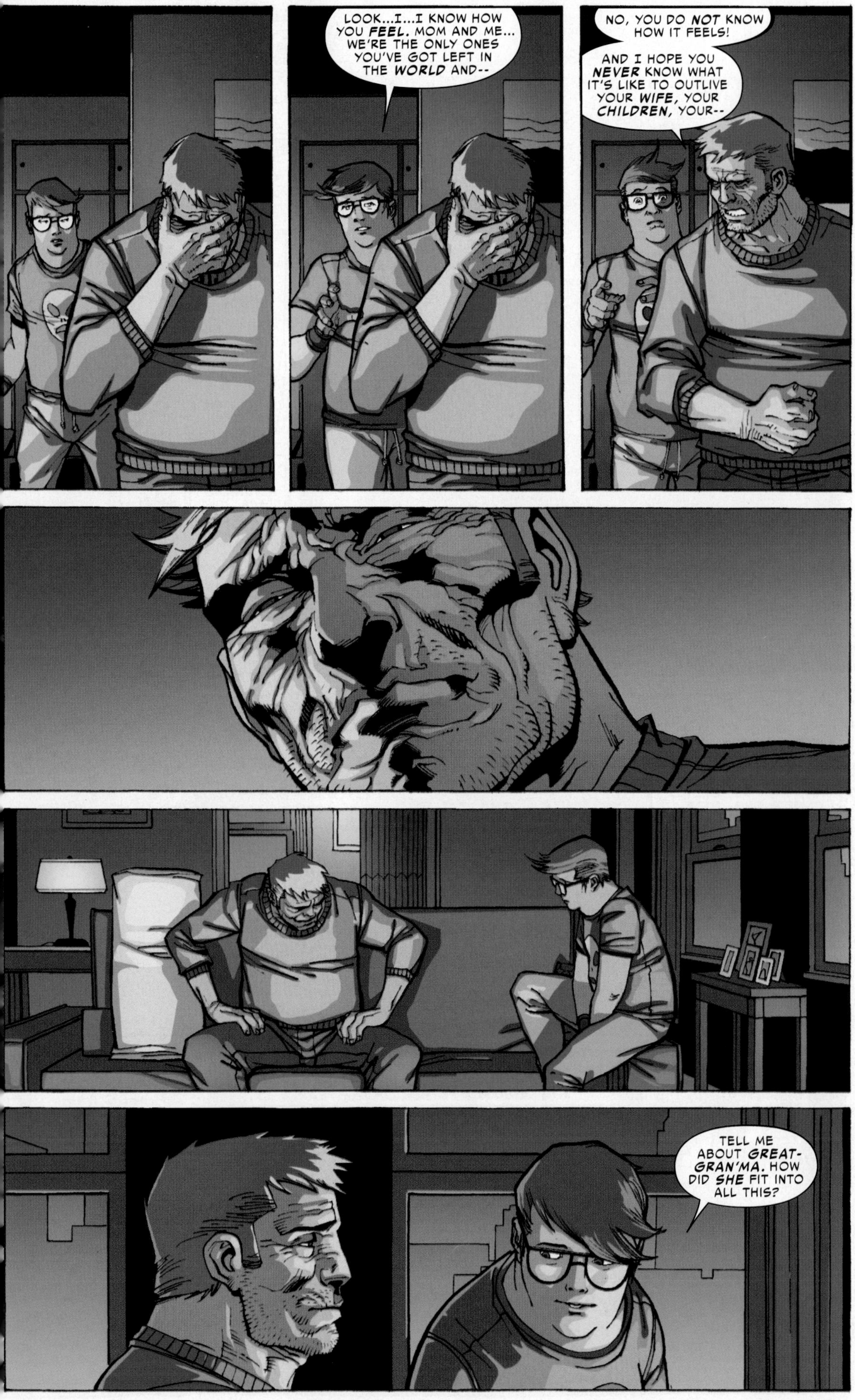
LOOK...I...I KNOW HOW YOU FEEL. MOM AND ME... WE'RE THE ONLY ONES YOU'VE GOT LEFT IN THE WORLD AND--
NO, YOU DO NOT KNOW HOW IT FEELS!
AND I HOPE YOU NEVER KNOW WHAT IT'S LIKE TO OUTLIVE YOUR WIFE, YOUR CHILDREN, YOUR--
TELL ME ABOUT GREAT-GRAN'MA. HOW DID SHE FIT INTO ALL THIS?

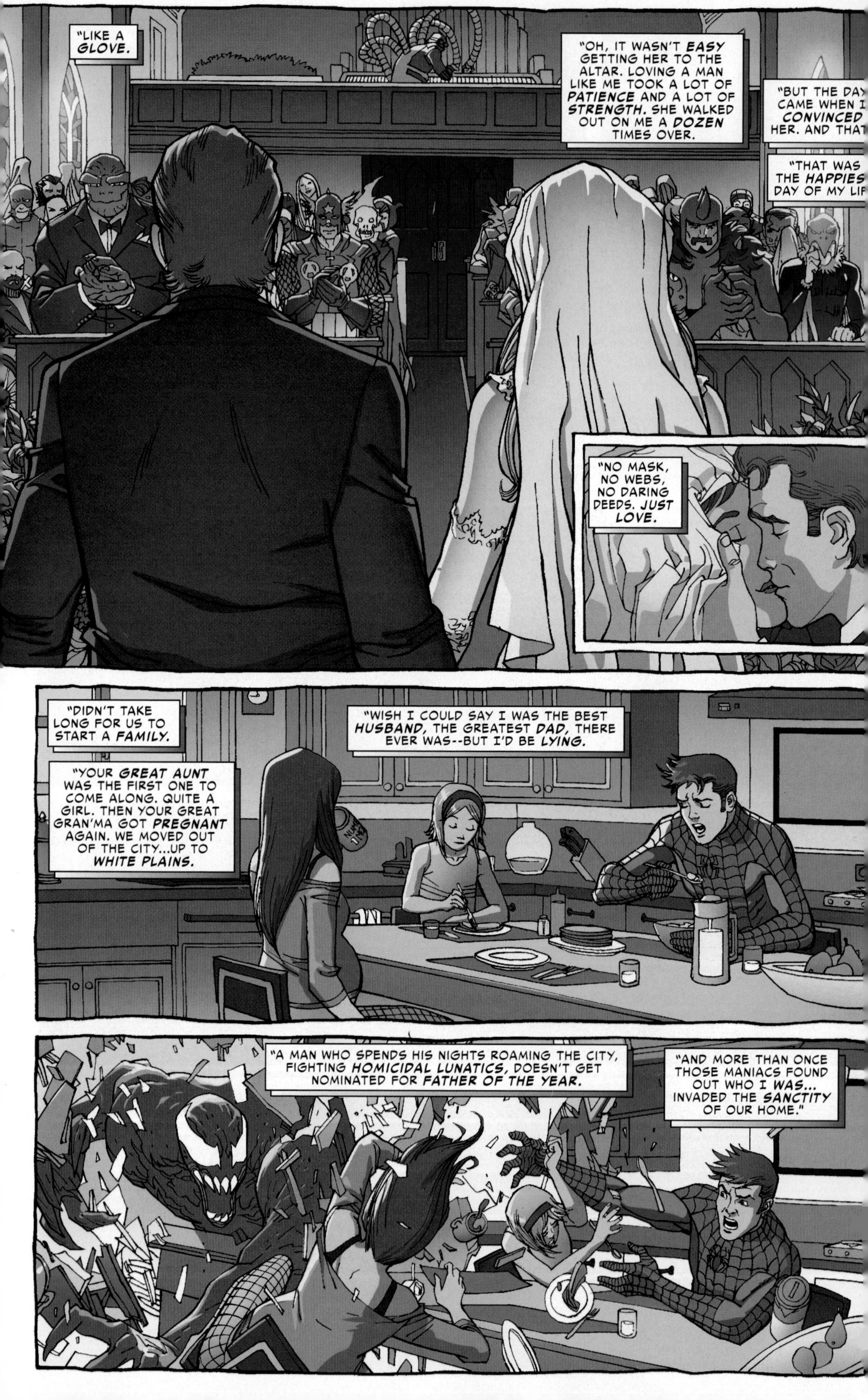
"LIKE A GLOVE.
"OH, IT WASN'T EASY GETTING HER TO THE ALTAR. LOVING A MAN LIKE ME TOOK A LOT OF PATIENCE AND A LOT OF STRENGTH. SHE WALKED OUT ON ME A DOZEN TIMES OVER.
"BUT THE DAY CAME WHEN I CONVINCED HER. AND THAT
"THAT WAS THE HAPPIES DAY OF MY LIF
"NO MASK, NO WEBS, NO DARING DEEDS. JUST LOVE.
"DIDN'T TAKE LONG FOR US TO START A FAMILY.
"YOUR GREAT AUNT WAS THE FIRST ONE TO COME ALONG. QUITE A GIRL. THEN YOUR GREAT GRAN'MA GOT PREGNANT AGAIN. WE MOVED OUT OF THE CITY...UP TO WHITE PLAINS.
"WISH I COULD SAY I WAS THE BEST HUSBAND, THE GREATEST DAD, THERE EVER WAS--BUT I'D BE LYING.
"A MAN WHO SPENDS HIS NIGHTS ROAMING THE CITY, FIGHTING HOMICIDAL LUNATICS, DOESN'T GET NOMINATED FOR FATHER OF THE YEAR.
"AND MORE THAN ONCE THOSE MANIACS FOUND OUT WHO I WAS... INVADED THE SANCTITY OF OUR HOME."

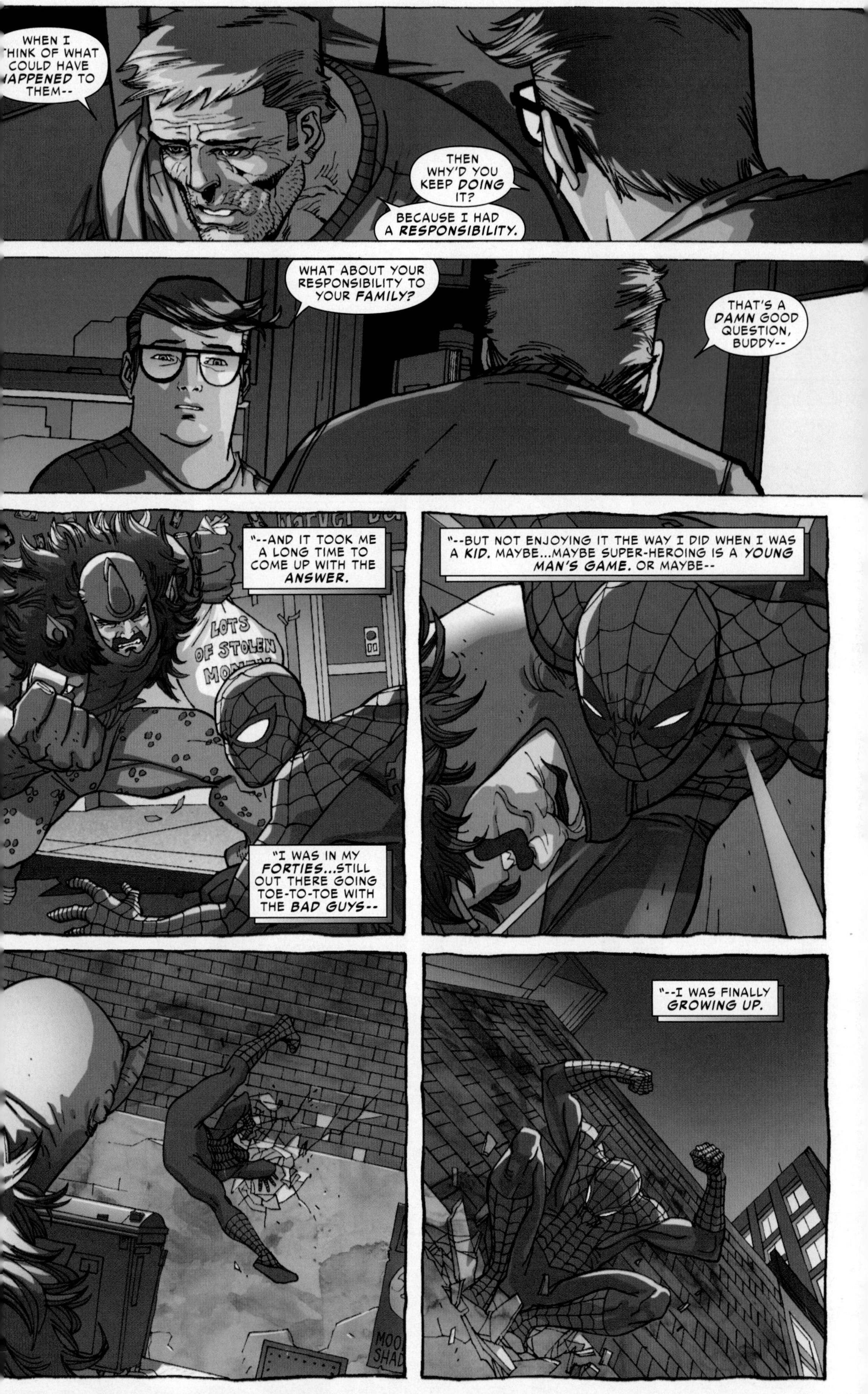
WHEN I THINK OF WHAT COULD HAVE HAPPENED TO THEM--
THEN WHY'D YOU KEEP DOING IT?
BECAUSE I HAD A RESPONSIBILITY.
WHAT ABOUT YOUR RESPONSIBILITY TO YOUR FAMILY?
THAT'S A DAMN GOOD QUESTION, BUDDY--
"--AND IT TOOK ME A LONG TIME TO COME UP WITH THE ANSWER.
LOTS
OF STOLEN
"I WAS IN MY FORTIES...STILL OUT THERE GOING TOE-TO-TOE WITH THE BAD GUYS--
"--BUT NOT ENJOYING IT THE WAY I DID WHEN I WAS A KID. MAYBE...MAYBE SUPER-HEROING IS A YOUNG MAN'S GAME. OR MAYBE--
"--I WAS FINALLY GROWING UP.

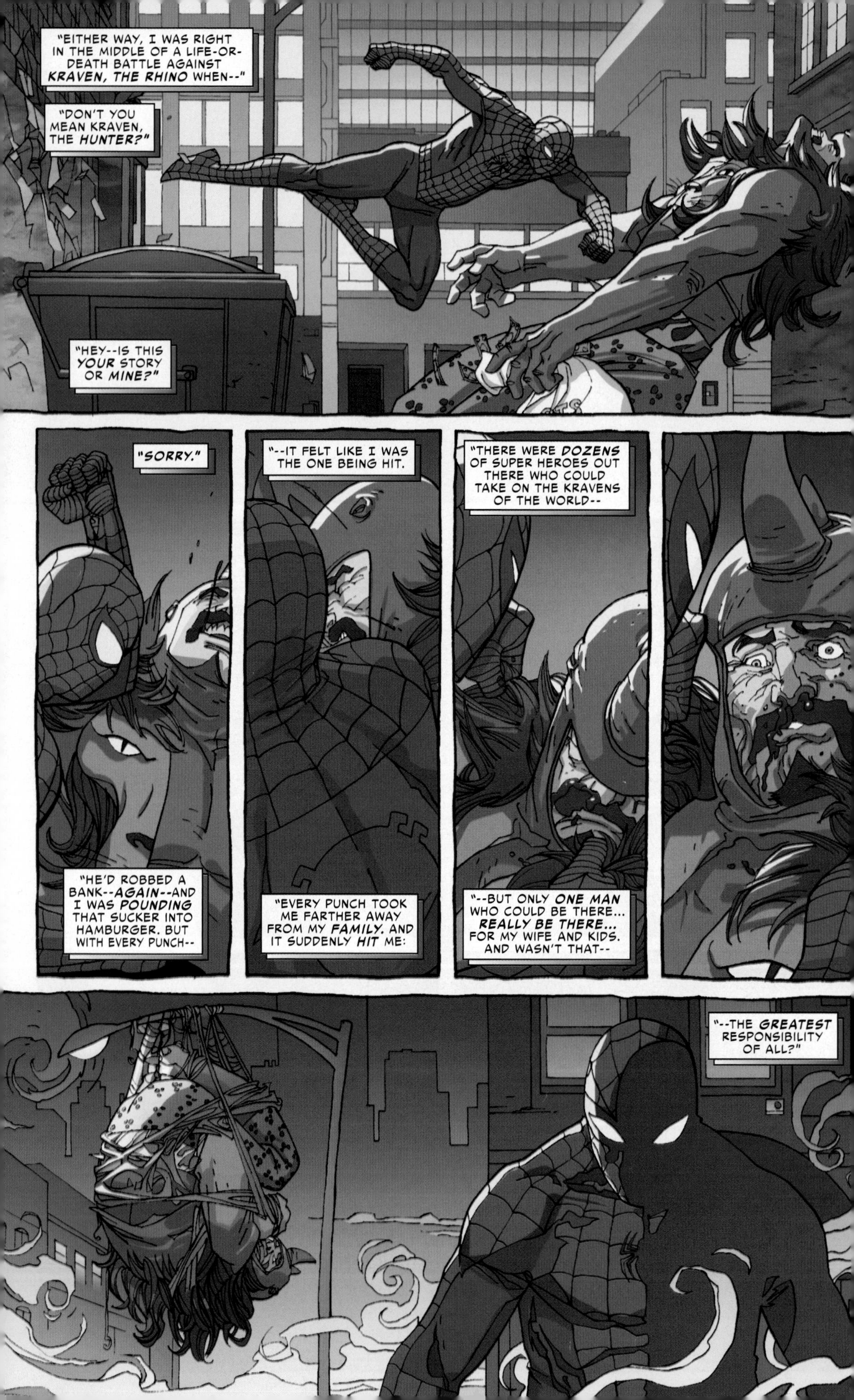
"EITHER WAY, I WAS RIGHT IN THE MIDDLE OF A LIFE-OR-DEATH BATTLE AGAINST KRAVEN, THE RHINO WHEN--"
"DON'T YOU MEAN KRAVEN, THE HUNTER?"
"HEY--IS THIS YOUR STORY OR MINE?"
"SORRY."
"HE'D ROBBED A BANK--AGAIN--AND I WAS POUNDING THAT SUCKER INTO HAMBURGER. BUT WITH EVERY PUNCH--
"--IT FELT LIKE I WAS THE ONE BEING HIT.
"EVERY PUNCH TOOK ME FARTHER AWAY FROM MY FAMILY. AND IT SUDDENLY HIT ME:
"THERE WERE DOZENS OF SUPER HEROES OUT THERE WHO COULD TAKE ON THE KRAVENS OF THE WORLD--
"--BUT ONLY ONE MAN WHO COULD BE THERE... REALLY BE THERE... FOR MY WIFE AND KIDS. AND WASN'T THAT--
"--THE GREATEST RESPONSIBILITY OF ALL?"

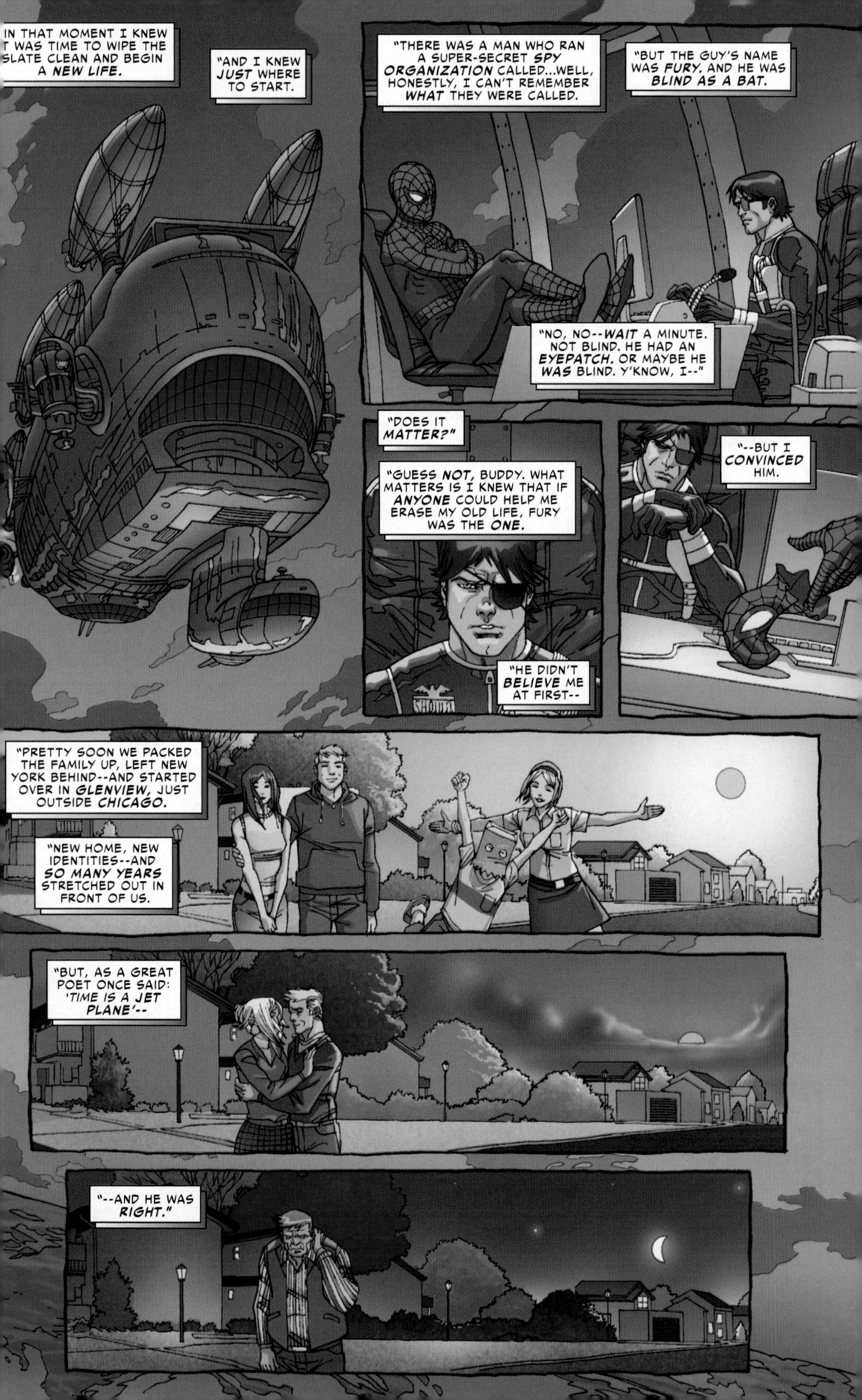
IN THAT MOMENT I KNEW T WAS TIME TO WIPE THE SLATE CLEAN AND BEGIN A NEW LIFE.
"AND I KNEW JUST WHERE TO START.
"THERE WAS A MAN WHO RAN A SUPER-SECRET SPY ORGANIZATION CALLED...WELL, HONESTLY, I CAN'T REMEMBER WHAT THEY WERE CALLED.
"BUT THE GUY'S NAME WAS FURY. AND HE WAS BLIND AS A BAT.
"NO, NO--WAIT A MINUTE. NOT BLIND. HE HAD AN EYEPATCH. OR MAYBE HE WAS BLIND. Y'KNOW, I--"
"DOES IT MATTER?"
"GUESS NOT, BUDDY. WHAT MATTERS IS I KNEW THAT IF ANYONE COULD HELP ME ERASE MY OLD LIFE, FURY WAS THE ONE.
"HE DIDN'T BELIEVE ME AT FIRST--
"--BUT I CONVINCED HIM.
"PRETTY SOON WE PACKED THE FAMILY UP, LEFT NEW YORK BEHIND--AND STARTED OVER IN GLENVIEW, JUST OUTSIDE CHICAGO.
"NEW HOME, NEW IDENTITIES--AND SO MANY YEARS STRETCHED OUT IN FRONT OF US.
"BUT, AS A GREAT POET ONCE SAID: 'TIME IS A JET PLANE'--
"--AND HE WAS RIGHT."

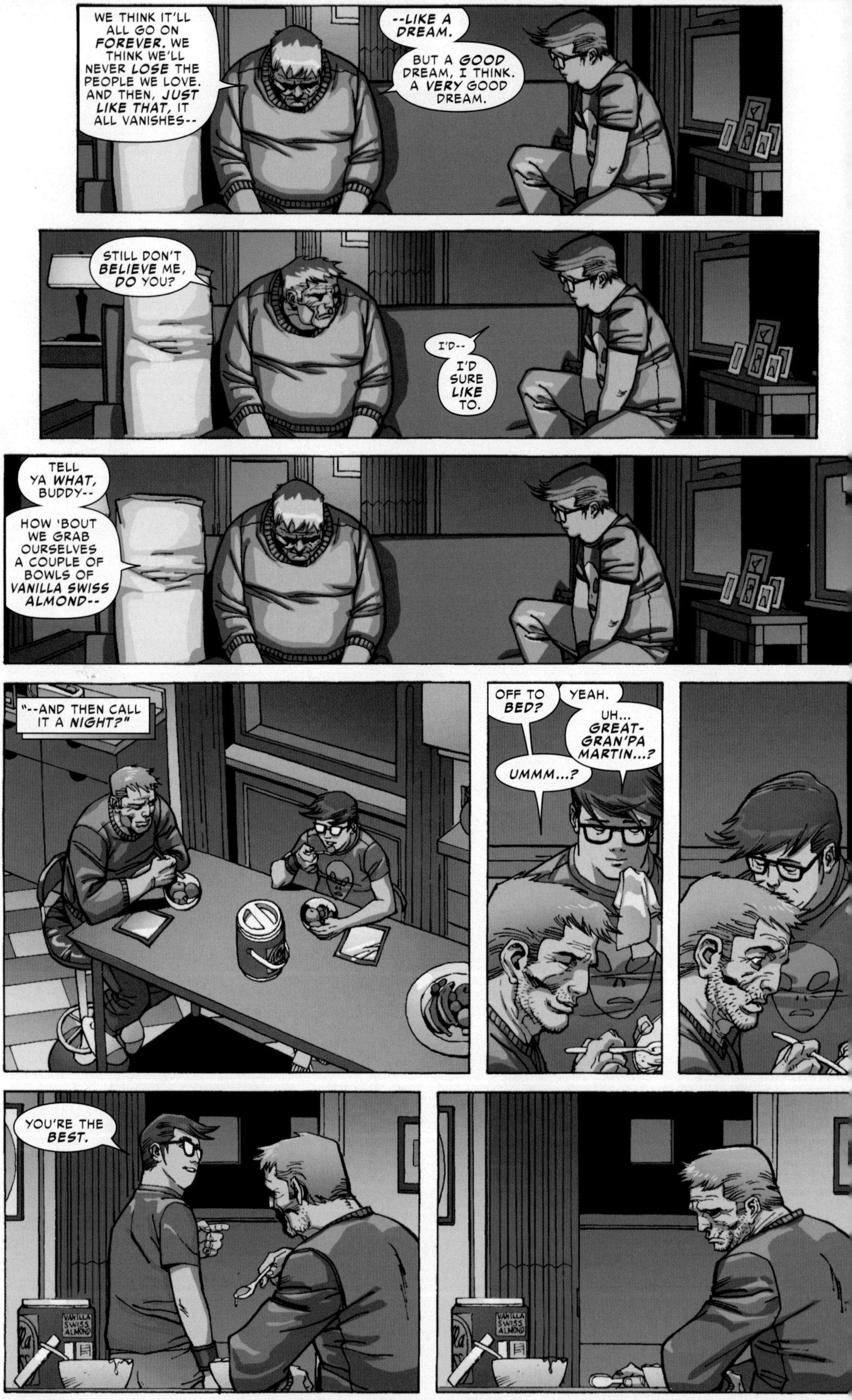
WE THINK IT'LL ALL GO ON *FOREVER.* WE THINK WE'LL NEVER *LOSE* THE PEOPLE WE LOVE. AND THEN, *JUST LIKE THAT,* IT ALL VANISHES--
--*LIKE A DREAM.*
BUT A *GOOD* DREAM, I THINK. A *VERY* GOOD DREAM.
STILL DON'T *BELIEVE* ME, *DO* YOU?
I'D--
I'D SURE *LIKE* TO.
TELL YA *WHAT,* BUDDY--
HOW 'BOUT WE GRAB OURSELVES A COUPLE OF BOWLS OF *VANILLA SWISS ALMOND--*
"--AND THEN CALL IT A *NIGHT?"*
OFF TO *BED?*
YEAH.
UH... *GREAT-GRAN'PA MARTIN...?*
UMMM...?
YOU'RE THE *BEST.*
VANILLA SWISS ALMOND
VANILLA SWISS ALMOND

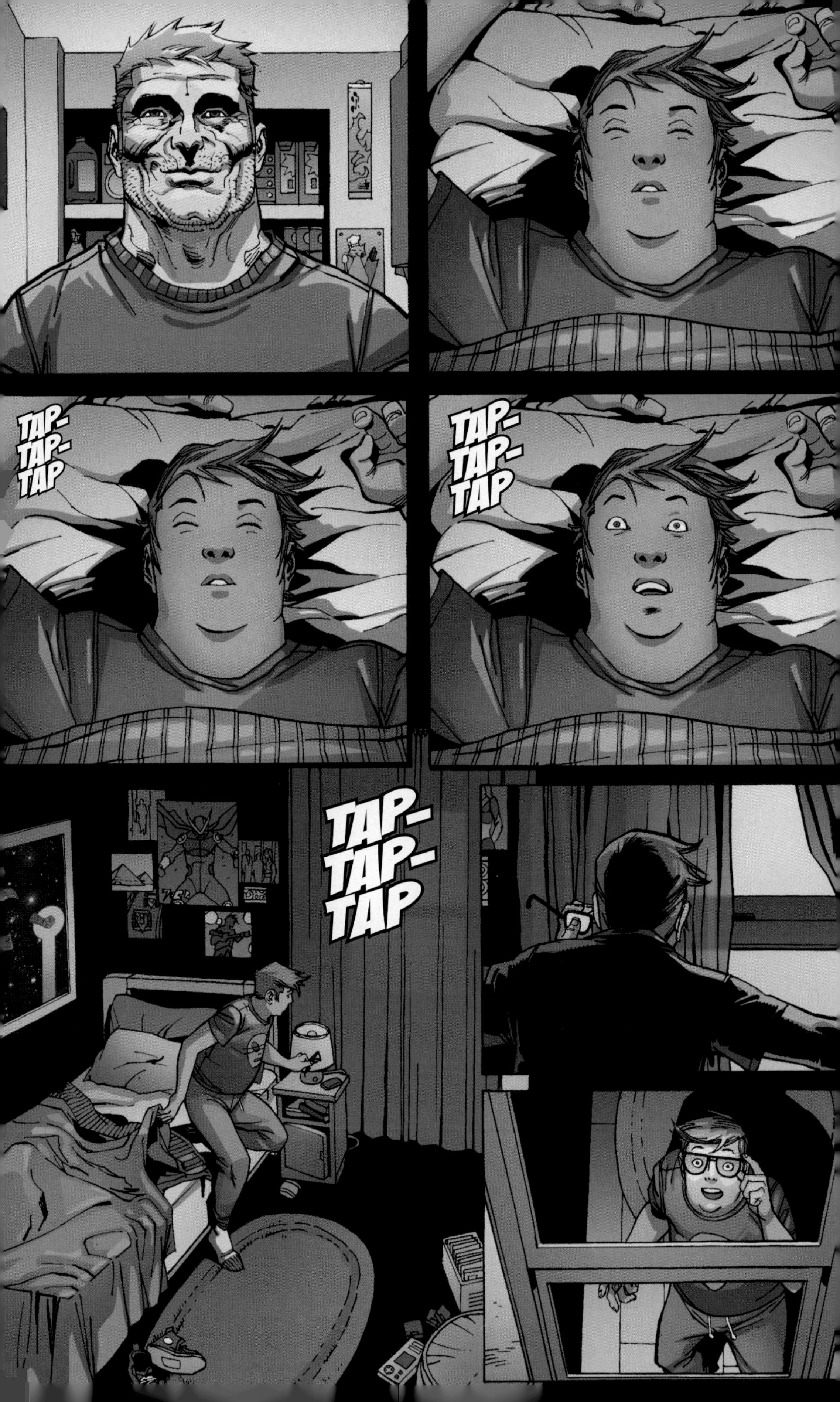
TAP-
TAP-
TAP
TAP-
TAP-
TAP
TAP-
TAP-
TAP

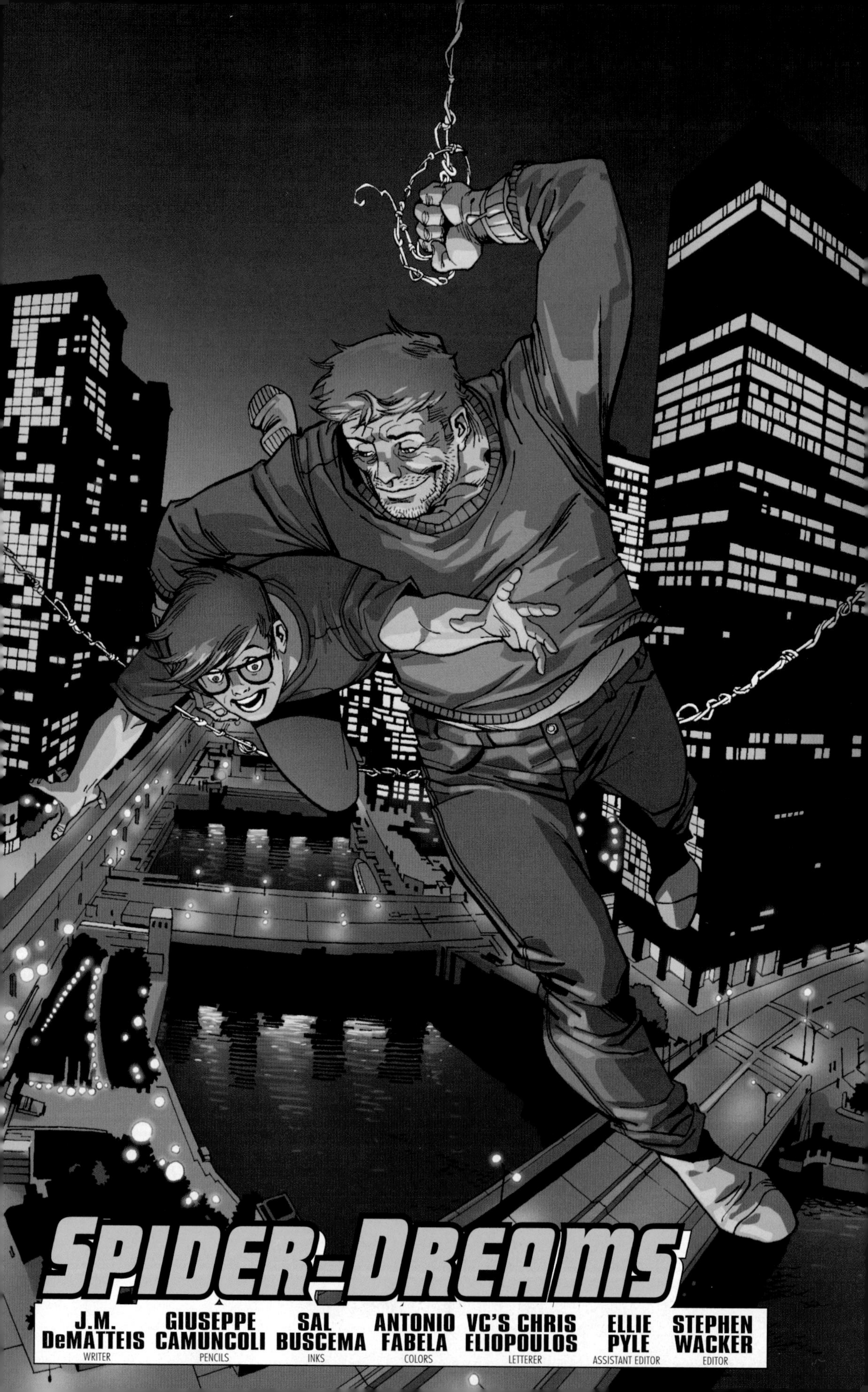
SPIDER-DREAMS
J.M. DeMATTEIS WRITER
GIUSEPPE CAMUNCOLI PENCILS
SAL BUSCEMA INKS
ANTONIO FABELA COLORS
VC'S CHRIS ELIOPOULOS LETTERER
ELLIE PYLE ASSISTANT EDITOR
STEPHEN WACKER EDITOR

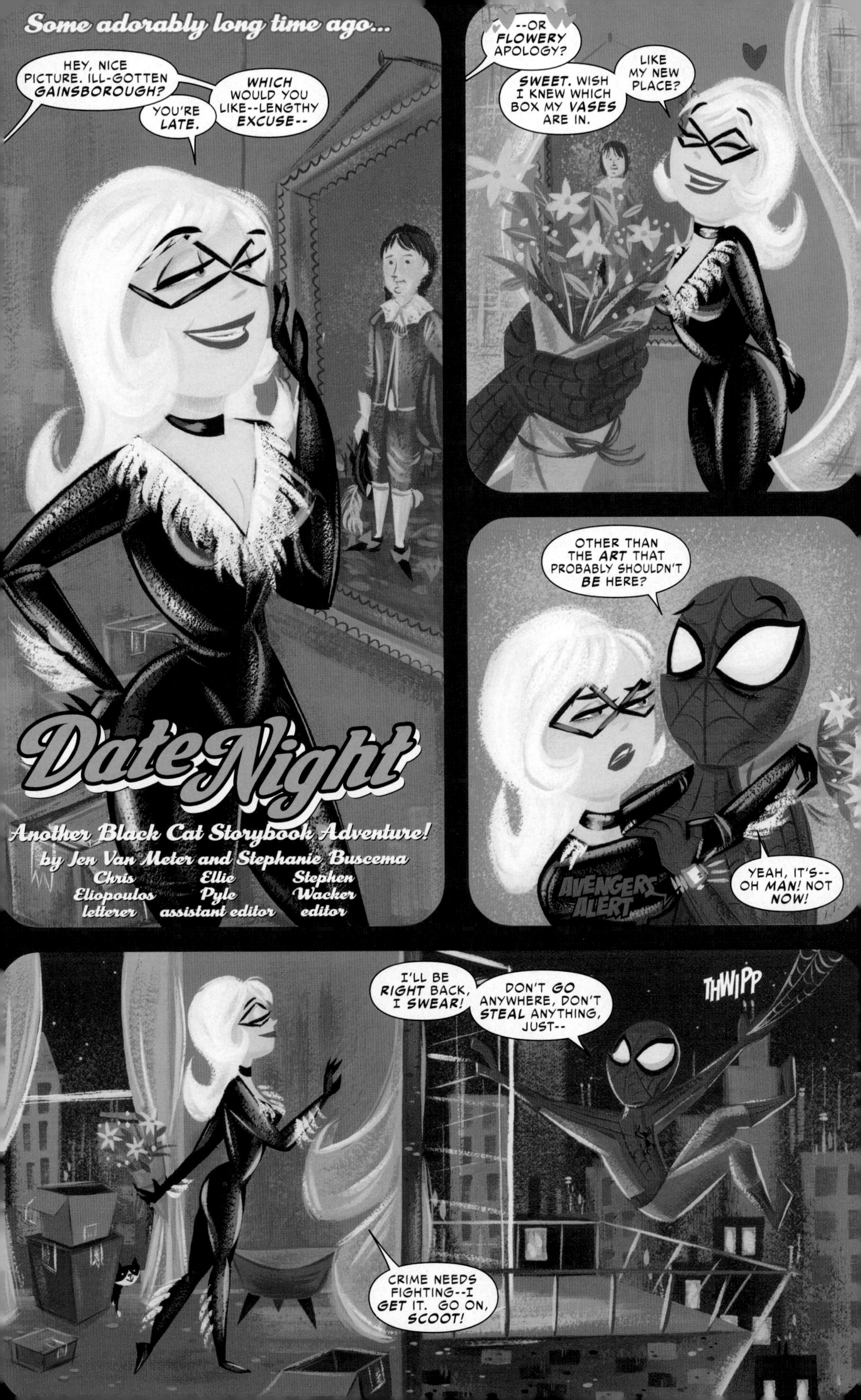
Some adorably long time ago...
HEY, NICE PICTURE. ILL-GOTTEN GAINSBOROUGH?
YOU'RE LATE.
WHICH WOULD YOU LIKE--LENGTHY EXCUSE--
--OR FLOWERY APOLOGY?
SWEET. WISH I KNEW WHICH BOX MY VASES ARE IN.
LIKE MY NEW PLACE?
OTHER THAN THE ART THAT PROBABLY SHOULDN'T BE HERE?
YEAH, IT'S-- OH MAN! NOT NOW!
AVENGERS ALERT
Date Night
Another Black Cat Storybook Adventure!
by Jen Van Meter and Stephanie Buscema
Chris Eliopoulos letterer
Ellie Pyle assistant editor
Stephen Wacker editor
I'LL BE RIGHT BACK, I SWEAR!
DON'T GO ANYWHERE, DON'T STEAL ANYTHING, JUST--
THWIPP
CRIME NEEDS FIGHTING--I GET IT. GO ON, SCOOT!

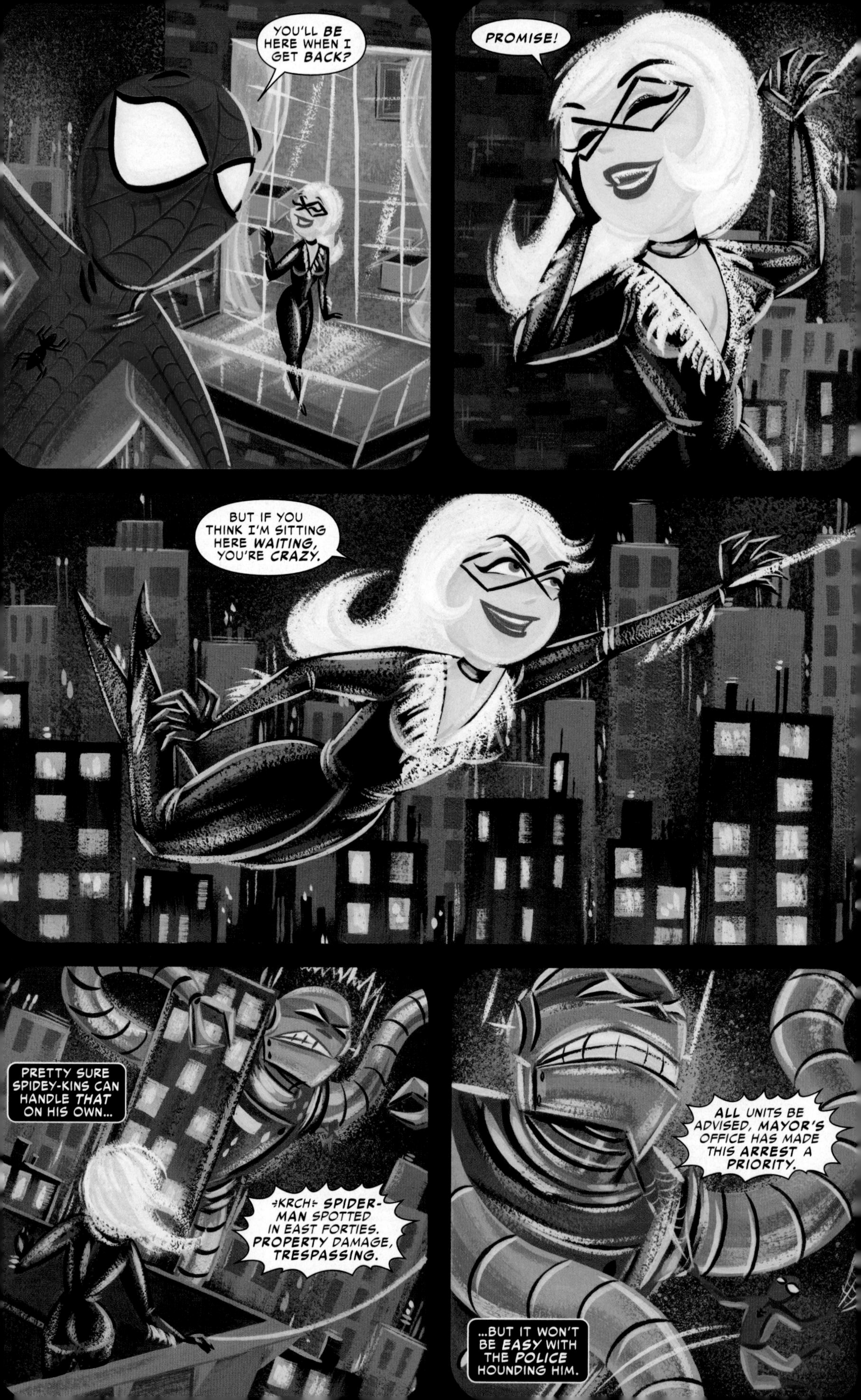
YOU'LL BE HERE WHEN I GET BACK?
PROMISE!
BUT IF YOU THINK I'M SITTING HERE WAITING, YOU'RE CRAZY.
PRETTY SURE SPIDEY-KINS CAN HANDLE THAT ON HIS OWN...
KRCH SPIDER-MAN SPOTTED IN EAST FORTIES. PROPERTY DAMAGE, TRESPASSING.
ALL UNITS BE ADVISED, MAYOR'S OFFICE HAS MADE THIS ARREST A PRIORITY.
...BUT IT WON'T BE EASY WITH THE POLICE HOUNDING HIM.

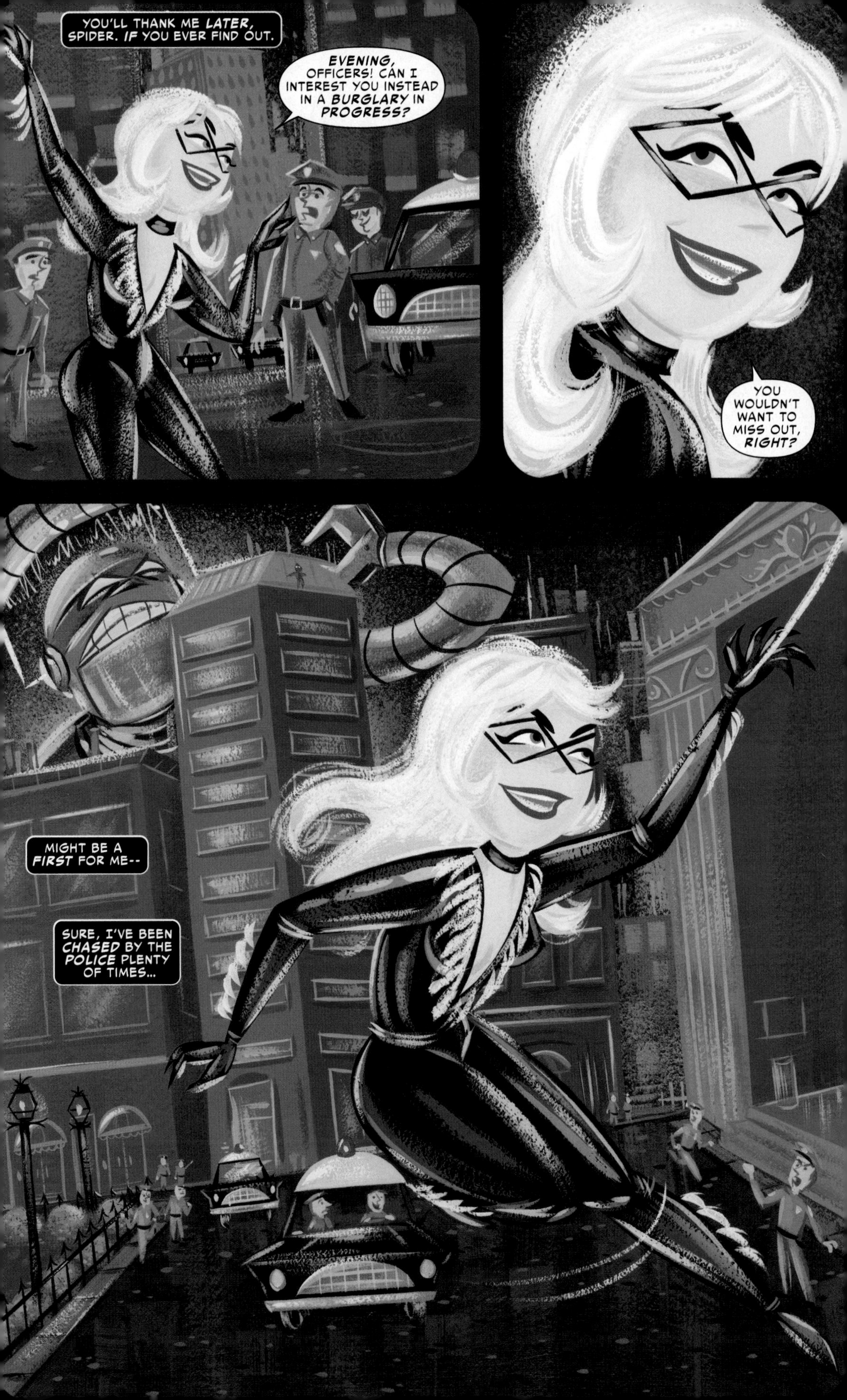
YOU'LL THANK ME LATER, SPIDER. IF YOU EVER FIND OUT.
EVENING, OFFICERS! CAN I INTEREST YOU INSTEAD IN A BURGLARY IN PROGRESS?
YOU WOULDN'T WANT TO MISS OUT, RIGHT?
MIGHT BE A FIRST FOR ME--
SURE, I'VE BEEN CHASED BY THE POLICE PLENTY OF TIMES...

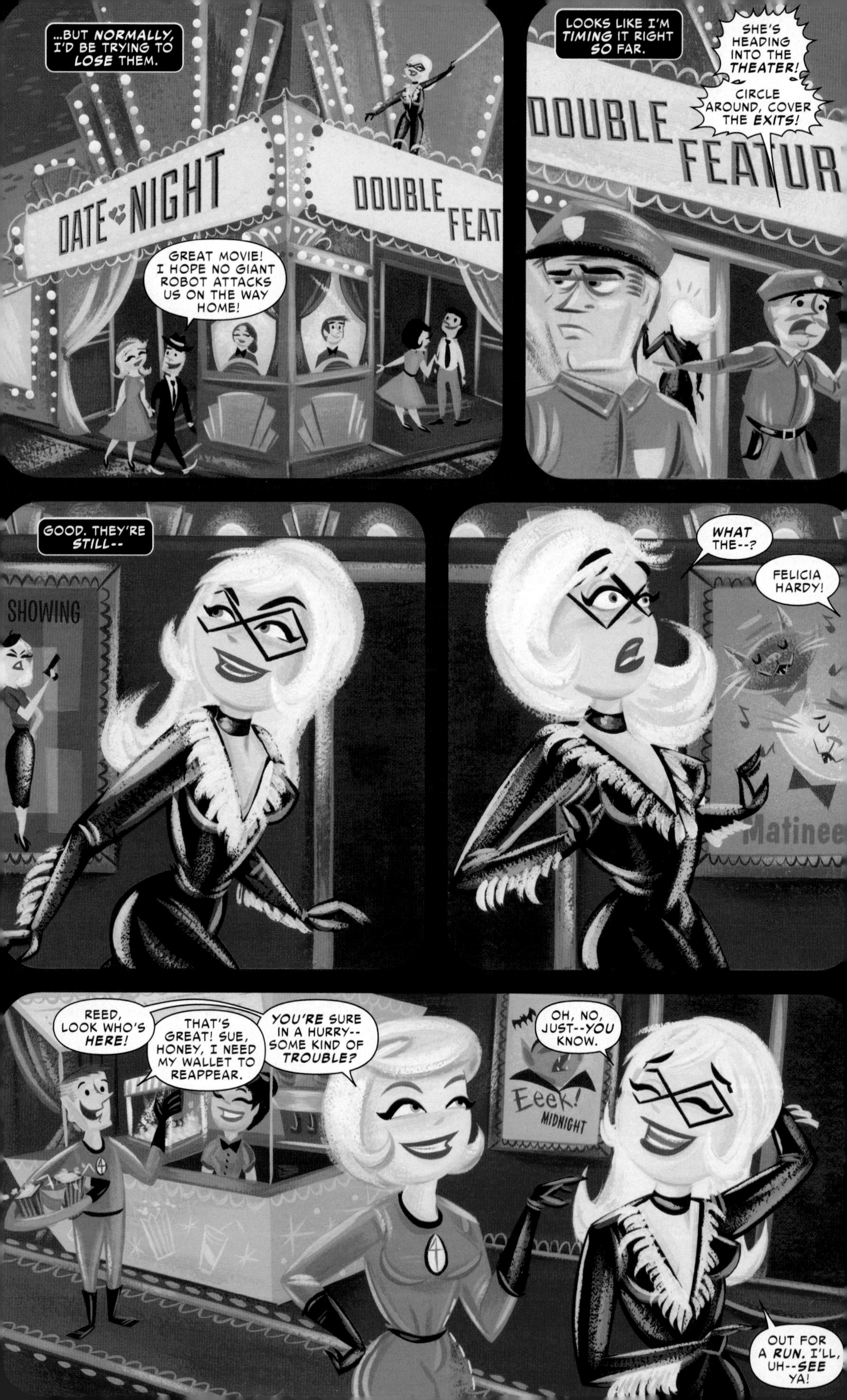
...BUT NORMALLY, I'D BE TRYING TO LOSE THEM.
DATE NIGHT
DOUBLE FEAT
GREAT MOVIE! I HOPE NO GIANT ROBOT ATTACKS US ON THE WAY HOME!
LOOKS LIKE I'M TIMING IT RIGHT SO FAR.
SHE'S HEADING INTO THE THEATER!
CIRCLE AROUND, COVER THE EXITS!
DOUBLE FEATUR
GOOD. THEY'RE STILL--
SHOWING
WHAT THE--?
FELICIA HARDY!
Matinee
REED, LOOK WHO'S HERE!
THAT'S GREAT! SUE, HONEY, I NEED MY WALLET TO REAPPEAR.
YOU'RE SURE IN A HURRY--SOME KIND OF TROUBLE?
OH, NO, JUST--YOU KNOW.
Eeek! MIDNIGHT
OUT FOR A RUN. I'LL, UH--SEE YA!

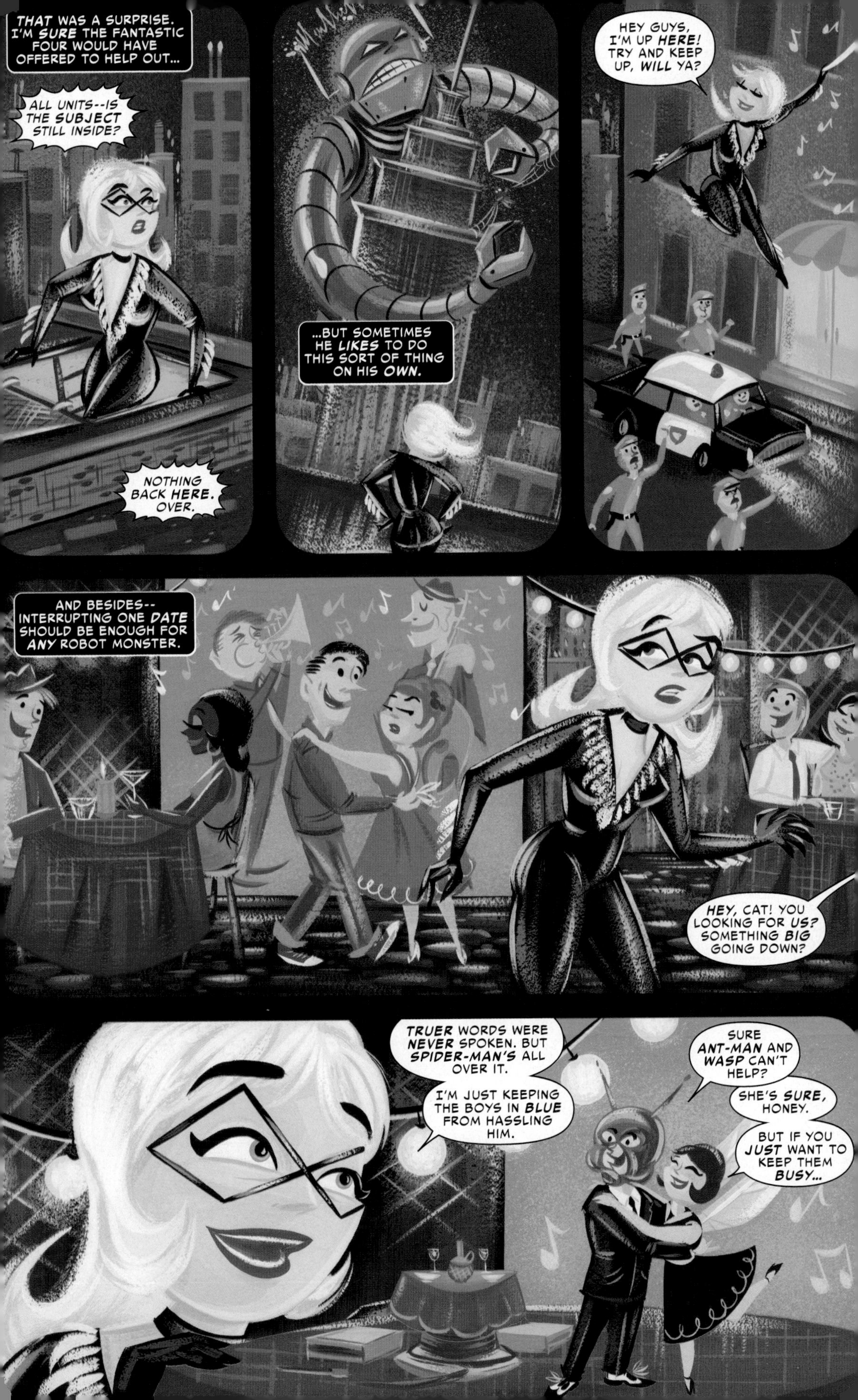
THAT WAS A SURPRISE. I'M SURE THE FANTASTIC FOUR WOULD HAVE OFFERED TO HELP OUT...
ALL UNITS--IS THE SUBJECT STILL INSIDE?
NOTHING BACK HERE. OVER.
...BUT SOMETIMES HE LIKES TO DO THIS SORT OF THING ON HIS OWN.
HEY GUYS, I'M UP HERE! TRY AND KEEP UP, WILL YA?
AND BESIDES--INTERRUPTING ONE DATE SHOULD BE ENOUGH FOR ANY ROBOT MONSTER.
HEY, CAT! YOU LOOKING FOR US? SOMETHING BIG GOING DOWN?
TRUER WORDS WERE NEVER SPOKEN. BUT SPIDER-MAN'S ALL OVER IT.
I'M JUST KEEPING THE BOYS IN BLUE FROM HASSLING HIM.
SURE ANT-MAN AND WASP CAN'T HELP?
SHE'S SURE, HONEY.
BUT IF YOU JUST WANT TO KEEP THEM BUSY...

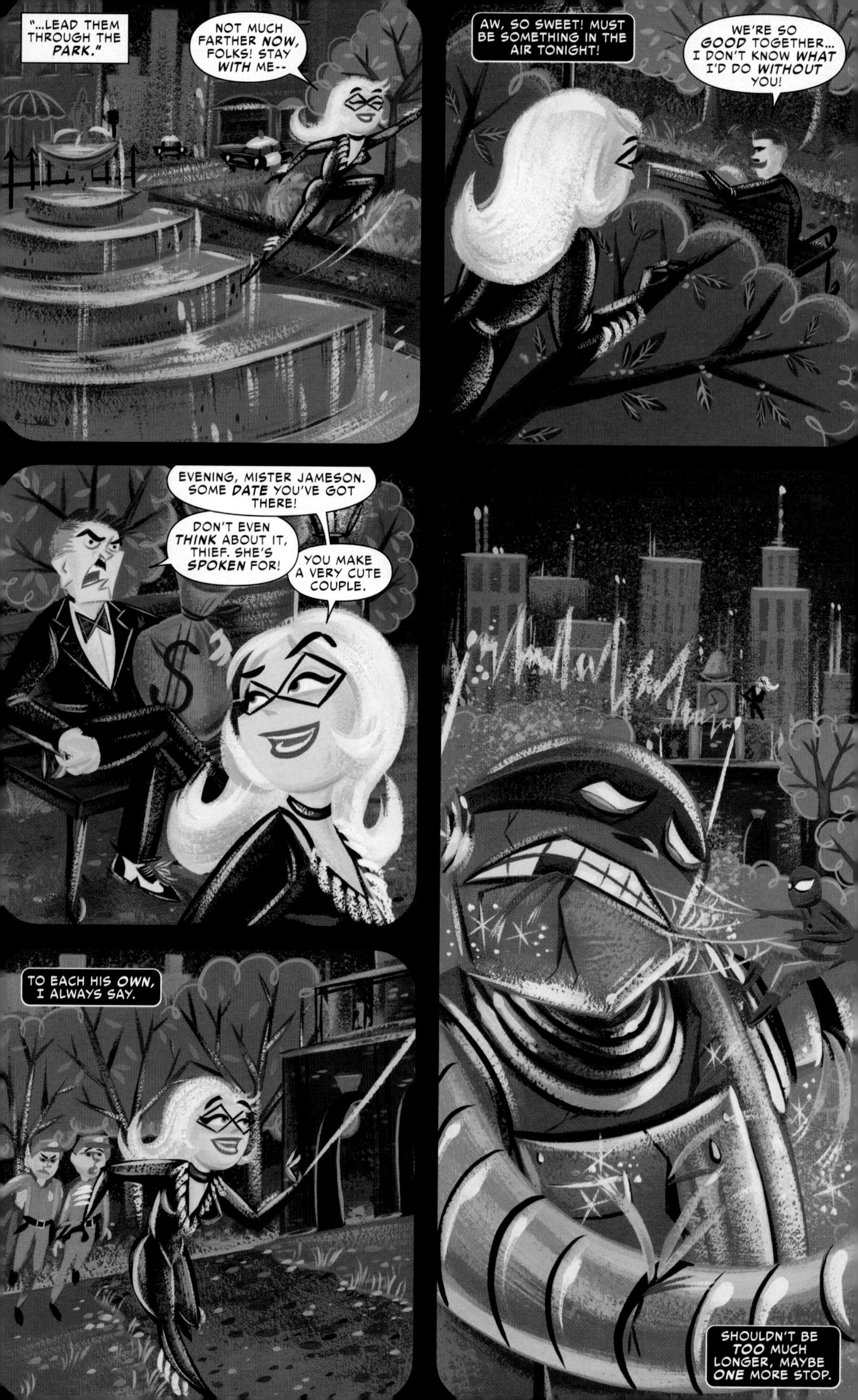
"...LEAD THEM THROUGH THE PARK."
NOT MUCH FARTHER NOW, FOLKS! STAY WITH ME--
AW, SO SWEET! MUST BE SOMETHING IN THE AIR TONIGHT!
WE'RE SO GOOD TOGETHER... I DON'T KNOW WHAT I'D DO WITHOUT YOU!
EVENING, MISTER JAMESON. SOME DATE YOU'VE GOT THERE!
DON'T EVEN THINK ABOUT IT, THIEF. SHE'S SPOKEN FOR!
YOU MAKE A VERY CUTE COUPLE.
TO EACH HIS OWN, I ALWAYS SAY.
SHOULDN'T BE TOO MUCH LONGER, MAYBE ONE MORE STOP.

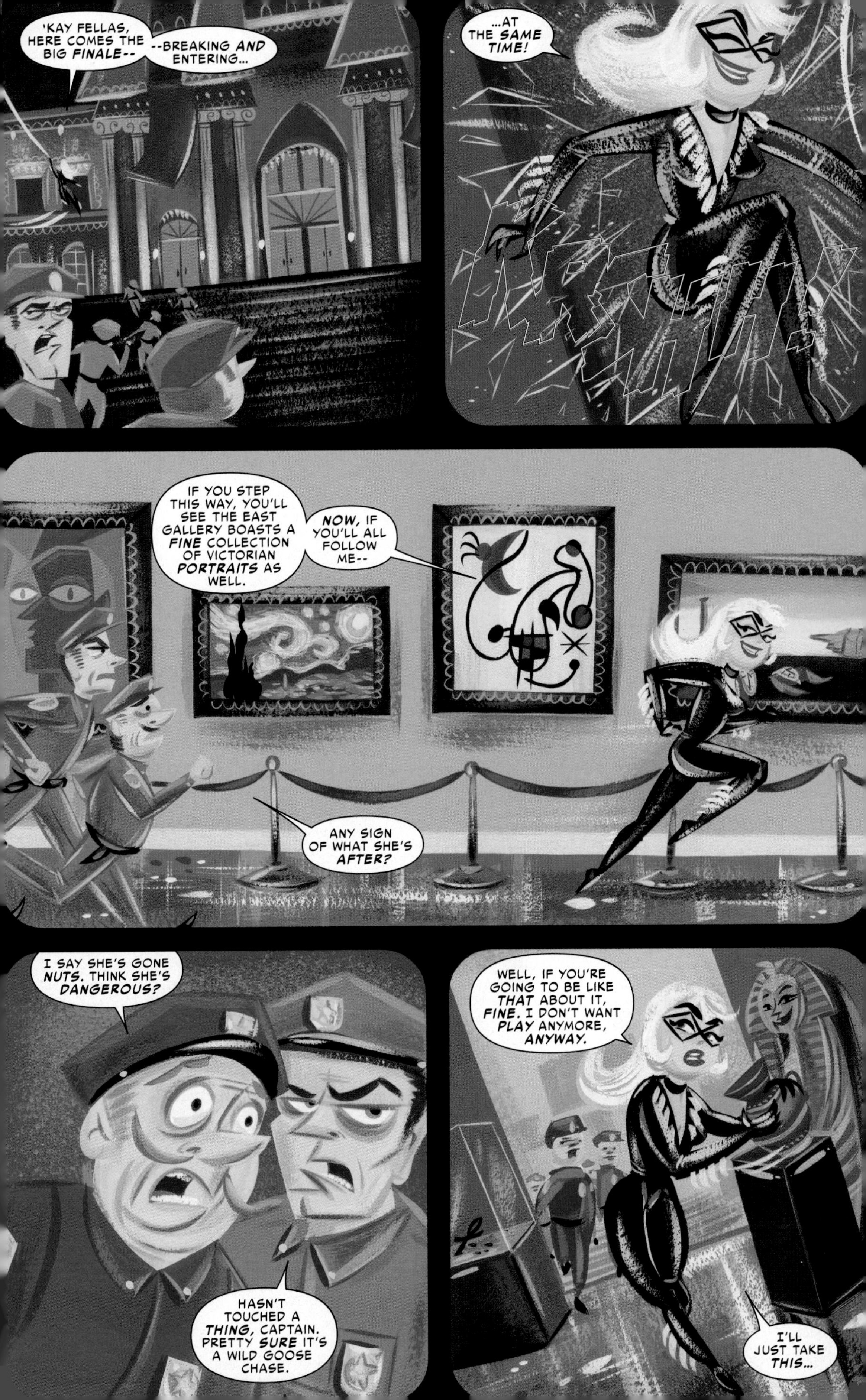
'KAY FELLAS, HERE COMES THE BIG *FINALE*--
--BREAKING *AND* ENTERING...
...AT THE *SAME TIME!*
IF YOU STEP THIS WAY, YOU'LL SEE THE EAST GALLERY BOASTS A *FINE* COLLECTION OF VICTORIAN *PORTRAITS* AS WELL.
NOW, IF YOU'LL ALL FOLLOW ME--
ANY SIGN OF WHAT SHE'S *AFTER?*
I SAY SHE'S GONE *NUTS*. THINK SHE'S *DANGEROUS?*
HASN'T TOUCHED A *THING*, CAPTAIN. PRETTY *SURE* IT'S A WILD GOOSE CHASE.
WELL, IF YOU'RE GOING TO BE LIKE *THAT* ABOUT IT, *FINE*. I DON'T WANT *PLAY* ANYMORE, *ANYWAY*.
I'LL JUST TAKE *THIS*...

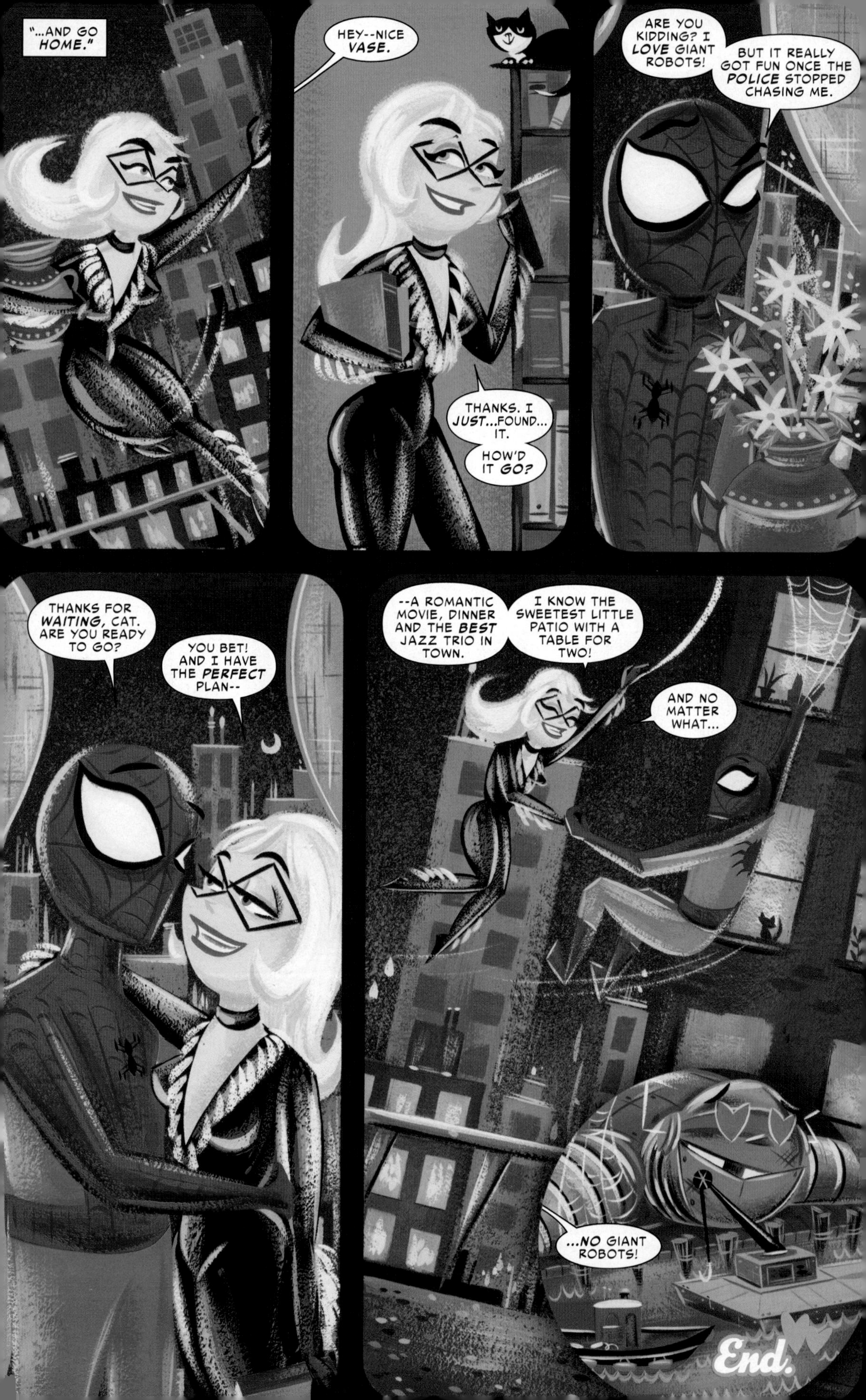
"...AND GO HOME."
HEY--NICE VASE.
THANKS. I JUST...FOUND... IT.
HOW'D IT GO?
ARE YOU KIDDING? I LOVE GIANT ROBOTS!
BUT IT REALLY GOT FUN ONCE THE POLICE STOPPED CHASING ME.
THANKS FOR WAITING, CAT. ARE YOU READY TO GO?
YOU BET! AND I HAVE THE PERFECT PLAN--
--A ROMANTIC MOVIE, DINNER AND THE BEST JAZZ TRIO IN TOWN.
I KNOW THE SWEETEST LITTLE PATIO WITH A TABLE FOR TWO!
AND NO MATTER WHAT...
...NO GIANT ROBOTS!
End.

AMAZING SPIDER-MAN #1-700 COVER GALLERY

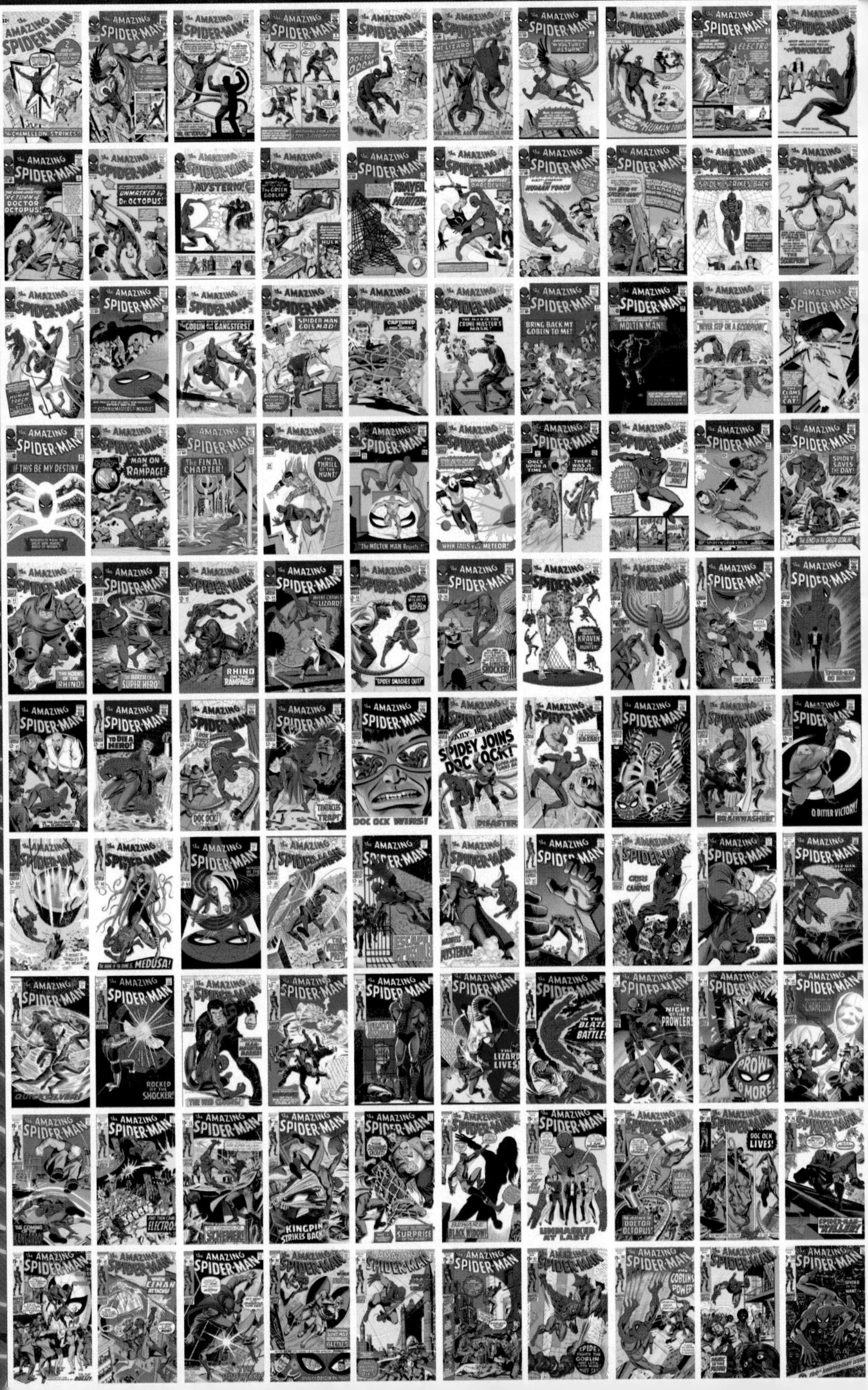

The Amazing Spider-Man
The Chameleon Strikes!
Doctor Doom
The Lizard
The Vulture's Return
Electro
The Human Torch
Return of Doctor Octopus
Unmasked by Dr. Octopus!
Mysterio!
The Green Goblin
Hulk
Kraven the Hunter
Human Torch
Spidey Strikes Back!
Scorpion
Human Torch
The Goblin and the Gangsters!
Spider-Man Goes Mad!
Captured
The Man in the Crime-Master's Mask!
Bring Back My Goblin to Me!
Molten Man!
Never Step on a Scorpion!
The Claws of the Cat!
If This Be My Destiny
Man on a Rampage!
The Final Chapter!
The Thrill of the Hunt!
The Molten Man Regrets
When Falls the Meteor!
Once Upon a Time
There Was a Robot!
Spidey Saves the Day!
The End of the Green Goblin!
The Horns of the Rhino!
The Birth of a Super Hero!
Rhino on the Rampage!
Where Crawls the Lizard!
Spidey Smashes Out!
Shocker!
Kraven the Hunter
This One Got It!
Spider-Man No More!
To Die a Hero!
Doc Ock!
Tentacles and Traps!
Doc Ock Wins!
Spidey Joins Doc Ock!
Disaster
Kazar
The Brainwasher!
O Bitter Victory!
Medusa!
Escape Impossible
The Madness of Mysterio!
Crisis on the Campus!
Quicksilver!
Rocked by the Shocker!
The Web Closes!
The Lizard Lives!
In the Blaze of Battle!
The Night of the Prowler!
Prowl No More!
Chameleon
The Coming of the Kingpin!
And Then Came Electro!
Schemer!
Kingpin Strikes Back!
Surprise
Black Widow!
Unmasked at Last!
The Arms of Doctor Octopus
Doc Ock Lives!
Spider-Man Wanted!
Ka-Zar Attacks!
Goblin's Power
Spidey and the Goblin

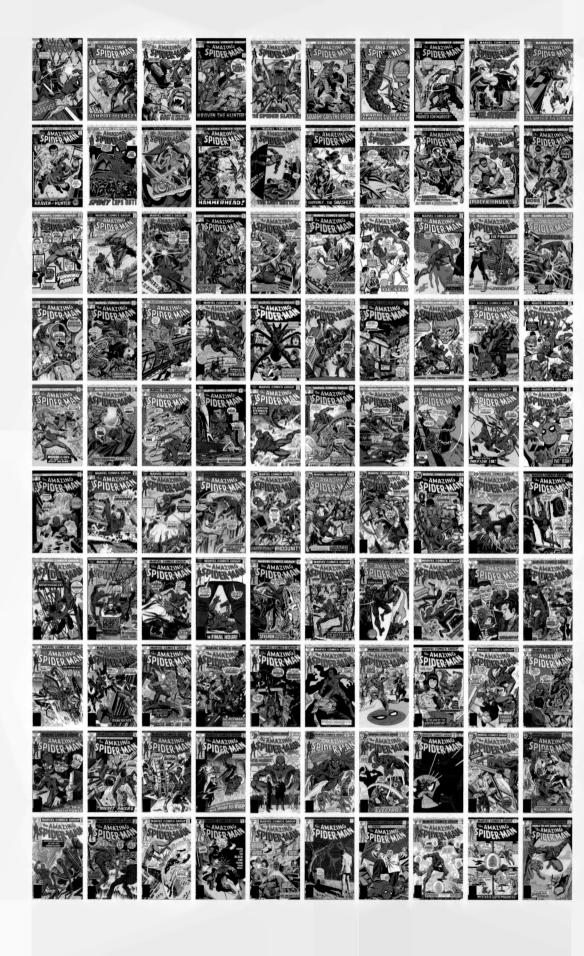

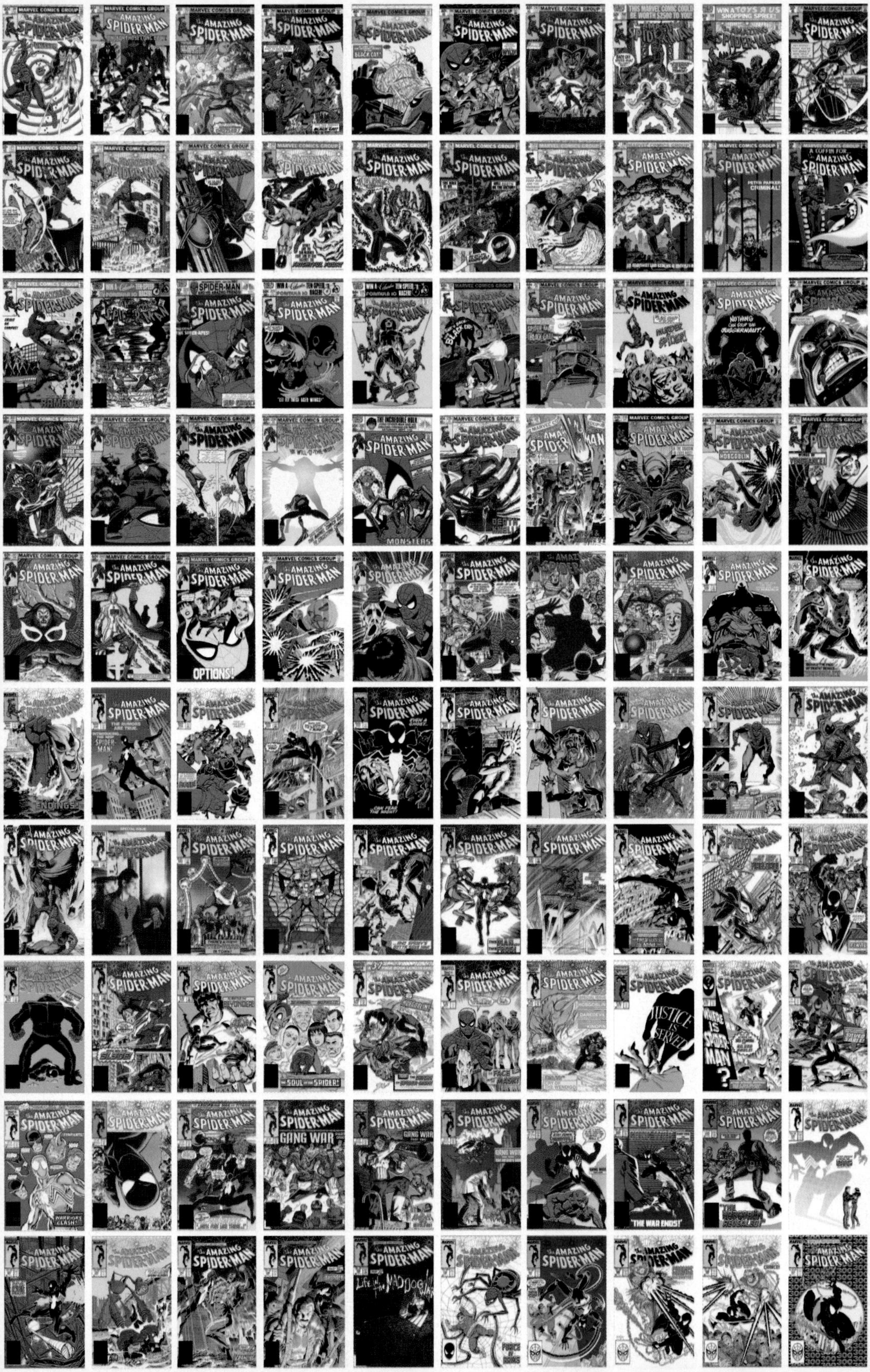

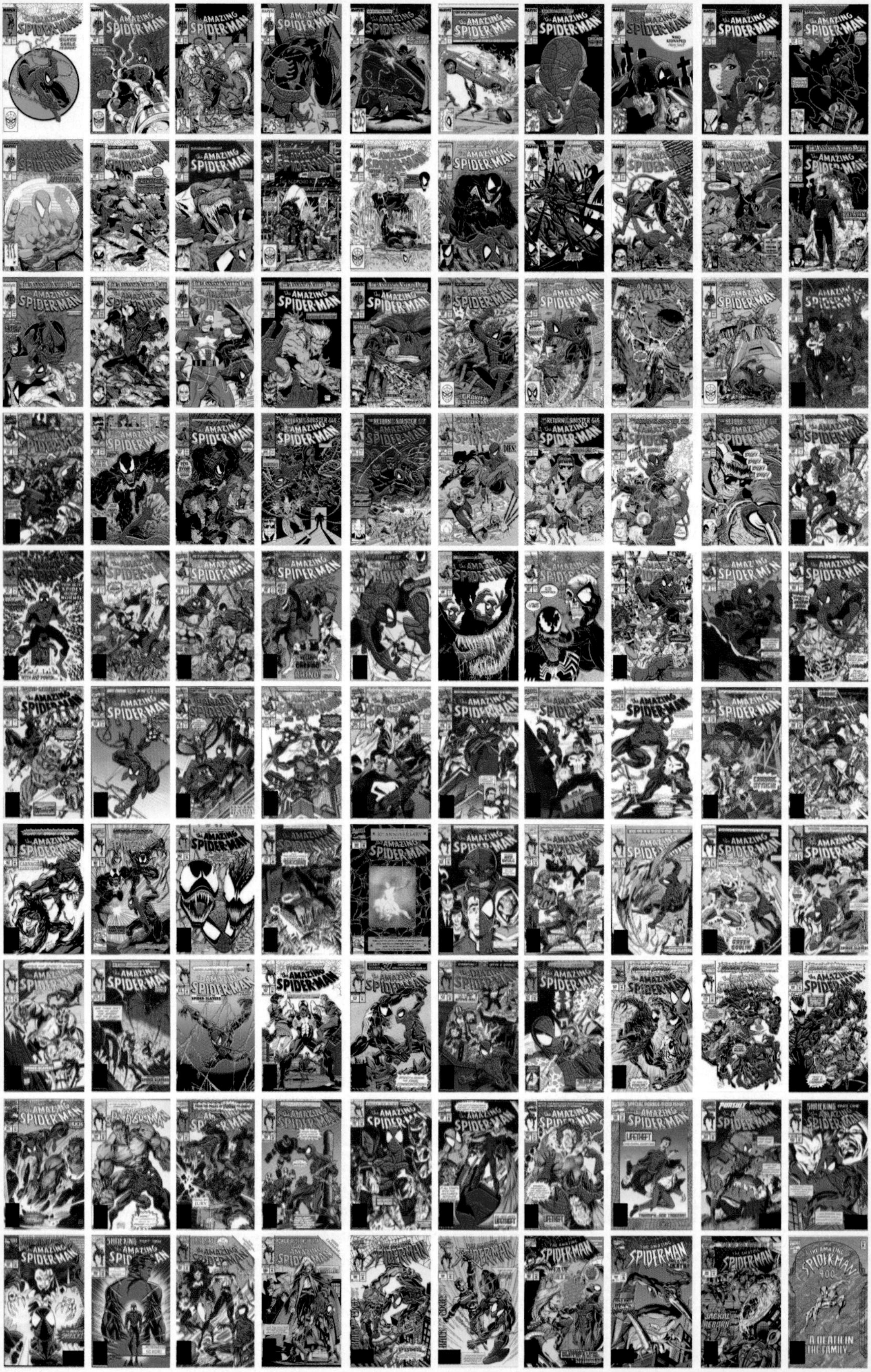
THE AMAZING SPIDER-MAN
400
A DEATH IN THE FAMILY

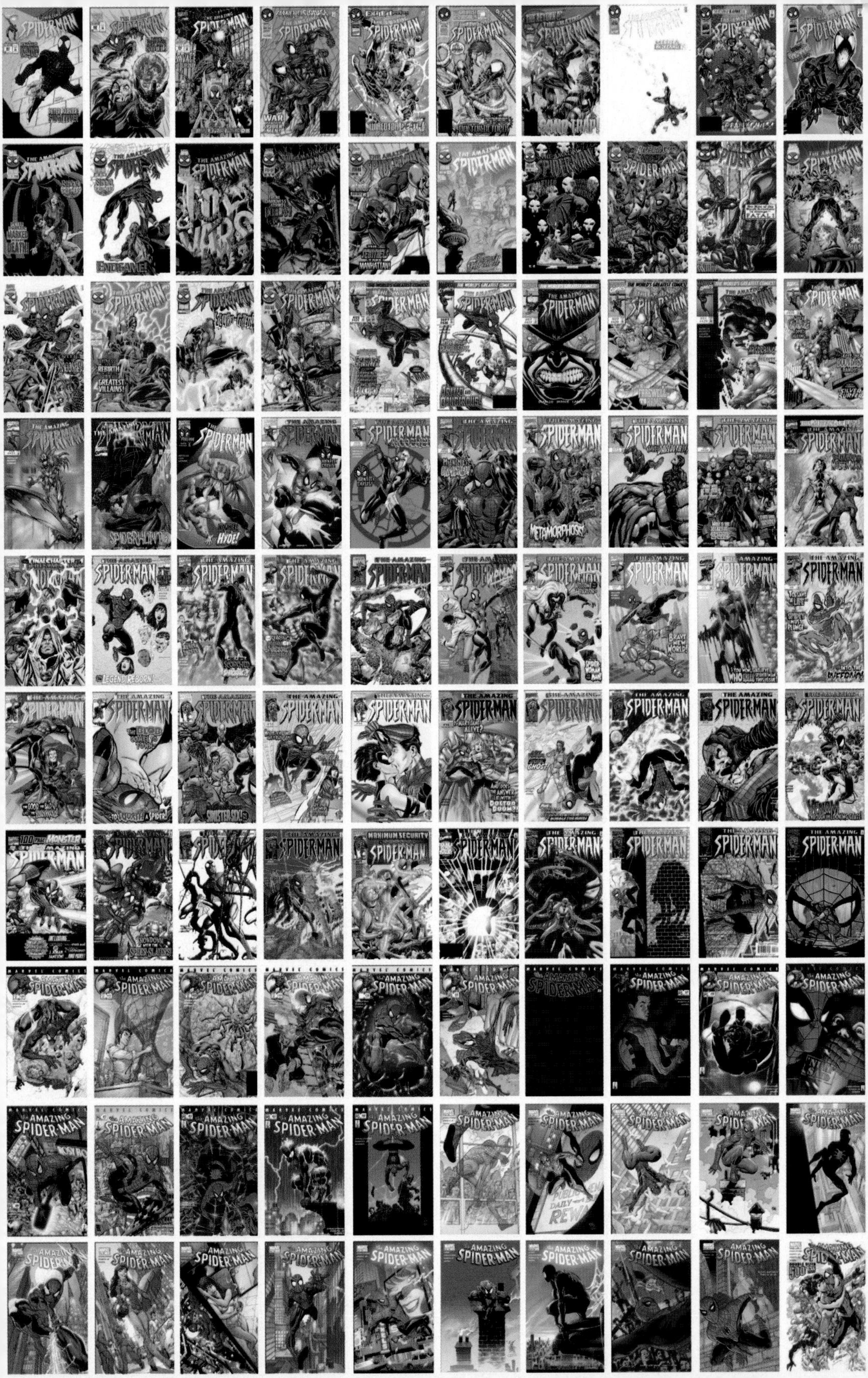

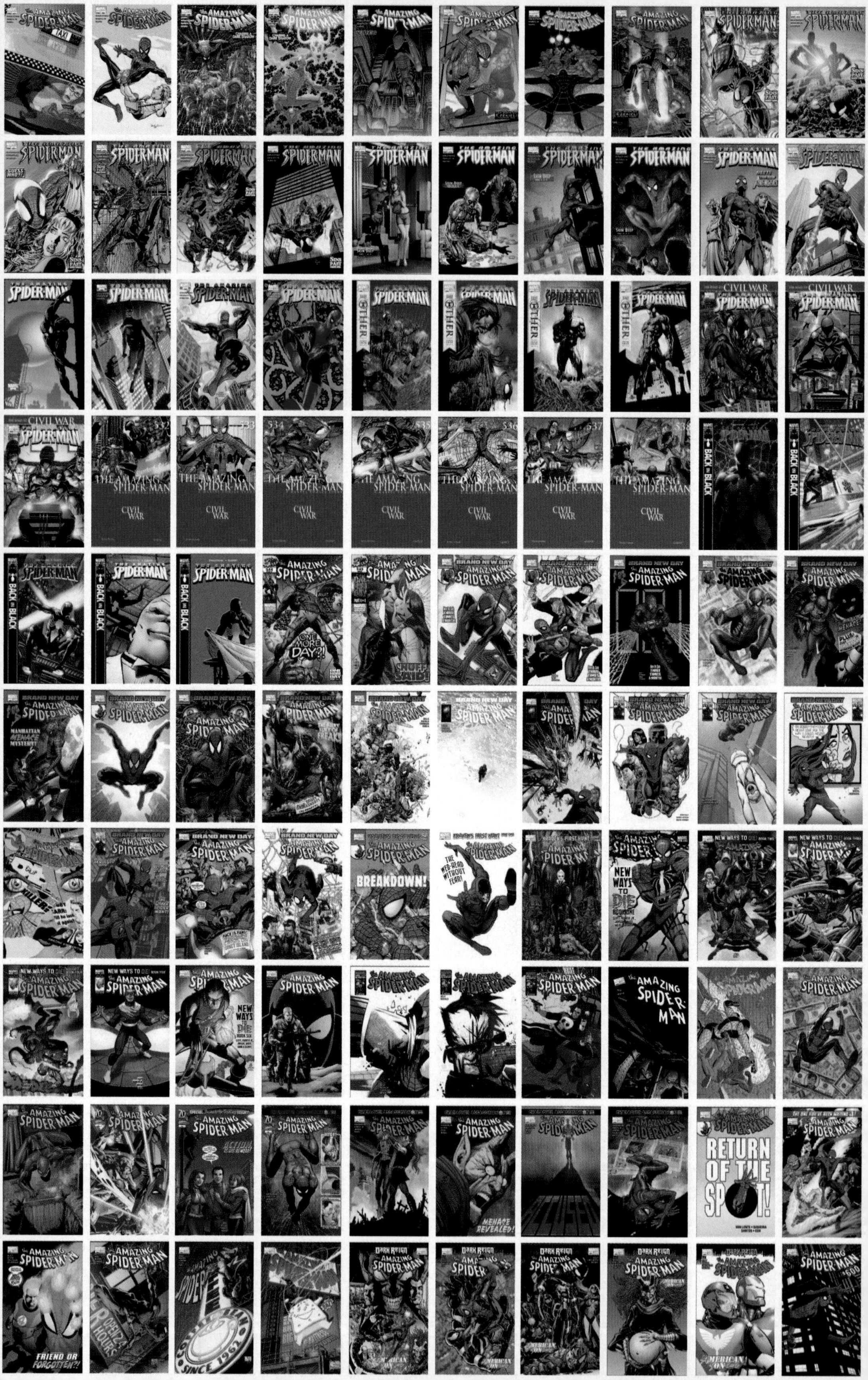

CIVIL WAR
THE AMAZING SPIDER-MAN
BACK IN BLACK
ONE MORE DAY?!
BRAND NEW DAY
BREAKDOWN!
NEW WAYS TO DIE
RETURN OF THE SPOT!
FRIEND OR FORGOTTEN?!
SINCE 1962

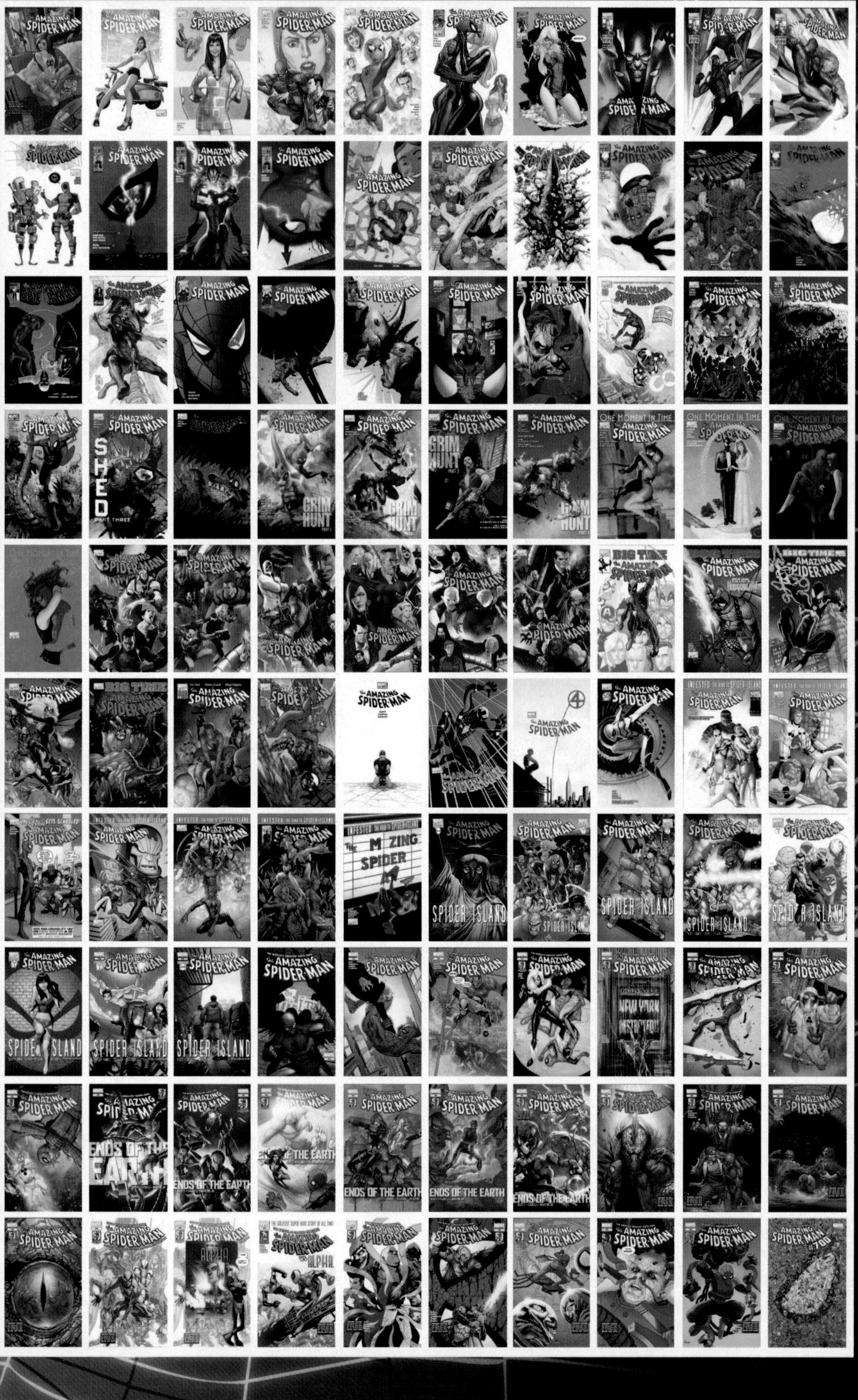

THE AMAZING SPIDER-MAN
SHED
PART THREE
GRIM HUNT
ONE MOMENT IN TIME
BIG TIME
INFESTED THE ROAD TO SPIDER-ISLAND
SPIDER ISLAND
NEW YORK DESTROYED!
ENDS OF THE EARTH
THE GREATEST SUPER HERO STORY OF ALL TIME!
ALPHA
#700

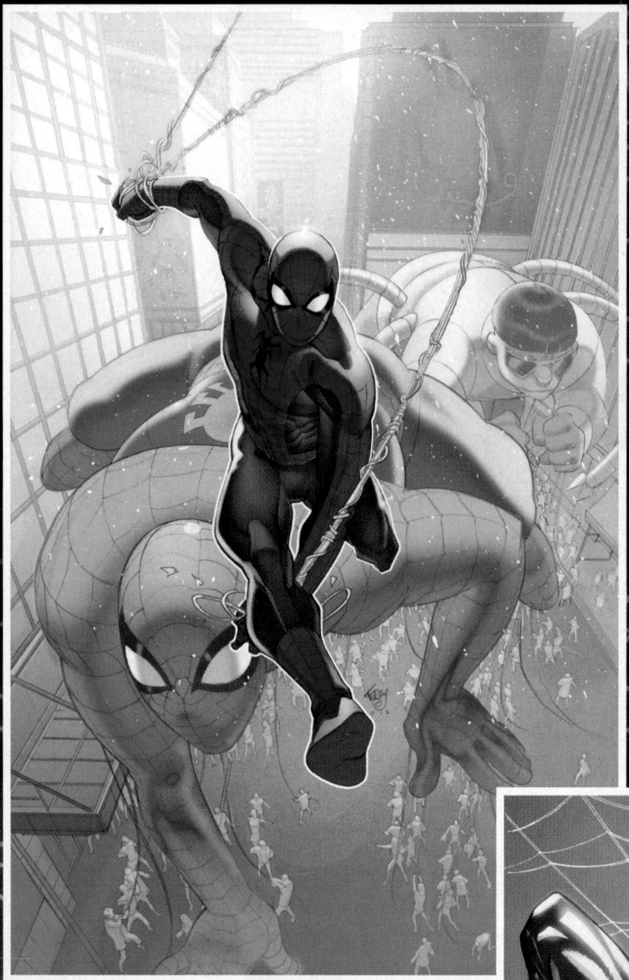

AMAZING SPIDER-MAN #698 VARIANT
COVER BY PASQUAL FERRY & MARTE GRACIA

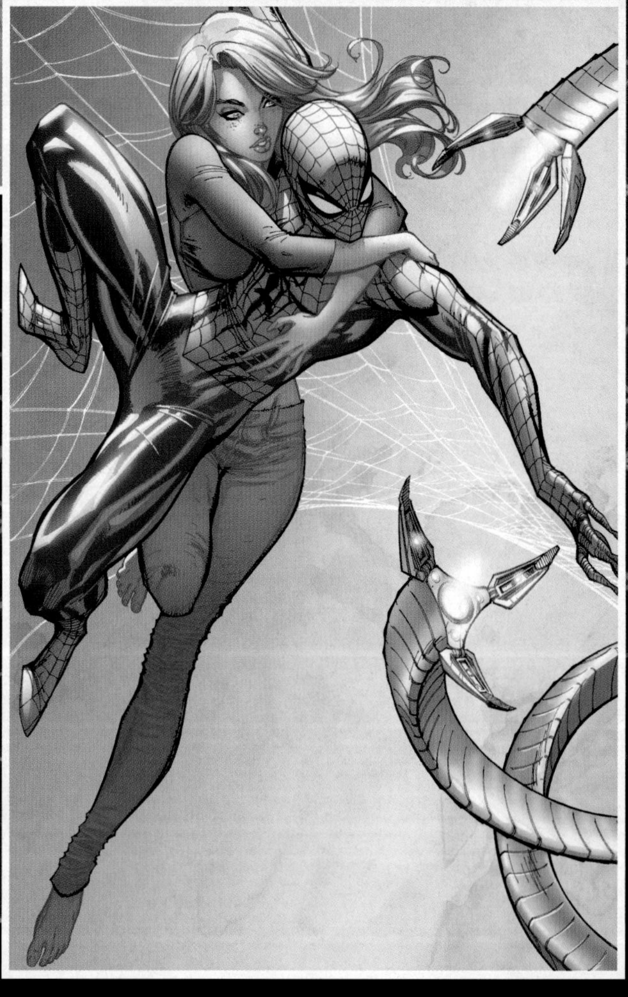

AMAZING SPIDER-MAN #700 MIDTOWN COMICS VARIANT
COVER BY J. SCOTT CAMPBELL & EDGAR DELGADO